Gedion Onyango
Editor

Designing Artificial Intelligence for Public Policy and Governance in Africa

palgrave
macmillan

Editor
Gedion Onyango
Firoz Lalji Institute for Africa
London School of Economics
and Political Science
London, UK

ISSN 2524-6291 ISSN 2524-6305 (electronic)
Studies in National Governance and Emerging Technologies
ISBN 978-3-031-83444-8 ISBN 978-3-031-83445-5 (eBook)
https://doi.org/10.1007/978-3-031-83445-5

The inclusion of papers within the volume was facilitated through invitations extended by Wits Tayarisha, South Africa

This Palgrave Macmillan imprint is published by the registered company Springer Nature Switzerland AG
The registered company address is: Gewerbestrasse 11, 6330 Cham, Switzerland

Contents

Notes on Contributors

Odilile Ayodele is a Senior Research Specialist at the Human Sciences Research Council (HSRC) within the Developmental, Capable & Ethical State (DCES) research division. Dr. Ayodele has a Ph.D. in Political Studies from the University of Johannesburg and a background that includes a BA, BA (Hons), and MA in International Relations from the University of the Witwatersrand. Her research focuses primarily on public and private sector responses to the unique needs of African states, particularly within the context of the Fourth Industrial Revolution and Africa's digital evolution. Dr. Ayodele's research aims to understand further, how Africa adapts to contemporary challenges and opportunities. Her forthcoming book, The Political Economy of Mobile Telephony in South Africa (Zed Books/Bloomsbury, September 2024) explores these themes. Email: oayodele@hsrc.ac.za

Adama Sow Badji is a senior lecturer and researcher at the Faculty of Economics and Management at Cheikh Anta Diop University in Dakar, Senegal. She is also a pedagogical director at the University Centre for Research and Training in Internet Technologies (CURI). She has a Ph.D. in Economics and extensive experience teaching and conducting research in Economics. In addition to her teaching activities, she is the coordinator of the Master E-learning program and was Senegal's focal point for the Sustainable Development Solutions Network in the Sahel (SDSN-SAHEL) from 2014 to 2021.

François Joseph Cabral is a Full Professor at the Université Cheikh Anta Diop de Dakar (UCAD) and outgoing Director of the Ecole Doctorale des Legal, political, economic and Management Sciences (EDJPEG) of Cheikh Anta Diop University, Dakar (UCAD), which he headed from 2014 to 2020. Prof. Cabral heads the Research Laboratory on Institutions and Growth (LINC) at UCAD. He has been a member of the Pep network since 2004 and of IFPRI's African growth and modelling consortium (Agrodep). He is also a research associate at the International Development Research Group (GREDI), University of Sherbrooke, Québec. He has carried out research and studies in collaboration with several institutions (AERC, CIRPEE, GDN, IDRC, Brookings Institute, ECOWAS, ADB, ILO, World Bank, UNCTAD, Ministries of Senegal, Guinea-Bissau, Cape Verde, and Niger). Email: joecabral7@gmail.com

Krish Chetty is a Senior Research Manager at the Equitable Education and Economies Division of the HSRC. He holds a master's Qualification in Knowledge and Information Management from the University of Stellenbosch) and is a Ph.D. candidate in the Computing Science Department at Nelson Mandela University. His Ph.D. study concentrates on developing partnership strategies for South African and Chinese incubators and accelerators to accelerate entrepreneurship development across the African continent. His research interests lie in the social applications of smart technologies that contribute to eradicating poverty, inequality, and unemployment. He previously worked in the HSRC's BRICS Research Centre, representing South Africa in several BRICS academic events. Before joining academia, he worked as a Data Architect for various South African financial institutions.

Lewis Edwin Chigova is a post-doctoral fellow under the Afrocentric Governance of Public Affairs research entity at North-West University's Vanderbjilpark campus, South Africa. He holds a Ph.D. in Public Management and Governance from North-West University—Potchefstroom, a master's degree in public administration and an Honours in Administration degree from the University of Zimbabwe. His research interests include civic crowdfunding, public sector innovation, diaspora philanthropy, co-production, digital transformation, and policy innovation. Lewis has written several peer-reviewed articles and book chapters and has presented many research papers at academic conferences. Lewis

Edwin Chigova was once a teaching assistant at the University of Zimbabwe's Governance and Public Management Department. Orcid number: 0000-0001-7357-2091, Email: lewisec47@gmail.com

Emmanuel Fundisi is a Geospatial Specialist in the HSRC's eRKC Division, Geo-Analytics Unit. He holds a Ph.D. in Remote Sensing from the University of Johannesburg (2021). He has lectured GIS and Remote Sensing at the University of Johannesburg and supervised and co-supervised honours to Master's students in the same field. He has authored and co-authored 10 publications. At HSRC, he has played a pivotal role in numerous projects, providing expert advice and input in geospatial modelling applications across various divisions. His collaborative efforts have significantly enhanced the quality and accuracy of geospatial data analysis and interpretation. Recently (2023), he was invited to join the prestigious Harvard University—Center for Geographic Analysis. As a member of the Remote Sensing Community affiliated with the Harvard University—Center for Geographic Analysis, he is actively involved in developing advanced modules for Geospatial Artificial Intelligence (GeoAI). Dr. Emmanuel's contributions are instrumental in advancing the field of geospatial analysis and its practical applications in Africa.

Tshidi Green is a master's student at the University of Witwatersrand with a keen focus on security sector reform. Her research includes examinations of alternative solutions to combat urban gang violence and conflicts, risks to human security in the Sahel region, and, most recently, the examination of states' diplomatic commitments to combating conflict-related sexual violence. Her work demonstrates her vast and diverse interest in promoting a more peaceful, stable, and cooperative global community.

Costa Hofisi is a distinguished NRF-rated professor of Public Administration at North-West University. He is also the founding Research Director at North-West University's Afrocentric Governance of Public Affairs. Professor Hofisi's research interests are public sector innovation, public policy, monitoring and evaluation, and research methods. Additionally, he works as a consultant, focusing on innovation leadership, strategy development, monitoring, and evaluation. With over 50 publications and more than 40 master's and Ph.D. students, Professor Costa Hofisi has extensive experience in teaching and has developed training modules for the National School of Government, Orcid: https://orcid.org/0000-0002-2571-6991

Shaun Kinnes is a Climate, Peace, and Security fellow at the African Centre for the Constructive Resolution of Disputes. He holds a master's in international relations from the University of Witwatersrand. His research interests include private military corporations, climate security, and human security in an African context. Email: shaunkinnes@yahoo.com

Nondumiso Masuku is a Researcher in the Education and Livelihoods theme of the Equitable Education and Economies (EEE) unit at the Human Sciences Research Council (HSRC). She holds a B.Com Honours in Economics from the University of KwaZulu-Natal. Her research interests include youth unemployment, gender inequality in labour markets, skills development, school-to-work transitions, and technology shifts induced by Artificial intelligence (AI). Ms Masuku is experienced in quantitative research and has contributed to various projects, including youth employment policy interventions adopted by the South African government.

Thema Monroe-White is an Associate Professor of Artificial Intelligence and Innovation Policy at the Schar School of Policy and Government and the Department of Computer Science (joint) at George Mason University. Her interests include bias mitigation in artificial intelligence (AI), critical quantitative and computational methods, and racial equity in innovation and entrepreneurship (I&E). She is concerned with understanding the pathways to achieving social and economic empowerment for minoritised groups via I&E, AI literacy, and emancipatory data science. She has received multiple NSF awards to investigate issues of racial equity in the STEM ecosystem, including serving as a lead member of the research team for the Inclusion in Innovation Initiative (i4), a $3.5 million cooperative partnership to develop a national infrastructure for diversity and inclusion within the NSF Innovation Corps (I-Corps™) Program. Inspired by her work on intersectional inequalities in science, she has also received funding to investigate the harms of structural racism on the scientific enterprise and the benefits derived from including historically marginalised groups in the scientific workforce. Thema holds a Ph.D. in Science, Technology, and Innovation Policy from the Georgia Institute of Technology and a master's and bachelor's degree in psychology from Howard University. Email: tmonroew@gmu.edu

Tahiya Moosa is a Researcher, policy advocate, and humanitarian currently working at the Human Sciences Research Council (HSRC). With over a decade of experience spanning the non-profit, for-profit, and corporate sectors, she specialises in international relations, equitable economies, global governance, and the empowerment of marginalised communities. Her research encompasses artificial intelligence (AI) and renewable energy. She explores AI's role in combating corruption, its impact on global governance, and its applications in secondary education. Tahiya's work in renewable energy addresses advancements and policy challenges within South Africa's renewable energy sector and includes contributions to a policy assessment on renewable energy financing in BRICS nations. Her research provides critical insights into leveraging AI and sustainable energy to drive societal progress.

Souleymane Ndao is an Associate Professor of Economics at the Université Cheikh Anta Diop de Dakar (UCAD). Before his recruitment at UCAD in 2020, Dr. NDAO was a post-doctoral fellow at the Banque de France and a lecturer in economics at the University of Picardie Jules Verne (France). He also worked as a researcher from 2014 to 2018 at the Amiens Research Center on Industry, Institutions and Economic Systems (CRIISEA). He has published his research in the Economic Alternatives, la Revue de la Regulation, and the Portuguese Economic Journal, among others. His research focuses on monetary integration, central banks, and monetary policies.

Ben Omar Ndiaye is a Full Professor of Economics at the University Cheikh Anta Diop (UCAD) with extensive experience in teaching and research in Economics and engaging at the highest levels with governments, leading figures from academia, civil society, the private sector, and international organisations. Prof. Ndiaye holds a bachelor's and master's degree in economics with an option in Corporate Management, an M. Phil. in Macroeconomics specialising in Money, Finance, and Banking, a Ph.D. in economic science, and a Post-Doctoral Diploma in Economics.

Japheth Otieno Ondiek is a Ph.D. student at the Department of Political Science and Public Administration, University of Nairobi, Kenya. He is a researcher focusing on digital transformation and technology, particularly how digital policies influence public sector institutions' accountability, decision-making, and service delivery. Japheth has extensive experience in analysing digital policies, artificial intelligence, blockchain, open government data, and ICT for transparency and accountability. Moreover, he has authored numerous book chapters and articles on public policy, artificial intelligence in public administration, blockchain for public sector accountability and decision-making, open government data, and digitalisation policies for public sector innovation. His recent publications include chapters in the books "Public Policy and Technology in Africa" edited by Gedion Onyango, and "Think Tank and Governments in Africa" edited by Frank Ohmeng and Joseph Ayee, "Routledge Handbook of Public Policy in Africa" edited by Gedion Onyango. Additionally, he has published an article on the digitalisation and integration of Sustainable Development Goals (SDGs) in public organisations in Kenya in the Public Organization Review-Journal, among other works. Email: japhondiekh@gmail.com

Gedion Onyango is a Research Fellow at the Firoz Lalji Institute for Africa at the London School of Economics and Political Science (LSE) in the United Kingdom. He is also a Senior Research Associate at the University of Johannesburg in South Africa. Previously, Gedion worked as a Senior Lecturer at the University of Nairobi and has served as a Guest Lecturer at various universities in Africa, Europe, and Canada. His work has been published in reputable public administration and policy journals. He has edited several reputable works on African Public Policy, such as "Routledge Handbook of Public Policy in Africa, London: Routledge", "State Politics and Public Policy in Eastern Africa: A perspective. London: Palgrave Macmillan", and "Public Policy and Technological Transformation in Africa: Nurturing Policy Entrepreneurship, Policy Tools and Citizen Participation, London: Palgrave Macmillan". Email: onyangojr@gmail.com

Mandla J. Radebe is an Associate Professor in the Department of Strategic Communication and is the Director of the Centre for Data and Digital Communications within the School of Communication. He instructs undergraduate and postgraduate students and supervises master's and Ph.D. candidates. He holds a Ph.D. (Media Studies), MA (Journalism & Media Studies), and BA Honours (Journalism & Media Studies) from the University of Witwatersrand, Johannesburg, South Africa, and a B.Sc. Degree (Statistics and Computer & Information Technology) from Vista University, Soweto, South Africa. An award-winning author, Mandla is the author of The Lost Prince of the ANC: The Life and Times of Jabulani Nobleman 'Mzala' Nxumalo 1955–1991 (Jacana Media, 2022) and Constructing Hegemony: The South African Commercial Media and the (Mis)Representation of Nationalisation (UKZN Press/ Routledge, 2020). He is also the editor of Public Sector Communication in the Digital Age (UJ Press, 2024). He has authored various book chapters, journal articles, and columns on the Critical Political Economy of Communication, Digital Capitalism, and National Question. https:// orcid.org/0000-0003-0329-9776. Email: mradebe@uj.ac.za

Danda Rawat is an Associate Dean for Research and Graduate Studies and a Full Professor in the Department of Electrical Engineering and Computer Science at Howard University in Washington, DC, USA. He is the Founding Director of the Howard University Data Science & Cybersecurity Center and the DoD Center of Excellence in Artificial Intelligence and Machine Learning. Dr. Rawat has secured over $110 million in research funding and received several awards, including the NSF CAREER Award 2016. He has published over 300 scientific articles and 11 books and has supervised and graduated 33 Ph.D. students, including 27 under-represented/minority students. He has served as an Editor/Guest Editor for over 100 international journals and has been involved in organising committees for several IEEE flagship conferences. Dr. Rawat received his Ph.D. from Old Dominion University, Norfolk, Virginia. He is a Senior Member of IEEE, a Lifetime Professional Senior Member of ACM, a Lifetime Member of AAAI, a life member of SPIE, a member of ASEE and AAAS, and a Fellow of IET. Additionally, he is an ACM Distinguished Speaker and an IEEE Distinguished Lecturer (FNTC and VTS).

Gabriella Razzano is the co-founder and Executive Director of OpenUp, a social impact technology hub based in Cape Town. She is a Doctoral Fellow in the Trust Program at WISER, the University of Witwatersrand. She is also a Senior Atlantic Fellow on Social and Income Inequality and an Advisor to the African AI Observatory. She is a human rights activist, lawyer, and researcher, specialising in themes of data and AI governance, digital rights and inequalities. She clerked with Justice Yacoob of the Constitutional Court and has worked with domestic and international non-governmental partners on various law and research projects. She was the Executive Director of a legal non-profit, the Open Democracy Advice Centre. She has contributed to drafting several regional instruments, such as the African Model Law on Access to Information, the African Declaration on Internet Rights and Freedoms, and the African Union Data Policy Framework. She was an Internet Governance Fellow, an alumnus of the International Visitor Leadership Program (Global Digital Leader), and one of the Mail and Guardians Young South Africans, 2013. Email: gabriella@openup.org.za

Petronella Saal is a Research Specialist in the HSRC's Equitable Education and Economies research division. She completed a doctorate in computer-integrated education with honorary colours at the University of Pretoria (2020). She also holds an honours degree in education management, law, and policy from the University of Pretoria (2015). Saal specialises in computer-integrated education in primary and secondary schools. Her research interests are comparative education, cross-sectional studies, educational technology, and mathematics education. Before her academic career, Saal was an educator who taught Computer Applications Technology, Economic Management Sciences, Economics, and Business Studies at multi-racial secondary schools in South Africa. Before joining the HSRC in 2021, she supervised honours students in Assessment and Quality Assurance in Education and Training at the University of Pretoria, and she is also a German Academic Exchange Service alumni.

Cesa Salaam is a Ph.D. Candidate at Howard University, specialising in Artificial Intelligence with a focus on fairness and bias mitigation in Natural Language Processing (NLP), NLP for low-resourced languages, and the role of culture in AI. As a research fellow at the DoD Center of Excellence in AI/ML under Dr. Danda Rawat's advisement, Cesa contributes to advanced AI research in many areas. His dedication to the field is further recognised by receiving the prestigious GEM Engineering Fellowship. Cesa's research spans various critical areas, as evidenced by his publications on topics such as AI applications in microaggression detection, sentiment analysis of code-switched text, ethical considerations in AI-based security applications, and AI value alignment. Cesa's work makes AI systems fairer, culturally aware, and applicable to diverse linguistic contexts. His publications, including "Self-Efficacy Sydney: An EHWLT for Young Children with Chronic Illness", "ABL-MICRO: Opportunities for Affective AI Built Using a Multimodal Microaggression Dataset", and "When the occasion comes, the proverb comes: Aligning LLM with moral values via proverbial knowledge bank", showcase his commitment to addressing ethical and cultural dimensions in AI development. As he progresses in his doctoral studies, Cesa aims to further bridge the gap between cutting-edge AI technologies and their ethical and cultural implications. His research promises to shape AI's future in more inclusive, fair, and attuned to diverse global contexts, with implications for enhancing AI ethics, improving NLP capabilities for underrepresented languages, and developing culturally grounded AI applications. Email: cesa.salaam@bison.howard.edu

Zanele Sokatsha is a trained clinical psychologist and ethicist pursuing her MA in Clinical Psychology at the University of Witwatersrand. With experience in two state hospitals serving under-resourced communities, she brings a deep understanding of community dynamics and mental health. As a transdisciplinary researcher, Zanele adopts an intersectional approach to investigating harm, well-being, and negotiating with the public. Her current research project focuses on tracing the experiences of Black women in South African universities. Previously, she studied undergraduate students' well-being and coping strategies during the COVID-19 pandemic and mapped human rights discourse in post-1994 South Africa. Zanele is currently working with Open Cities Lab on building civic technology that is equitable and inclusive of marginalised communities in South Africa.

Mardiya Siba Yahaya is a digital sociologist, researcher, and community movement builder and works as a Global Community Manager, Team CommUNITY at Article 19. She is also a Violence, Inequality and Power Fellow (VIP Lab) at the University of San Diego Kroc Institute of Peace and Justice. Working at the intersection of digital labour, gender and cybersecurity, surveillance, and counter public and digital identities, they investigate the implications of technology-facilitated surveillance and datafied societies on minoritised communities in the global South. Email: mardiyasiba@gmail.com

List of Figures

List of Tables

CHAPTER 1

Artificial Intelligence (AI) for Public Policy and Governance in Africa

Gedion Onyango

Introduction

Artificial Intelligence (AI) is rapidly gaining traction in policy innovation on the global stage, yet it is also raising concerns about how it can be leveraged responsibly to build more inclusive and accountable governance processes, which continue to be a challenge in Africa. The most critical concern, however, is whether African countries are ready for AI and whether governments have the capacity to design it in a manner that would fully leverage its potential without jeopardising existing gains or exacerbating current challenges like human rights abuse and inequality. This volume broadly explores these issues while drawing public policy insights from specific empirical case studies across Africa. It comes at a time when more practical engagements are

G. Onyango (✉)
London School of Economics and Political Science, London, UK
e-mail: onyangojr@gmail.com

University of Johannesburg, Johannesburg, South Africa

G. Onyango (ed.), *Designing Artificial Intelligence for Public Policy and Governance in Africa*, Studies in National Governance and Emerging Technologies, https://doi.org/10.1007/978-3-031-83445-5_1

needed and when governments, international development organisations, African Development Bank (AfDB) and businesses strive to find effective ways to leverage AI technologies in Africa and other countries globally. Unlike in the last decade, more concerted investments are being made by governments, non-governmental organisations and business corporations towards AI integration in public policy and governance processes. This has featured bolder regional collaborations and national policies, as well as research agendas informing how AI can be appropriately leveraged in African governments. AI institutions and adoption frameworks are being established to focus on designing responsible AI, the fit-to-context frameworks and regulation of AI for governance purposes. This aspect of AI adaptation is also referred to in this volume as *AI for Government*—focused on leveraging AI technologies as reforms or public policy and service enablers. There is no doubt that AI has brought about significant changes and presents greater opportunities in African public policy ecosystem, including health, security, education, energy, and agriculture, among others, and it is being hoisted as a formidable tool for economic growth (Amankwah-Amoah & Lu, 2024; Mlambo & Mhlanga, 2022). The role of AI became more prominent during the pandemic, and it is anticipated that these gains could be consolidated or expanded to drive a sustainable development agenda—the United Nations' Agenda 2030 and the African Union's Agenda 2063. The result of such efforts has recently witnessed the creation of several AI Labs across major African cities by international corporations such as Google and IBM Labs in Johannesburg, Accra and Nairobi. IBM has also partnered with African Risk Capacity (ARC), an African Union agency, on how to leverage AI to mitigate the impacts of climate change, such as flood risks, through modelling large-scale geospatial data and analytics systems. We also saw how AI technologies were at the centre of innovations behind vaccine optimisation in Botswana and South Africa, as well as the delivery of vaccines to remote areas in countries like Ghana, Rwanda and Malawi through unmanned aerial vehicles or drones (Leedom, 2024; Mathaha et al., 2022; Mellado et al., 2021; World Bank, 2021). AI technologies are increasingly being adopted to enhance security in African countries through border control reforms (Smart Borders), boost agriculture with Climate Smart Agriculture, and improve housing with Smart Cities initiatives, among others, as discussed in detail by different contributions in this volume.

These developments show that while much of the discussions and empirical works about the impact of AI technologies in society have concentrated on experiences from Anglo-Saxon countries, such as the United States, United Kingdom, Continental Europe, and the New Industrial Countries in Asia, African countries are also actively exploring the potential benefits of AI. Nevertheless, this has come with varying institutional performances, governance opportunities and risks to human rights across countries and sectors in Africa. Examining these dynamics underscores the importance of this volume. Each chapter aims to provide critical analysis of how these emerging AI systems should be designed and integrated into governance and policy frameworks in developing countries, particularly in Africa. According to the OECD-AI Policy Observatory statistics, the AI African experiences are driven by its youthful population aged between 25 and 34 (OECD-AI, 2024). The World Bank's programs such as the *Digital Economy Initiative for Africa* (DE4A) and latest studies (e.g., Barasa & Kiiru, 2023), have shown that this age group is actively involved in defining digital economic development across the world, with Africa being at the forefront because of its primarily youthful population.

Nevertheless, despite AI's significant potential, its adoption in Africa, like in other regions, has come with complex challenges mainly due to a lack of societal consensus and norms to guide its integration into public policy, algorithmic bias, the predatory nature of external actors' engagement, mainly the BigTechs and a weak regulatory state, among others. From this perspective, AI poses fundamental risks to essential political values such as representation, accountability, responsibility, equality, and equity, which are crucial for ongoing governance reforms in Africa. Again, most African governments, like many globally, have not yet developed clear guidelines for AI implementation. Besides, the digital infrastructure in most African countries is only developing and is yet to foster the establishment of effective AI systems. Furthermore, risks associated with leveraging AI pose a problem to Africa's weak regulatory state and are most likely to exacerbate structural problems of inequality and human rights abuse, as seen in the lawsuits against Meta in Kenya, Ghana and Nigeria, recently. Conventional policy challenges, such as the lack of contextual specificity of most global policies, poor digital infrastructure, insufficient national investment in AI, and algorithmic bias—which may be exacerbating rather than addressing colonial and other structural inequality connotations—remain critical concerns, as well (Ayana et al., 2024).

This notwithstanding, AI is now a reality that African governments, citizens and other key stakeholders in governance can no longer wish away, and it is set to expand exponentially in the next decade with the increasing applications in various sectors. While many governments in the region remain suspicious and hesitant towards embracing AI, a handful are taking proactive steps to develop national strategies and policies that would leverage AI into public policy and governance. As of September 2024, more African countries are engaged in a process of drafting their own AI national policies or strategies. So far, countries with national policies or strategies for implementing AI include Rwanda, Ghana, Algeria, Mauritius, Benin, Egypt, South Africa, Tunisia, Senegal and Nigeria. Others, like Botswana, Namibia, and Kenya, have initiated AI strategy development processes to guide the adoption and implementation of AI in governance processes. There is no doubt that in the coming years, more countries will be joining this trend as continental organisations spearhead policy designs for leveraging AI in carrying out public affairs.

Indeed, on February 29, 2024, the African Union published a draft AI policy, and the AU Strategy on Artificial Intelligence (AI) was adopted in July 2024 in Ghana. This could be seen as an action by the continent following the step of the framework established by the European Union's AI Act 2024. This draft policy could significantly influence discussions surrounding national AI policies across member states. Its primary aim is to guide and promote the integrated adoption and governance of AI technologies. The policy focuses on creating an environment that fosters data-driven innovation and value creation while addressing potential risks. It tackles critical issues such as data inequality, inadequate digital infrastructure, and data governance. Additionally, the AU draft policy encourages the development of sector-specific approaches and establishes essential conditions for AI implementation. This includes defining data types, classifications, and the necessary infrastructure to create legitimate and trustworthy data systems in accordance with the needs of the context. Furthermore, the policy encourages a design that promotes collaborative engagements between African governments and NGOs to leverage AI into various sectors—such as immigration, healthcare, climate change adaptation, and education policies—to improve public service delivery and policymaking. Leveraging AI needs sound data governance infrastructure that ensures the following design issues of AI policy are realised.

These design issues should be anchored in effective legislation, privacy principles, etc., as summarised in Table 1.1.

These data governance aspects have been considered foundational pillars and guiding principles for developing AI governance and regulation in different national policies, like Rwanda's and national strategies like South Africa's, as well as in the fifteen priority areas of the African Union's Continental AI strategy, as seen in Fig. 1.1.

Despite these notable continental and national efforts in developing AI adoption guidelines, most African countries have yet to *catch up* with the fast-paced manner in which advanced technologies like AI are being integrated into governing systems. The main reason for this lag stems from the significant amount of resources and expensive investment needed to fully integrate advanced technologies in governance processes. These kind of resources are unavailable for most African countries that are also still grappling with realising effective and sustainable revenue collection systems (Onyango, 2024). Moreover, these countries' political systems are only acquiring their policy capabilities (Onyango, 2022, 2023) and remain relatively underdeveloped to adopt AI for policy processes effectively. The differences in AI strategy development among countries, therefore, stem from their varying levels of digital infrastructure and investments or digital maturity, as discussed in *Chapter 6* below. The ongoing digital governance reforms and emerging trends in AI strategy development in Africa should be seen as a response to 'catch up' with global initiatives to integrate AI into government systems (Onyango, 2023). This globalisation effect and *catch-up position* of African countries in the international political economy offers them unique opportunities but also assign them specific vulnerabilities and risks associated with AI adoption.

This book is informed by such realities while similarly contributing to the overall trajectories in AI research and practice across the globe. It is now evident that research on the real-world impact of AI in public policy and governance is still in its early stages, indicating that more work is needed in this area. This volume is a moderate attempt to contribute to this agenda from a public policy perspective. It examines policy design issues around AI and how these policies are currently and should be crafted within the context of the historical and present challenges faced by African countries. In doing so, different contributors also present empirical case studies on how AI is being implemented in various governance sectors and across different African countries while identifying gaps

Table 1.1 Core aspects of AI policy design

Key aspects	*Definitional components*
Regulation frameworks	• *Privacy* involves protecting privacy rights while encouraging innovation. Balanced data collection for AI with safeguards against misuse should be implemented, following standards like the GDPR and Data Protection laws • *Transparency and accountability* in AI governance are essential. This requires clear explanations of algorithmic decisions and holds developers accountable for ethical data use • *Trustworthiness underscores* safe and secure data systems based on functional cybersecurity and data protection rules and practices. Addressing ethical concerns like bias and promoting diversity in AI development will ensure that algorithms reflect diverse community values
Privacy-by-design principles	• *Privacy-by-design principles*, integrating privacy and data protection measures from the start • *Domestication* articulating clear roles between different actors and authorities locally • *Utility and balancing* innovation with privacy protection. There is a need to encourage locally driven entrepreneurialism, competition and innovation. Establish cloud storage and processing solutions for sensitive and proprietary data

(continued)

Table 1.1 (continued)

Key aspects	*Definitional components*
Responsible data sharing and collaboration	• *Prioritising individual privacy rights,* which underscores access based on demand for data and incident reporting, promotes consumer choice and legitimacy • *Compliance* with legal and ethical standards and norms in data-sharing practices. Anchored on promoting integrity, representativity, non-discrimination and data quality • *Drafting guidelines* for data-sharing agreements • *Collaboration* with stakeholders and the Data Protection Agency. The design should create co-jurisdictional, cooperative and collaborative frameworks. Proactively engaging in collaborative regional processes and mechanisms
Monitoring and enforcement mechanisms	• *Auditing* compliance with data privacy and governance standards • *Penalties* for noncompliance will deter data misuse and maintain trust in AI systems • *Capacity-building and awareness* initiatives. Promote research, development, and innovation in various data-driven areas • *Data stewardship* among AI developers, users, and policymakers. Promotion of interoperability, portability

Source Authors

and opportunities for delivering AI-enabled public services and executing public policy.

A public policy perspective is essential in different ways. For one, it audits practical initiatives by governments and other stakeholders aimed at leveraging AI in governance processes. It also takes stock of the impact of AI in shaping public value, mapping potential opportunities and risks to deeply socially embedded values, especially, in developing political contexts where public institutions grapple with serving societal

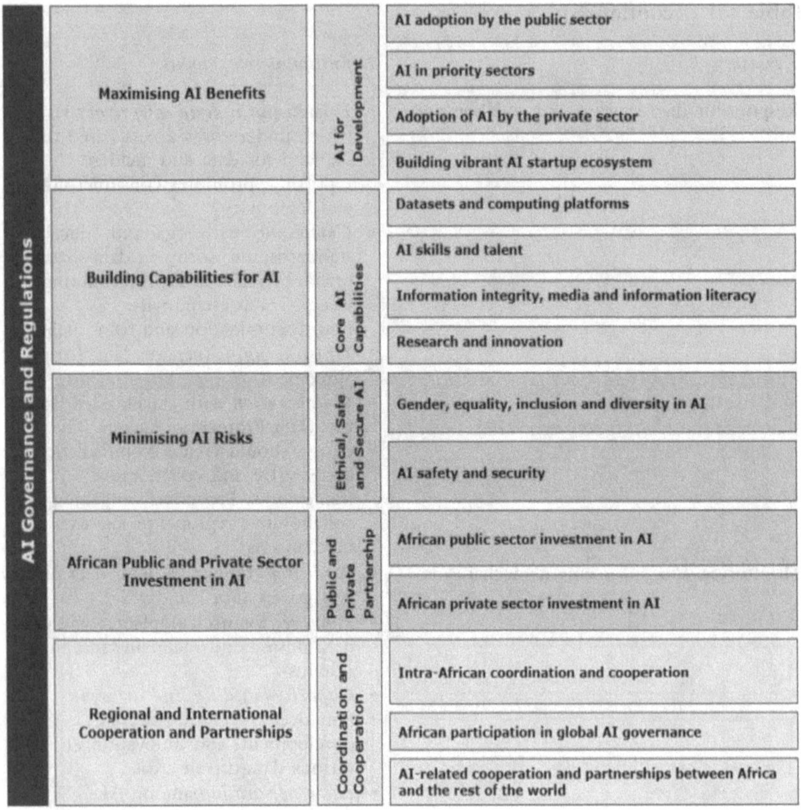

Fig. 1.1 Priority areas for AU's Continental AI strategy (*Source* AU Continental Artificial Intelligence Strategy)

needs effectively. To this end, a focus on public policy helps us put into context the role of AI in fashioning government-citizen relations, which remain highly dynamic. Further to this, a public policy perspective sets out a more transdisciplinary research agenda on various aspects of AI, the state, and society. This, for example, builds on the growing interest in AI policy and research regarding African countries, particularly focusing on how governments and policy actors can develop responsible AI while addressing underlying algorithmic biases. We believe the essence of developing responsible AI should be framed within the broader understanding of political, historical and socio-economic contexts that characterise current challenges and efforts to formulate national AI policies in Africa. This book assembles a multidisciplinary authorship with expertise in public policy and governance, including, academic and policy practitioners, students, and consultants interested in African politics, governance, and public policy. The aim is to provide updated teaching and training materials on digital governance transformation in Africa while drawing lessons for other developing regions.

Organisation of the Book

Different chapters in this volume explore and present the conceptual developments, practical dynamics, benefits, and challenges of AI in African governance contexts and the implications of these to public policy. Eleven chapters are structured into two parts. Part I focuses on issues around designing AI frameworks in Africa. Part II contains chapters showcasing implementation experiences and potentials of AI in Africa, reflecting on key principles and priority areas as articulated in the AU's AI strategy (see AU Continental AI Strategy, 2024, pp. 35–58). These include holistic implementation strategy, devising responsible AI, public sector AI investments, addressing safety and security, gender equality and diversity in AI, among others.

Following this introductory chapter, **Chapter 2** explores efforts to establish a holistic AI governance framework in Africa. In this chapter, *Cesa Salaam, Danda Rawat, and Thema Monroe-White* present an AI governance framework that can be tailored to various African contexts. They point out that most AI policies rely heavily on data governance structures foreign to Africa. This could mean that AI applications need to be decolonised, highlighting the urgent need for an African-centred data governance paradigm to ensure local and regional equity and inclusivity. The effort by the African Union Data Policy Framework could be a step in the right direction. This landmark document has already proven invaluable and is expected to greatly influence the future of AI and data governance across the continent. However, despite some successes in implementing various initiatives and policies, persistent challenges remain across African states. These challenges include inadequate data protection measures, difficulties establishing effective oversight frameworks to support sustained sector growth, and limited governance and economic resources for technological and workforce development.

These notwithstanding, the authors view AI as a tool for socio-technical empowerment and upliftment that African countries need to pursue to optimise policy implementation. Doing so would require African governments to challenge the "enduring hegemony of Northern theory," which has historically influenced African public policy and governance systems. A relevant AI policy for African countries should be anchored on an emancipatory approach to decolonisation that emphasises and prioritises African identity, contributing to a more inclusive AI governance landscape. This should integrate participatory governance techniques with indigenous knowledge systems; the A3IG framework supports the responsible design, development, adoption, and deployment of AI technologies grounded in local environmental and sociocultural contexts.

While exploring this local environmental and sociocultural context dimension,**Chapter 3** focuses on how AI can be designed responsibly for the future. Gabriella Razzano argues that such an endeavour would benefit tremendously from the existing localised efforts and skills already established by civic technologists who have advocated inclusive governance processes through digital technologies. She presents an empirical argument based on the experiences of South Africa's Civic Technology Community, specifically the Vulekamali project to establish the intersection between Civic technologies and AI. In doing so, the chapter addresses challenges in AI governance, including the issue of the law's pace in relation to digital technology advancements, as well as the Collingridge Paradox. Razzano hinges on the need for sound data governance by pointing out that effective data management is crucial for securing information. Ultimately, the chapter highlights the valuable contributions civic technologists can make to discussions about AI's future, drawing from their experiences in social impact innovation. The chapter relies on these experiences to propose alternative solutions for establishing responsible AI practices in contexts where governance reforms lag behind technological development. In the end, it emphasises the importance of creating a shared agenda focused on human flourishing in AI development and underscores the critical role of the civic technology community in shaping future narratives around AI.

Chapter 4 expands on these arguments by exploring what Ethical AI for Government in African public administration would look like. They highlight the importance of navigating and ensuring that adopting AI would not threaten public values at the centre of public administration activities that have characterised government-citizen contestations over the years. In this chapter, *Japheth Otieno Ondiek and Gedion Onyango* underscore the importance of adopting human-centred and context-specific approaches in ethical AI design and its impacts. They argue that such designs should not only focus on efficiency and effectiveness but also on core political values—such as representation, accountability, and equality. Further to this, the chapter addresses critical issues related to misinformation, human rights abuses, and the needs of vulnerable groups to combat algorithmic biases commonly found in AI technologies. The chapter offers potential policy recommendations for AI's effective and ethical design in public administration. Overall, the authors advocate holistic engagement with stakeholders to ensure regulatory compliance and incorporate the perspectives of diverse groups, particularly marginalised communities. This will uphold transparency and other public administration values at the centre of public sector reforms.

Still, on ethical concerns, particularly focusing on equality and how algorithmic biases in AI technologies seem to affect African Nigerian women, **Chapter 5**, by *Mardiya Siba Yahaya and Zanele Sokatsha*, explores how AI for governance can be developed through an Afro-feminist lens. Such a lens should incorporate design justice principles and intersectional policymaking. The chapter argues that for AI to be ethical and safe, it is essential to integrate design justice and feminist AI principles throughout all phases—from research and design to deployment and usage. The authors further raise the fundamental question of what an African feminist approach to AI development, deployment, and governance would entail to benefit marginalised communities in African policymaking contexts. As such, the chapter advocates for meaningful civic participation in designing emerging technologies, such as AI, which disproportionately affect marginalised groups. They contend that the integration of AI in governance processes should consider the consequences for those often harmed by an increasingly data-driven state and society. At the same time, this should prioritise gender aggregated data to facilitate more inclusive policymaking that acknowledges diverse social identities and benefits people who are socioeconomically and politically marginalised.

This chapter concludes the first part of this volume, focusing on issues related to AI design, with a particular emphasis on policymaking in Africa. The second part, which addresses the realities of implementation, begins with **Chapter 6**, "Digital Maturity as AI Governance Pathways: Public

Sector Challenges and Opportunities in South Africa." In this chapter, Odilile Ayodele, Petronella Saal, Tahiya Moosa, Krish Chetty, Emmanuel Fundisi, and Nondumiso Masuku argue that the implementation of AI is closely linked to the structural transformation towards digital maturity. This argument rightly underscores the need for an effective data governance structure, as discussed in Part I. By examining South African experiences, this chapter demonstrates that AI governance involves optimising the digitalisation of public sector processes. Therefore, a digital maturity pathway can help identify specific AI implementation strategies that government agencies can adopt to improve public service efficiency and address socioeconomic disparities. Within this digital maturity index, the chapter provides critical AI implementation insights generalisable to other developing or middle-income economies in Africa and elsewhere. First, the government needs a unified framework for data standards and integrated digital platforms to enhance data sharing. Securing dedicated funding for AI and fostering public–private partnerships are crucial, alongside strong leadership, to clarify roles and responsibilities. Second, capacity building is essential, including training programs to boost civil servants' digital literacy and AI skills. Change management strategies should be adopted to address resistance, promote regular communication, and foster a culture of innovation. Third, bridging the digital divide is necessary for equitable ICT access, requiring investment in IT infrastructure and reliable Internet access. Policymakers must stay updated on technological advancements, engage local leaders, and implement social programs to combat poverty and inequality. Fourth, prioritising cybersecurity is vital through strict measures, regular audits, staff training, and compliance with data protection regulations. African governments can effectively implement AI by addressing these areas and enhancing service delivery and efficiency.

Chapter 7, by François Joseph Cabral, Adama Sow Badji, Ben Omar Ndiaye, and Souleymane Ndao, examines the impact of artificial intelligence (AI) on economic growth, the labour market, and household welfare in African countries, with a specific focus on Senegal. The authors utilised a Computable General Equilibrium (CGE) approach to model AI based on the endogenous growth literature. This framework treats total factor productivity (TFP) as an endogenous variable, influenced by research and development (R&D), AI, human capital, infrastructure, and public capital externalities across various market sectors. The chapter identifies the positive and negative effects of AI-enabled development on economic growth. They show that while AI can enhance productivity and yield short-term benefits for households, its role as a substitute for human labour may adversely affect household welfare. The long-term implications of AI on welfare are not consistently favourable, although it can improve human capital, R&D, and physical capital. The chapter highlights significant GDP growth, demonstrating that combining AI, laboratory research, and human capital can foster sustainable wealth creation. The chapter offers several policy recommendations: first, countries like Senegal should create a favourable business environment for AI startups. A successful AI strategy requires boosting the supply of essential skills. The labour market must adapt to the increasing demand for qualifications and skills related to AI. Lastly, as demonstrated by countries like Canada or Mauritius, supporting an AI strategy could significantly improve total factor productivity (TFP) and create new economic opportunities in technology-intensive sectors. However, to achieve this, the government needs to master and initiate highly effective partnerships with various actors who could invest in and develop AI applications that are suitable to the context.

In **Chapter 8**, Gedion Onyango and Japheth Otieno Ondiek explore how AI can be leveraged to enhance public accountability by adhering to ethical decision-making principles and promoting transparency in the public sector of Kenya and South Africa. The chapter emphasises that implementing AI in African public administration presents unique opportunities and challenges, each specific to the context of the country and the sector in which it is applied. To effectively harness AI for public accountability, the government needs to engage in a collaborative approach to implementation. AI-enabled public accountability should be hinged on and improve regulation oversight, auditability and transparent participation and decision-making. This necessitates having in place clear roles and responsibilities among stakeholders in AI development, as well as algorithmic modelling, deployment, and oversight to ensure accountability. There is also a need for public education and skill training in the public sector to help identify misinformation and disinformation. The current emphasis on transparency in the creation of AI systems allows stakeholders to assess the reasoning behind AI decisions and identify any biases, prejudices, or errors in the process. The chapter concludes with policy recommendations for governance practitioners and decision-makers on how to use AI systems effectively to enhance public accountability standards within public sector institutions.

Chapter 9 by Lewis Edwin Chigova and Costa Hofisi examines how AI tools can help the police prevent crime, enhance investigations, manage traffic, and conduct surveillance in public places and streets. Focusing on Johannesburg, the authors empirically analyse AI's role in ensuring public safety and security. By implementing AI methods such as preventive policing, smart policing, criminal investigations, traffic control, and public area surveillance, AI has the potential to improve safety in crime-prone cities like Johannesburg. The chapter aligns its discussion with Sustainable Development Goal 11 (SDG 11) and South Africa's comprehensive policy frameworks. These frameworks, along with various policy documents—including NDP 2030 and multiple White Papers on Policing, Safety, and Security—emphasise the importance of creating safe cities and advocating for adopting AI-supported technologies. The authors establish that while the benefits of using AI technologies to enhance safety in Johannesburg are evident, integrating AI into urban environments requires careful consideration of its challenges. It is crucial to address ethical issues related to AI usage, ensuring compliance with the country's constitutional provisions. The authors recommend that future research should explore how residents in high-crime areas perceive AI-enabled surveillance. This could involve conducting surveys and longitudinal studies to understand the perspectives of individuals navigating the difficult balance between living in a surveillance state and the desire for safety in their communities. Lastly, the chapter addresses ethical concerns associated with AI use and advocates for implementing clear institutional and legal frameworks to ensure appropriate checks and balances.

Chapter 10 addresses a growing concern in Africa regarding the rise of electronic voting (e-voting system) administration. *Mandla J. Radebe* examines the role of AI in electoral processes, using South Africa as a case study. The chapter starts with the idea that AI has the potential to disrupt democracies. It shows that the 2024 elections in South Africa reflected both local political dynamics and global trends. This chapter argues that AI manipulation may have influenced these elections, which poses a significant threat. The increase in fake news in South Africa is fueled by high internet usage, as well as social media platforms like Facebook and X and messaging apps such as WhatsApp. Low voter turnout has had a considerable impact on the ruling African National Congress (ANC), causing it to receive less than 50% of the vote for the first time since 1994, potentially due to intentional sabotage. Although it is too early to establish a direct link between these issues and AI manipulations like the Cambridge Analytica scandal, caution is warranted. It concludes that policymakers should prioritise addressing the negative aspects of AI in electoral reforms while promoting its positive uses to safeguard democracy. This should align with the principles of the rule of law as a foundation for policy formulation and regulation. The discourse on the social economy should also be considered to achieve equitable wealth distribution and reduce representative deficits common in countries like South Africa. Policymakers have a responsibility to guide the discussion surrounding AI technology, focusing on inclusivity and development for everyone.

In **Chapter 11**, Shaun Kinnes and Tshidi Green examine the role of AI in state-building with a focus on peacebuilding, which remains a significant challenge in countries like the Democratic Republic of the Congo (DRC) and Mali. They demonstrate how AI can potentially mitigate and even eradicate the rise of terrorism, rebel groups, and civil conflict in Mozambique, Mali, and the DRC. The duo argue that intelligence agencies and hostile actors have historically viewed the physical landscape as a dynamic factor in conflict. Studies suggest that it is time for stakeholders to consider technology as an equally important factor that can be leveraged to end violence and promote stability in Africa.

By citing practical operational cases in these countries and comparing them with those from other regions, Kinnes and Green demonstrate that AI could be particularly beneficial in addressing conflicts across African countries' fragile borders and inaccessible hostile territories. For example, peacekeeping forces supported by the Southern African Development Community (SADC) and the Wagner Group often struggle to access extremist strongholds due to challenging terrains and inadequate road infrastructure. In this context, AI could play a crucial role. The chapter shows that drones equipped with AI could be deployed in Mozambique's Cabo Delgado province to navigate difficult terrains that traditional vehicles cannot access. This capability would enable peacekeeping forces to reach remote areas where extremist groups operate and could help implement battlefield technologies to restore peace in the region. However, it is essential to establish effective policies to ensure that human agencies and decision-making are not reduced to mere statistics, in order to prevent potential human rights violations.

In all, these chapters collectively illustrate the unimaginable potential of AI in all governance sectors, underscoring its essence in driving the state reform projects that developing African countries are grappling with. We can see that in relatively stable countries with more consolidated policy systems like South Africa, Kenya, and Mauritius, AI can transform these systems to deliver governance outcomes in a more effective and efficient fashion. This is whether AI is used as a means of delivering public services (AI for Government), ensuring urban safety, and designing evidence-informed policies. AI also remain highly relevant in state construction. If designed effectively to fit purpose and context, AI technologies can help in peacekeeping processes to stabilise fragile states such as Mali and the DRC. However, the design of AI systems remains a critical phase in developing responsible AI solutions that would effectively leverage these potential benefits and support policy implementation. Each chapter tackles these challenges in different policy sectors and country contexts.

References

Amankwah-Amoah, J., & Lu, Y. (2024). Harnessing AI for business development: A review of drivers and challenges in Africa. *Production Planning & Control, 35*(13), 1551–1560.

AU Continental AI Strategy (2024). *Continental Artificial Intelligence strategy: Harnessing AI for Africa's development and prosperity*. African Union. https://au.int/en/documents/20240809/continental-artificial-intelligence-strategy

Ayana, G., Dese, K., Daba Nemomssa, H., Habtamu, B., Mellado, B., Badu, K., Yamba, E., Faye, S. L., Ondua, M., Nsagha, D., & Nkweteyim, D. (2024). Decolonizing global AI governance: Assessment of the state of decolonized AI governance in Sub-Saharan Africa. *Royal Society Open Science, 11*(8), 231994.

Barasa, L., & Kiiru, J. M. (2023). The digital economy and youth employment in Africa. In*Public policy and technological transformations in Africa: Nurturing policy entrepreneurship, policy tools and citizen participation* (pp. 161–182). Palgrave Macmillan.

Leedom, M. (2024). *Drones deliver humanitarian aid in Africa*. ThinkGlobalHealth. https://www.thinkglobalhealth.org/article/drones-deliver-humanitarian-aid-africa#:~:text=Drones%2C%20or%20unmanned%20aerial%20vehicles%20(UAVs)%2C%20have,and%20blood%20to%20solve%20last%20mile%20hurdles

Mathaha, T., Mafu, M., Mabikwa, O. V., Ndenda, J., Hillhouse, G., & Mellado, B. (2022). Leveraging artificial intelligence to optimize COVID-19 robust spread and vaccination roll-out strategies in Southern Africa. *Frontiers in Artificial Intelligence, 5*, 1013010. https://doi.org/10.3389/frai.2022.1013010

Mellado, B., Wu, J., Kong, J. D., Bragazzi, N. L., Asgary, A., Kawonga, M., Choma, N., Hayasi, K., Lieberman, B., Mathaha, T., Mbada, M., Ruan, X., Stevenson, F., & Orbinski, J. (2021). Leveraging artificial intelligence and big data to optimize COVID-19 clinical public health and vaccination roll-out strategies in Africa. *International Journal of Environmental Research and Public Health, 18*(15), 7890. https://doi.org/10.3390/ijerph18157890

Mlambo, F., & Mhlanga, D. (2022). Artificial intelligence and machine learning for energy in South Africa. *AfricaGrowth Agenda, 19*(4), 20–23.

OECD.AI. (2024). *Visualisations powered by Tableau using data from StackOverflow*. https://oecd.ai/en/dashboards/countries/Kenya

Onyango, G. (2022). *Routledge handbook of public policy in Africa*. Routledge.

Onyango, G. (2023). State entrepreneurship in Africa: Realising digital transformation for policy effectiveness in selected countries. In *Public policy and technological transformations in Africa: Nurturing policy entrepreneurship, policy tools and citizen participation* (pp. 29–66). Palgrave Macmillan.

Onyango, G. (2024). Improving the public purse: The Kenya Revenue Authority as an example of positive public administration in Africa. In *Pathways to Positive Public Administration* (pp. 187–204). Edward Elgar Publishing. https://doi.org/10.4337/9781803929170.00020

World Bank. (2021). *Harnessing artificial intelligence for development in the post-COVID-19 era: A review of national AI strategies and policies*. Analytical Insights. https://thedocs.worldbank.org/en/doc/2e658ef2144a05f30e254221ccaf7a42-0200022021/original/DD-Analytical-Insights-Note-4.pdf

PART I

Designing Artificial Intelligence (AI) Framework for Africa

SECTION 1: DESIGNING ARTIFICIAL INTELLIGENCE (AI) FRAMEWORK FOR AFRICA

SECTION OVERVIEW

This part of the volume contains chapters that outline and analyse aspects of the architectural design of Artificial Intelligence (AI) technologies for African governance and public policy. These chapters highlight and discuss, theoretically and empirically, the potential benefits and challenges of implementing AI in public policy in Africa. They address questions such as what AI for African society and governance would involve, with a focus on design considerations for developing AI strategy frameworks within African political contexts. Additionally, this section explores ethical issues around the realisation of AI in public policy and governance processes in Africa. Such discussions further delve into how AI can be harnessed responsibly going forward, including how AI impacts gender and racial relations and geographical inequality concerns pointing to issues of algorithmic bias.

Highlights for Practitioners and Researchers

- AI systems should reflect local values, reduce anti-African and anti-Black biases, and be tailored to the needs of their populations.

- Sound AI governance relies foremostly on sound data governance and governance practice

- Adopting AI design templates from successful drafters like the EU may make it difficult for African governments to customise and align AI implementation with citizens' needs

- Formulation of clear policies is crucial for integrating and adopting AI for Government, especially, in the public sector amid the growth of automated services.

- AI Strategy frameworks need to implement an *anticipatory rather than reactionary AI governance model* that will ensure sustainable and culturally contextualised AI systems.

- Restructuring government systems to allow integration of AI laws and regulations from the onset to foster responsible innovation and governance procedures that support moral and secure AI systems. This should reduce potential risks

- Ensure interoperability in AI architecture design for government operations

- Holistic and collaborative assessment and understanding of the *complex integrations* of moral, ethical, technological, and legal principles.

- Establish a shared agenda for human agency and a whole-of-government approach to AI development through the Civic Technology community to shape future AI narratives.

CHAPTER 2

Towards Holistic AI Governance in Africa

Cesa Salaam, *Danda Rawat*, *and Thema Monroe-White*

Introduction

The rapid development of artificial intelligence (AI) technologies has created a world seemingly racing to bring every facet of science fiction to life. Every day, there is a new announcement of AI technology purported to change the world for "the better." These advancements span various domains, including public administration, education, the creative sector, and healthcare, among others (Akgun & Greenhow, 2022; Al-Zahrani & Alasmari, 2024; Anantrasirichai & Bull, 2022; Mergel et al., 2024; Rajpurkar et al., 2022). However, these changes, typically, are not guided or monitored by a larger governing body designed to ensure the safety and benefits of these systems are as real as they claim. The

C. Salaam · D. Rawat
Howard University, Washington, DC, USA
e-mail: cesa.salaam@bison.howard.edu

T. Monroe-White (✉)
George Mason University, Fairfax, VA, USA
e-mail: tmonroew@gmu.edu

Schar School of Policy and Government, Hopewell, VA, USA

G. Onyango (ed.), *Designing Artificial Intelligence for Public Policy and Governance in Africa*, Studies in National Governance and Emerging Technologies, https://doi.org/10.1007/978-3-031-83445-5_2

lack of comprehensive oversight heightens concerns about potential risks, ethical implications, and unintended consequences of rapidly deployed AI technologies. Issues such as algorithmic bias, privacy concerns, and the potential for job displacement are often overlooked in the rush to innovate (Scherer, 2015; Zaidan & Ibrahim, 2024). Additionally, the direction of research and development of these systems is generally not grounded in a governing paradigm focused on the actual challenges facing the very people they claim to help (Birhane, 2020). Rather, it is focused on following Western developmental trends that tend to prioritise technological advancement for its own sake, often neglecting communities' diverse needs and cultural contexts. As Birhane (2020) argues, this approach often leads to the development of technologies that are misaligned with the real-world problems faced by marginalised communities and developing nations. Western AI development often emphasises efficiency, automation, and economic growth, sometimes at the expense of social equity, cultural preservation, and environmental sustainability. This narrow focus can result in AI solutions that exacerbate existing inequalities or create new ones rather than addressing the root causes of societal challenges.

Subsequently, other nations across the world, specifically in the Global South, are focused on "catching up" rather than charting their own path forward. This approach often leads to the uncritical adoption of AI technologies and development strategies that may not be suitable for their specific contexts, cultural values, or economic realities. The pressure to keep pace with global technological trends can result in neglecting local innovation and overlooking Indigenous knowledge systems that could inform more appropriate and sustainable technological solutions (Olaopa & Ayodele, 2022). For Africa to utilise any technology in a beneficial manner, it must first be brave enough to stray away from following a foreign path of development (Soumonni & Monroe-White, n.d.). This requires a fundamental shift in mindset and action, moving from a position of technological consumption and imitation to one of innovation and leadership. African nations must critically evaluate AI technologies' applicability and potential consequences within their unique socio-economic contexts. It must look inward to determine the "what," "why," "when," and "how" of an African technological development that is grounded in the actual needs of its communities on both a micro and macro level.

This chapter focuses on African AI governance systems and policy, offering frameworks and perspectives for guiding technological development from a community-centric approach. In doing so, the chapter delves into three interconnected perspectives (see Fig. 2.1): first, we critically examine the current state of AI governance and policy in Africa; second, we highlight who stands to benefit and who is harmed under existing global AI governance frameworks; and third, we propose a holistic framework for AI governance in Africa, drawing on lessons from dynamic and adaptable policy models that would enable African states to leapfrog existing global powers. A central argument of this chapter is the need to integrate indigenous governance systems into AI policy and governance systems. By applying principles from African cultural frameworks, such as the complimentary leadership structures of Indigenous Akan states, African countries can ensure that AI systems reflect local values, reduce anti-African and anti-Black biases, and are tailored to the needs of their populations. Furthermore, we argue that AI development and innovation in Africa need not follow the patterns established by Western or Eastern nations; instead, it should be based on African societies' unique needs, desires, and cultural contexts. Through this approach, Africa can develop a distinct, forward-thinking, pan-African AI governance model that is not reactionary but anticipatory, ensuring sustainable and culturally contextualised AI systems.

The State of AI Governance and Policies in Africa

The landscape of artificial intelligence (AI) in Africa is rapidly evolving, significantly impacting policy development, implementation, and outcomes across the continent. As Asiegbu and Okolo (2024) highlight, companies are adopting AI tools to address various challenges and opportunities. This accelerated adoption is evident in Kenya, where 27% of the population uses ChatGPT daily, ranking the country third globally in usage. The AI ecosystem in Africa has expanded considerably, with a growing number of startups developing diverse AI applications, from healthcare diagnostics to natural language processing for African languages. Major tech companies like Microsoft, Google, and IBM have further bolstered the continent's AI capabilities by establishing research labs in various African countries, including Kenya, South Africa and Egypt (Asiegbu & Okolo, 2024; Ondiek & Onyango, 2023). However,

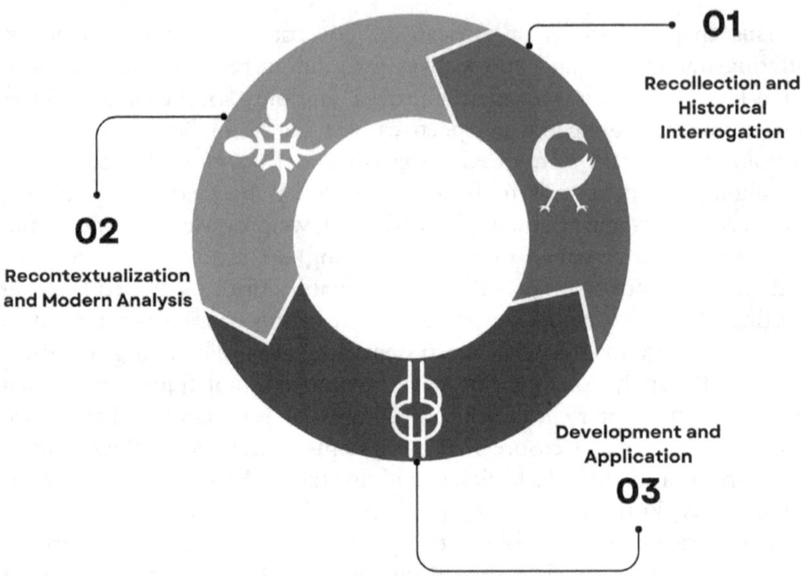

Fig. 2.1 The three stages of the African Adaptive AI Governance Framework

like most digital technologies today, this rapid AI adoption brings challenges and an urgent need for effective governance measures. As seen in other contributions to this volume, the major challenge is found around regulation and the capacity of the relevant institutions to effectively leverage them to improve public policy (also see Hanson, 2023; Ondiek & Onyango, 2023).

In the bid to improve policy directions to leverage AI, efforts have gone beyond the national policy designs to develop regional blueprints. The African Union has taken steps to address this by ratifying the Malabo Convention in 2023 (Data Guidance, 2024), which serves as a benchmark for AI policy in Africa. The African Union Development Agency has also developed a draft policy framework (*Technology Review*, 2024) for individual countries' AI regulatory regimes. Despite these initiatives, only seven African countries have developed national AI programs with varying levels of implementation. Recently, several nations have been proactive in developing and adopting policies, laws, and guidelines on data governance in relation to AI (Adeniran, 2024). Others are contemplating similar implementations (Hlaka, 2024). However, most of these

AI policies rely on data governance structures drawn primarily from non-African-based initiatives, emphasising the critical need for an African-centred data governance paradigm to ensure local and regional equity and inclusivity.

African countries are witnessing a gradual but significant rise in Robust AI initiatives, primarily supported and guided by the 2022 African Union (AU) Data Policy Framework. This landmark document has already proven invaluable and is expected to significantly impact the future of AI and data governance across Africa (Hanson, 2023). The Framework serves as a comprehensive blueprint for developing and regulating Africa's growing data market, assisting member states in navigating the intricate landscape of data regulation while fostering innovation and protecting individual and national interests. While some successes have been achieved in implementing various initiatives and policies, consistent challenges persist across African states. These include insufficient data protection regimes, complications in achieving robust oversight frameworks to support sustained sector growth, and limited governance and economic resources for technological and workforce development (Diallo et al., 2024).

In addition to the Malabo Convention, the AU developed the AU Convention on Cyber Security and Personal Data Protection in 2023. Several individual African states, including Ghana, Mauritius, Egypt, Senegal, Rwanda, Benin, and Tunisia, have also developed their own AI data policies (Effoduh, n.d.), further contributing to the evolving landscape of AI governance in Africa.

Gaps in Policy & Research

As shown above, most research and initiatives have focused on developing AI policy and governance structures. However, very little research has explored the intersection of AI governance with culture, indigenous governance structures, and indigenous knowledge systems. This gap represents a significant oversight in Africa's current approach to AI governance. Cultural Considerations in AI Current AI systems and policies often adopt a one-size-fits-all paradigm based on non-African cultural realities, failing to account for the nuanced cultural contexts across the continent. African AI governance policies modelled after foreign systems may fail to capture the unique landscape of African governmental structures. This oversight can lead to significant challenges in the implementation and effectiveness of AI technologies and policies in African contexts.

Indigenous Governance Structures Traditional African governance systems, which have evolved over centuries, offer valuable insights that could inform AI governance. However, these systems are often overlooked in favour of imported governance models (Khumalo & Baloyi, 2017). Indigenous decision-making processes, which often prioritise community consensus, complimentary leadership, and long-term sustainability, could provide alternative frameworks for AI governance. Indigenous Knowledge Systems and AI Indigenous knowledge systems have long been recognised as valid sources of expertise for science and environmental policy (UNESCO, 2018). African indigenous knowledge systems, encompassing traditional practices, beliefs, and ways of understanding the world, remain largely unexplored in the context of AI technology and governance. These knowledge systems could offer unique perspectives on ethical AI development and deployment. For example, African philosophies such as Ubuntu, emphasising interconnectedness and collective well-being, could inform more holistic approaches to AI ethics and governance. We address these major gaps in research by providing a framework and a set of guidelines that centre on the intersection of culture, Indigenous African governance structures, and Indigenous African knowledge systems.

A Framework for Governing AI in Africa

To address the dynamic nature of African governmental structures and the development of substantive AI governance policies, we propose the African Adaptive AI Governance (A3IG) (Work in progress) Framework. This framework is rooted in indigenous African wisdom and designed to be flexible enough to accommodate the diverse cultural and political landscapes across the continent while providing a robust structure for AI governance. The foundational principle of the A3IG Framework is built upon the indigenous Akan Adinkra symbol of Sankofa. Sankofa is represented by a bird in flight with its head turned backwards and an egg in its mouth. This powerful symbol encapsulates the understanding that it is imperative to actively look backwards to retrieve desired knowledge, experiences, and lessons of the past to move forward wisely and build a prosperous future.

The Three Phases of the A3IG Framework

The A3IG Framework operates through three interconnected phases, each building upon the previous to ensure a comprehensive and community-grounded approach to African AI governance in Africa, as captured in Fig. 2.1.

Phase 1: Recollection and Historical Interrogation

This initial phase focuses on understanding the historical context and experiences of a given community or nation regarding the challenge that AI aims to address. It emphasises the importance of not assuming ignorance on the part of community members and instead valuing their historical knowledge and experiences. Key questions to be addressed in this phase include:

- What is the historical relationship the community has with the challenge?
- What historical solutions has the community applied to the problem?
- What are the historical and present-day aspirations of the community in relation to the problem?

Researchers and developers should conduct thorough research and engage in meaningful discussions with community members to comprehensively understand the problem's historical context and previous solution attempts.

Example: *Historical Interrogation Biometrics*

In the context of biometric identification in Africa, Recollection and Historical Interrogation reveal that many African nations have been grappling with challenges such as ghost workers in government payrolls and inefficient public service delivery (Toesland, 2021). Additionally, African nations have faced difficulties and institutional negotiations accompanying the desire to develop a centralised population data infrastructure (Thiel, 2020). The aspirations of African communities and governments in relation to this challenge are centred around improving data security, preventing fraud, and providing reliable identification to citizens.

Phase 2: Recontextualization and Modern Analysis

Building upon the historical understanding gained in Phase 1, this phase applies a contemporary perspective to the set of experiences and knowledge gathered. It aims to bridge the gap between historical solutions and modern technological possibilities. Key considerations in this phase include:

- How does the problem manifest uniquely in the present day?
- What modern factors influence the effectiveness of historical solutions?
- How can AI technologies complement or enhance traditional approaches to the problem?

This phase critically analyses how historical solutions can be adapted or reimagined using AI while respecting cultural values and community preferences.

Example: *Modern Analysis of Biometrics*

In the modern context, the identification challenge has evolved, influenced by factors such as the COVID-19 pandemic and technological advancements. The pandemic necessitated contactless solutions, leading to innovations like facial recognition systems replacing fingerprint IDs to reduce virus transmission. The effectiveness of historical solutions, such as manual audits, has been surpassed by biometric systems that can more efficiently identify issues like ghost workers.

Phase 3: Development and Application

The final phase focuses on the practical development and implementation of AI solutions, which is informed by the insights gained from the previous two phases. This phase emphasises co-creation with community members and iterative development to ensure the AI solution aligns with community needs and values (Bourgeois et al., 2024).

Key aspects of this phase include:

- Collaborative design of policy and technology with community involvement.
- Pilot testing and iterative refinement based on community feedback.

- Development of locally relevant metrics for assessing policy effectiveness.
- Establishment of governance structures that incorporate indigenous oversight mechanisms and governance processes.

Throughout this phase, developers, policymakers, and community members should continuously dialogue to ensure that AI development remains aligned with community needs and respects cultural norms.

Example: *Development and Application of AI and Biometrics*

AI technologies are now complementing traditional approaches in various ways: for instance, in Kenya,'Robodocs' uses facial recognition to establish unique patient records, enhancing healthcare delivery. In Togo, the government leveraged its biometric electoral register to provide targeted cash transfers during COVID-19 lockdowns, demonstrating how AI can enhance social welfare programs. These examples show how AI and biometrics are being adapted to address longstanding challenges in identification and service delivery while responding to new, uniquely modern problems like contactless interactions during a pandemic.

By following these three interconnected phases, the A3IG Framework aims to create AI governance structures and solutions that are both technologically advanced, culturally appropriate, and socially beneficial. This approach ensures that AI development in Africa is grounded in historical wisdom, responsive to modern challenges, and aligned with the goals of African communities. Our A3IG framework seeks to be dynamic and adaptable in various environments; we propose four foundational aspects to consider when applying the framework.

An Argument for Indigenous Governmental Structures in AI Governance

Indigenous governance systems have consistently been overlooked for their validity and effectiveness in providing substantive structure and guidance to communities on both local and national levels (Wane et al., 2022). This oversight often comes in tandem with a hyper-fixation of Western governance structures, which are frequently perceived as more forward-thinking and modern. However, this perception ignores the long history of indigenous governments in effectively addressing the consistent needs of local and national communities (Noyoo & Campus, 2014).

Historical Context and Misconceptions

The marginalisation of Indigenous governance systems can be traced back to colonial periods when European powers systematically undermined and replaced traditional African governance structures. This historical context has led to several persistent misconceptions:

- Perceived primitiveness: Indigenous systems are often wrongly characterised as primitive or outdated, ignoring their sophisticated mechanisms for conflict resolution, resource management, and social cohesion (Eneyew & Ayalew, 2023).
- Lack of scalability: Despite evidence to the contrary, there is a common misconception that Indigenous governance models cannot scale to address the complexities of modern nation-states (Adjaye, 1985).

Strengths of Indigenous Governance Systems

Contrary to these misconceptions, Indigenous governance systems possess several strengths that make them particularly relevant in the contemporary context:

- *Holistic approach*: Many Indigenous systems take a holistic view of governance, integrating environmental, social, and spiritual considerations in decision-making processes (Basheka & Auriacombe, 2020). These broader perspectives are critical when developing technology to fundamentally change human-to-human and human-to-nature interactions (Zimmerman et al., 2023). Indigenous African governance systems are primed to be leaders in this regard.
- *Consensus-building*: Indigenous governance often emphasises consensus-building (Muo et al., 2012; Murithi, 2006; Onuoha, 2011) and inclusive decision-making, which can lead to more stable and widely accepted policies that are grounded in the best interests of the community rather than a select few. This methodology is crucial to establishing a set of AI policies and an overall AI Governance system that considers multi-faceted approaches to development grounded in the community's needs.

- *Participatory AI development*: The emphasis on community participation in many indigenous systems could inspire more inclusive approaches to AI development and deployment (Birhane et al., 2022; Bondi et al., 2021; Sahota, 2010). At a time when Africa is at a data privacy, data ownership, and worker rights crossroad, Indigenous African governance values centred on family/community and collective ownership can be beneficial in shaping policies in AI Governance.
- *Complementary Leadership*: Indigenous African governance structures often feature complementary leadership models, involving both men and women in co-leadership roles, offering a valuable paradigm for AI governance. Exemplified in systems like the dual-gender political organisations of the Akan (Amenyedzi, 2021; Annan, 2020; Baah-Ennumh et al., 2005; Stoeltje, 1997) and Yoruba (Adeboye, 2005; Afolabi & Olasupo, 2008; Falola, 1995) peoples, these models can significantly enhance AI governance by ensuring the integration of diverse viewpoints into AI policy decisions, thereby helping to mitigate gender-based biases in AI systems. Just as the Akan Governance structure maintains the roles of Ohene (male) and Ohemaa (female) in leadership, AI development teams and governance bodies should enforce mandatory roles for males and females at each level of leadership. This approach can lead to more comprehensive and nuanced decision-making processes, crucial for addressing AI technologies' complex ethical and societal implications. By adopting this indigenous approach to shared leadership, AI governance in Africa can become more inclusive, comprehensive, and culturally appropriate, not only addressing gender representation but also tapping into the complementary strengths and perspectives that diverse leadership brings. This model is crucial for managing the far-reaching impacts of AI on society and aligns with deeply rooted African cultural practices, potentially increasing the acceptance and effectiveness of AI policies.

By recognising and integrating the strengths of Indigenous governance systems, African nations have the opportunity to develop AI governance frameworks that are not only technologically advanced but also culturally grounded and socially responsive. This approach could lead to more effective, ethical, and widely accepted AI policies across the continent.

Culture in AI Systems and Governance

Integral to the A3IG framework is the consideration of culture as a fundamental reality that must consistently be emphasised in technological development and governance. Culture directly impacts the internal and external dynamics of AI systems and how they exist in their deployed communities (Salaam et al., n.d.). Internally, a culture or worldview is developed in an AI system. According to Salaam et al. (n.d.), this internal culture is determined by four primary activation points: Values, Behavioural Patterns, Decision Algorithms, and Experiences. This can manifest in various ways, from the selection of training data to the definition of fairness metrics and the prioritisation of certain outcomes over others. For instance, an AI system developed in a culture that values individual privacy may have different data handling protocols compared to one developed in a culture that prioritises communal knowledge sharing.

Externally, culture is crucial in how AI systems are perceived, adopted, and integrated into society. The effectiveness and acceptability of AI solutions are deeply intertwined with the cultural context of the communities they serve. This includes considerations such as language, societal relationships, traditional practices, and local knowledge systems. For example, an AI-driven healthcare solution might need to account for traditional healing practices (World Health Organization, 2023) to be fully effective and accepted in certain African communities. Moreover, the governance structures and policies surrounding AI must be culturally attuned to ensure they resonate with local values and practices. This could involve incorporating traditional decision-making processes into AI governance frameworks or ensuring that ethical guidelines for AI align with indigenous moral philosophies. By placing culture at the forefront of AI development and governance, the A3IG framework aims to create AI systems that are not only technically proficient but also culturally relevant, ethically aligned, and socially beneficial to African communities.

The Intersection of AI and Indigenous African Knowledge Systems

The integration of AI with Indigenous African Knowledge Systems (IAKS) represents a crucial frontier in the development of culturally appropriate and effective AI solutions for Africa. IAKS encompasses a wide range of traditional practices, beliefs, and knowledge accumulated over generations, guiding African communities in areas such as agriculture, healthcare, environmental management, and social organisation. AI systems can benefit significantly from incorporating IAKS in several ways. Firstly, IAKS can provide rich, contextual data that may not be captured in conventional datasets, enhancing the accuracy and relevance of AI models. For instance, traditional weather prediction methods could be integrated with AI-driven climate models to improve local forecasting. Secondly, the holistic and interconnected worldview often found in IAKS can inspire more comprehensive AI systems that consider the broader implications of their actions on communities and ecosystems. Conversely, AI can help preserve and propagate IAKS by digitising oral traditions, creating accessible traditional knowledge databases, and developing AI-powered translation tools for indigenous languages. This symbiotic relationship between AI and IAKS can lead to innovative solutions that are both technologically advanced and culturally rooted. However, this intersection also presents challenges, such as the risk of misappropriation or misinterpretation of indigenous knowledge. It is crucial to develop ethical frameworks and protocols for the respectful integration of IAKS into AI systems, ensuring that Indigenous communities maintain ownership and control over their knowledge. By carefully navigating this intersection, AI development in Africa can create unique, culturally resonant technologies that address local needs while preserving and celebrating indigenous wisdom.

It is crucial to ensure that the development of AI systems does not overshadow or supplant IAKS, which are deeply rooted in the intergenerational transmission of wisdom and experiences. In Indigenous cultural contexts, societal development is fundamentally based on relationships—both between humans and between humans and nature. Therefore, AI systems should be designed and implemented not to replace these essential aspects of indigenous societies but rather to support and enhance them. The goal should be to create AI technologies that complement and reinforce the existing knowledge structures and relational foundations of Indigenous communities rather than disrupting or superseding them.

African AI Development Does Not Need to Look Like Other People's AI Development

The A3IG framework emphasises that AI development in Africa should not be a mere replication of models and approaches used in other parts of the world. Instead, it should be a unique process that reflects the continent's diverse cultural, social, and economic realities. This principle is crucial for creating AI systems that are truly beneficial and sustainable in the African context.

African AI development can differentiate itself in several ways. Firstly, it can prioritise solving uniquely African challenges, such as improving agricultural yields in diverse climatic conditions or developing healthcare solutions for underserved rural areas. Secondly, it can incorporate African philosophical concepts, such as Ubuntu (human interconnectedness), into the ethical frameworks guiding AI development and deployment. Moreover, the development process itself can be structured differently. Instead of relying solely on top-down, tech-centric approaches, African AI development can embrace more participatory methods that involve local communities from the outset. This could include co-design sessions with traditional leaders, integrating local languages and communication styles into user interfaces, and developing AI systems that complement rather than replace existing social structures.

African AI development can also pioneer new data collection and usage approaches that respect communal ownership of information and prioritise data sovereignty. This might involve developing decentralised AI systems that keep data within local communities or creating new models for fair data sharing and compensation. By charting its own course in AI development, Africa can create technologies that are effective, culturally appropriate, ethically sound, and truly representative of African values and aspirations. This unique approach can contribute valuable perspectives to the global AI community, potentially leading to more diverse and inclusive AI technologies worldwide.

Conclusion and Policy Implications

The African governance literature has consistently highlighted the importance of context in the study and practice of public policy (Onyango, 2022). For African states, this requires (1) embracing Indigenous knowledge systems (Ayana et al., 2024), (2) contending with the history of colonisation across the continent, and (3) addressing the persistent global, regional, and racial inequities that are exacerbated in times of technological advances (Birhane, 2020). Subsequently, AI governance in Africa need not be viewed in terms of "catch-up" to any universal standard. Instead, this chapter echoes calls for a "paradigm shift in the conception and implementation of AI governance" (Ayana et al., 2024; Hanson, 2023) in favour of empowering portrayals of historically grounded, culturally situated African AI governance models.

In this chapter, we have outlined an AI governance framework capable of being adapted to various African state contexts as a mechanism for socio-technical empowerment and uplift. The A3IG framework's flexible design is intentional. While the organising tenets of the framework remain the same (i.e., Phases 1–3), the parameters of the governance model may require fine-tuning to meet the unique needs of the locales they aim to serve. This framework invites African governments to combat the "enduring hegemony of Northern theory" that has historically permeated African public policy and governance systems (Tapscott, 2022); by having them embrace an emancipatory form of decolonisation (Mbembe, 2015), whereby African identity is centred and prioritised contributing to a more inclusive AI governance landscape. Ultimately, by leveraging participatory governance techniques paired with indigenous knowledge systems, the A3IG framework supports the responsible design, development, adoption, and deployment of AI technologies grounded in local environmental and sociocultural contexts.

However, three things need to be true to effectively implement this framework: (1) policymakers will need access to deep expertise in AI capabilities and indigenous knowledge systems. Hiring and retaining this expertise is paramount. (2) AI technologies should be based on local infrastructure and materials as much as possible. Investment in broad local science and technology capacity building is paramount; (3) multiple points of connection (i.e., partnerships, agreements, coordination activities) among institutions and actors should be established to promote a reversible and interactive learning process between Indigenous knowledge and AI systems. These backbone characteristics will support the fluid exchange of information and collaboration, which are capable of keeping pace with rapid AI technological advancements.

It is against this backdrop that we invite avenues for future research to entail exploring challenges and opportunities in AI governance undertaken by specific African states via case studies and comparative research designs examining the extent to which IAKS principles are already being employed across African AI governance frameworks. By applying principles from African cultural frameworks, such as the complimentary leadership structures of Indigenous Akan states, African countries can ensure that AI systems reflect local values, reduce anti-African and anti-Black biases, and are tailored to the needs of their populations. Furthermore, we argue that AI development and innovation in Africa need not follow the patterns established by Western or Eastern nations; instead, it should be based on African societies' unique needs, desires, and cultural contexts. Through this approach, Africa can develop a distinct, forward-thinking, pan-African AI governance model that is not reactionary but anticipatory, ensuring sustainable and culturally contextualised AI systems.

References

Adeboye, O. (2005). Breaking through gender barriers: Religion and female leadership in Nigeria. *Journal of History and Diplomatic Studies, 2*(2), 142–150.

Adeniran, A. (2024, September 16). *Developing an effective data governance framework to deliver African digital potentials*. Brookings. https://www.brookings.edu/articles/developing-an-effective-data-governance-framework-to-deliver-african-digital-potentials/

Adjaye, J. K. (1985). Indigenous African diplomacy: An Asante case study. *The International Journal of African Historical Studies, 18*(3), 487–503.

Afolabi, M. M., & Olasupo, F. (2008). *The female gender in traditional leadership in Nigeria: A socio-cultural perspective*. Engendering Leadership Through Research and Practice Conference Proceedings, Vol. 21, p. 8. Perth.

Akgun, S., & Greenhow, C. (2022). Artificial intelligence in education: Addressing ethical challenges in K-12 settings. *AI and Ethics, 2*(3), 431–440.

Al-Zahrani, A. M., & Alasmari, T. M. (2024). Exploring the impact of artificial intelligence on higher education: The dynamics of ethical, social, and educational implications. *Humanities and Social Sciences Communications, 11*(1), 1–12.

Amenyedzi, S. B. (2021). Leadership roles for indigenous Ghanaian women: The case of Prof Jane Naana Opoku Agyemang as vice-presidential candidate for the national democratic congress (NDC). *African Thought: A Journal of Afro-Centric Knowledge, 1*(se1), 169–191.

Anantrasirichai, N., & Bull, D. (2022). Artificial intelligence in the creative industries: A review. *Artificial Intelligence Review, 55*(1), 589–656.

Annan, N. (2020). Women and political leadership in Africa. In *Pathways into the political arena: The perspectives of global women leaders* (pp. 87–144). Information Age Publishing.

Asiegbu, C., & Okolo, C. T. (2024). *How AI is impacting policy processes and outcomes in Africa*. Brookings.

Ayana, G., Dese, K., Daba Nemomssa, H., Habtamu, B., Mellado, B., Badu, K., Yamba, E., Faye, S. L., Ondua, M., Nsagha, D., et al. (2024). Decolonizing global AI governance: Assessment of the state of decolonized AI governance in sub-Saharan Africa. *Royal Society Open Science, 11*(8), 231994.

Baah-Ennumh, T., Owusu, S., & Kokor, J. (2005). Participation of women in local governance in Ghana: A case study of Ashanti region. *Journal of Science and Technology (Ghana), 25*(1), 95–107.

Basheka, B., & Auriacombe, C. (2020). Contextualising the regeneration of Africa's indigenous governance and management systems and practices. *Administratio Publica, 28*(3), 223–243.

Birhane, A. (2020). Algorithmic colonization of Africa. *Scripted, 17*, 389.

Birhane, A., Isaac, W., Prabhakaran, V., Diaz, M., Elish, M. C., Gabriel, I., & Mohamed, S. (2022). *Power to the people? Opportunities and challenges for participatory AI*. Proceedings of the 2nd ACM Conference on Equity and Access in Algorithms, Mechanisms, and Optimization, pp. 1–8.

Bondi, E., Xu, L., Acosta-Navas, D., & Killian, J. A. (2021). *Envisioning communities: A participatory approach towards AI for social good*. Proceedings of the 2021 AAAI/ACM Conference on AI, Ethics, and Society, pp. 425–436.

Bourgeois, R., Karuri-Sebina, G., & Feukeu, K. E. (2024). The future as a public good: Decolonising the future through anticipatory participatory action research. *Foresight, 26*(4), 533–549.

Data Guidance. (2024, September 23). *Africa: Malabo Convention—A pan-African strategy on data protection and cybersecurity*. https://www.dataguidance.com/opinion/africa-malabo-convention-pan-african-strategy-data

Diallo, K., Smith, J., Okolo, C. T., Nyamwaya, D., Kgomo, J., & Ngamita, R. (2024). *Case studies of AI policy development in Africa*. arXiv. https://arxiv.org/abs/2403.14662

Effoduh, J. O. (n.d.). *7 ways that African states are legitimizing artificial intelligence*. Open AIR. https://openair.africa/7-ways-that-african-states-are-legitimizing-artificial-intelligence

Eneyew, B. G., & Ayalew, M. (2023). The role and challenges of indigenous conflict resolution mechanism: The case of aboled in Borena Woreda, northeast Ethiopia. *Heliyon, 9*(6).

Falola, T. (1995). Gender, business, and space control: Yoruba market women and power. In *Gender in cross-cultural perspective* (pp. 246–261). Routledge.

Hanson, K. T. (2023). Technological leapfrogging and innovation: Re-imagining evaluation approaches and practice in Africa. In *Public policy and technological transformations in Africa: Nurturing policy entrepreneurship, policy tools and citizen participation* (pp. 67–84). Palgrave Macmillan.

Hlaka, T. (2024, September 17). *Advancing data governance in Africa*. MERL Tech. https://merltech.org/advancing-data-governance-in-africa/

Khumalo, N. B., & Baloyi, C. (2017). African indigenous knowledge: An underutilized and neglected resource for development. *Library Philosophy and Practice, 1663*, 1–15.

Mbembe, A. (2015). *Decolonizing knowledge and the question of the archive.*

Mergel, I., Dickinson, H., Stenvall, J., & Gasco, M. (2024). Implementing AI in the public sector. *Public Management Review*, 1–14.

Muo, I., Oghojafor, B., et al. (2012). Ohazurume: The philosophy and practice of decision making and consensus building among the Ndigbo of Nigeria. *American Journal of Business and Management, 1*(3), 154–161.

Murithi, T. (2006). African approaches to building peace and social solidarity. *African Journal on Conflict Resolution, 6*(2), 9–33.

Noyoo, N., & Campus, K. (2014). *Indigenous systems of governance and post-colonial Africa: The case of Barotseland.* Conference on African Indigenous Knowledge Systems, pp. 8–9. Indaba Hotel, Fourways, Johannesburg.

Olaopa, O. R., & Ayodele, O. A. (2022). Building on the strengths of African indigenous knowledge and innovation (AIK&I) for sustainable development in Africa. *African Journal of Science, Technology, Innovation and Development, 14*(5), 1313–1326.

Ondiek, J. O., & Onyango, G. (2023). Strengthening citizen agencies in policymaking through social media. In *Public policy and technological transformations in Africa: Nurturing policy entrepreneurship, policy tools and citizen participation* (pp. 257–278). Palgrave Macmillan.

Onuoha, B. (2011). Power, conflict and consensus building in Africa: Ideology revisited. *African Journal on Conflict Resolution, 11*(2), 8–31.

Onyango, G. (2022). *A public policy approach to governance in Africa.* Timothy M. Shaw, PhD, Faculty Fellow, Department of Conflict Resolution, Human Security, and Global Governance; McCormack Graduate School, USA, 1.

Rajpurkar, P., Chen, E., Banerjee, O., & Topol, E. J. (2022). AI in health and medicine. *Nature Medicine, 28*(1), 31–38.

Sahota, P. C. (2010). *Community-based participatory research in American Indian and Alaska Native communities*. NCAI Policy Research Center.

Salaam, C., Hagos, D., & Rawat, D. (n.d.). *Culture in artificial intelligence.* Unpublished manuscript.

Scherer, M. U. (2015). Regulating artificial intelligence systems: Risks, challenges, competencies, and strategies. *Harvard Journal of Law & Technology, 29*, 353.

Soumonni, O., & Monroe-White, T. (n.d.). *Endogenous innovation and digital inclusion: A global African perspective.* Unpublished manuscript.

Stoeltje, B. J. (1997). Asante queen mothers: A study in female authority. *Annals of the New York Academy of Sciences, 810*(1), 41–71.

Tapscott, C. (2022). Researching and teaching public policy and governance in Africa. In *Routledge handbook of public policy in Africa* (pp. 34–45). Routledge.

Technology Review. (2024, October 1). Africa's push to regulate AI starts now. https://www.technologyreview.com/2024/03/15/1089844/africa-ai-artificial-intelligence-regulation-au-policy/

Thiel, A. (2020). Biometric identification technologies and the Ghanaian 'data revolution.' *The Journal of Modern African Studies, 58*(1), 115–136.

Toesland, F. (2021). African countries embracing biometrics, digital IDs. *African Renewal*.

UNESCO. (2018). *UNESCO policy on engaging with indigenous peoples*.

Wane, N. N., Opondo, W., Alam, S., Kipkosgei, E., & Tarus, I. (2022). Indigenous governance in Africa: A decolonial dialogue. In *Decolonizing and indigenizing visions of educational leadership* (pp. 151–173). Emerald.

World Health Organization. (2023). *Traditional medicine has a long history of contributing to conventional medicine and continues to hold promise*. World Health Organization [Internet] [cited 25 Feb 2024]. Available: https://www.who.int/news-room/feature-stories/detail/traditional-medicine-has-a-long-history-of-contributing-to-conventional-medicine-and-continues-to-hold-promise

Zaidan, E., & Ibrahim, I. A. (2024). AI governance in a complex and rapidly changing regulatory landscape: A global perspective. *Humanities and Social Sciences Communications, 11*(1), 1–18.

Zimmerman, A., Janhonen, J., & Beer, E. (2023). Human/AI relationships: Challenges, downsides, and impacts on human/human relationships. *AI and Ethics, 4*, 1555–1567.

CHAPTER 3

Shaping a Responsible AI Future: Lessons from South Africa's Civic Technology Community

Gabriella Razzano

Introduction

How you build things matters, and designing Artificial Intelligence (AI) systems is no exception. Many speculative futures are being constructed in political and academic narratives about Artificial Intelligence (AI) in Africa. These futures range from the optimistic to the dystopian, depending largely on the incentives of those driving the narratives. One understated voice in this cacophony, largely because it is an understated voice in the manner it sits outside both academic and policy mainstreams, is the perspective of civic and social impact technologists—who are in fact key in designing AI systems that are tailored to the context of implementation. Civic technologists in Africa, as elsewhere, have significant

G. Razzano (✉)
OpenUp, Cape Town, South Africa
e-mail: gabriella@openup.org.za

University of Witwatersrand, Johannesburg, South Africa

G. Onyango (ed.), *Designing Artificial Intelligence for Public Policy and Governance in Africa*, Studies in National Governance and Emerging Technologies, https://doi.org/10.1007/978-3-031-83445-5_3

experience in developing social impact innovations that can benefit discussions on AI's future and, therefore, have experience across the gamut of design, implementation, and impact of technologies. Practical technical experience developing for social impact is a very particular learning curve. Using the case study of a South African civic technology project, Vulekamali, this Chapter will consider specific and implementable lessons for the future of AI development. To consider perspectives on civic technology for informing a responsible AI future, the chapter will first outline the key concepts of AI and civic technology, and briefly introduce the case study example that will be used to inform the rest of the Chapter. It will then introduce the African AI context from which the case study emerges. The case study will then be unpacked to outline key lessons from the civic technology experience for AI governance, development design practice, and then for collaborative design models. Finally, foundational issues of importance that were not extracted from the case study will be highlighted briefly (which also touches on some future visions for civic technology and AI) before high-level conclusions are outlined.

Understanding Artificial Intelligence and Civic Technologies

There are a variety of definitions of AI, but we will utilise one which identifies AI as software or hardware systems:

> [...] designed by humans that, given a complex goal, act in the physical or digital dimension by perceiving their environment through data acquisition, interpreting the collected structured or unstructured data, reasoning on the knowledge, or processing the information derived from this data and deciding the best action(s) to take to achieve the given goal. AI systems can either use symbolic rules or learn a numeric model, and they can also adapt their behaviour by analysing how the environment is affected by their previous actions. (High-Level Expert Group on Artificial Intelligence, 2019)

It is essential to appreciate that AI refers currently to a suite of technologies in the pursuit of a general AI—and that, whilst generative AI and natural language processing are, of course, a topical functional form, other areas of AI function that dominate literature include:

- Search and optimisation (e.g., Bland, 2024),
- Fuzzy systems (e.g., Gu et al., 2023),
- Planning and decision-making (e.g., Neumann et al., 2024),
- Natural language processing and knowledge representation (e.g., Liu et al., 2023),
- Computer Vision (e.g., Ayman & Fakhr, 2023),
- Machine learning (e.g., Mbunge & Batani, 2023), and
- Probabilistic reasoning and neuralnetworks (Stahl, 2021).

These definitions provide (some) clarity on the technical and functional parameters of AI. Yet, as will be unpacked in the chapter, the very definition of AI should also be an aspect of reinventing AI's future. As already demonstrated by previous chapters in this volume, values, ethics, and human-centred (rather than techno-centred) elements should be embedded into our understanding of AI designs or systems in African public policy and governance (Eke et al., 2023). It is critical to integrate an understanding of how technical capabilities intersect with ethical principles and societal values. An expanded definition should emphasise that AI is not just a technological tool but a socio-technical system that operates within a complex web of human values, cultural norms, and ethical considerations (Sartori & Theodorou, 2022). Understanding it as a socio-technical system means emphasising its social origins (learning from social systems and environments) and social impacts, an issue that will become increasingly relevant as this discussion considers the ultimate objectives that should define AI development.

There is no clear definition of Civic Technologies. However, it is a concept used to describe technologies concerned with leveraging social accountability or citizen engagement in governance processes (Peixoto et al., 2022). Civic technologies are primarily anchored in promoting citizen-centric engagement in order to drive a more transparent, open and collaborative public governance process (Onyango, 2023). According to the World Bank, civic technologies "broadly refers to the use of digital technologies to support a range of citizen engagement processes. From allowing individuals to report problems to local government to enable the crowdsourcing of national legislation, civic tech aims to promote better policies and services – whilst contributing to more inclusive democratic institutions" (Peixoto et al., 2022).

This summation is fairly consistent with the views proposed by the Civic Tech Field Guide (Stempeck, 2018), and the Civic Tech Innovation Network (CTIN)—though the CTIN ordinarily seeks to de-emphasise technology to exist as a means for achieving political and social goals around citizen empowerment. It is by actioning its own definition of civic technology that has led CTIN to a mission that:

> [...] supports its community towards the growth, development, and effective use of appropriate digital technologies and methodologies in connecting government and citizens, in public participation, in transparency and accountability and in delivering public services. (Civic Tech Innovation Network, n.d.)

Understanding the breadth of civic technology is important for understanding the baseline of its experience in unpacking the case study to come. There are typical methods and pursuits in civic technology practices, though these may not be definitional. In the African landscape, for instance, open data platforms, data sharing and data-driven solutions are strongly represented solutions, demonstrating the transparency and accountability ambitions of much of civic technology (Civic Tech Innovation Network, 2023a). In terms of adopted methods, significant amounts of the interventions are open source (and also use open-source solutions), with human-centred design often being a feature (Civic Tech Innovation Network, 2023a). Shaping a more responsible AI for the future needs to be integrated into structures and norms already consolidated within civic technologies. This would apply to AI technologies in a way that would fit the purpose and context of the application, making it more responsible. The next section explores how this might be done, using the case of Vulekamali in South Africa.

The Vulekamali Case Study

On 20 February 2018, Vulekamali—the South African government's online open budget portal—was launched in Parliament (OpenUp & South Africa National Treasury, 2017). OpenUp (a social impact technology non-profit organisation based in Cape Town) developed this open data platform after being awarded a tender by the National Treasury. However, it has been pursued through a relatively revolutionary development process. Vulekamali is a demonstration of multi-stakeholder development between the National Treasury of South Africa, OpenUp and Imali Yethu—which is an open coalition of civil society organisations driven by an interest in promoting budget transparency and public participation. All three stakeholders engaged in setting development priorities and raising community awareness around the portal. The engagement between the stakeholders was scheduled and regular and based on agile methodologies, which involve the development of a technology project management methodology that uses an iterative and flexible approach Beck et al. (2001). Scrum is a specific type of agile development that focuses on short, time-boxed sprints. The Vulekamali Phase 1 and Phase 2 development involved practically bi-weekly sprint planning and monthly Operational Working Group meetings.

Vulekamali is open source and provides open access to significant amounts of data. To drive transparency and accountability, the site boasts an organised information structure to help with navigation. It also strongly emphasises educational resources: it features a "Learning" section with videos, dataset guides, resources, a glossary, and Frequently Asked Questions. These tools are chiefly aimed at enhancing user understanding of the budget process and data. The portal is also acknowledged as an example of open data technologies. Vulekamali was awarded the 17th Public Sector Innovation Award of 2019 under the Innovations Enhancing 4IR Solutions Category (Matshediso, 2020). Since its launch (and up to February 2023), it has seen almost a quarter of a million users and almost half a million page views in 204,700 sessions. The Vulekamali CKAN—which is its open data store—provides access to 2409 open datasets (and users have an average session duration of an hour on the CKAN). Importantly, there are indications that the datastore is being accessed by civil society, government, and private sector users. It provides data whilst also being used as a platform by the National Treasury to drive public participation in the budget process itself (Kasa, 2021). To ensure effective data accessibility and explainability, the platform can be accessed in English, Afrikaans, isiZulu, isiXhosa, and Sesotho. Studies have shown the critical essence of local languages in enabling appropriate interpretations of digital data and developing more localised frames of the policy problem. In other words, the digitalisation process grounded in a language that policymakers properly understand is essential in designing public innovations like Vulekamali (see Onyango & Ondiek, 2022). The next section presents the AI context in Africa before a discussion that links it to the Vulekamali project.

The African AI Context

There is much discussion about the potential of AI in Africa for both economic and social development, with the AU-NEPAD stating, for instance, that there is "...overwhelming evidence that AI applications have the potential to dramatically transform the socio-economic development of African countries as well as globally" (African Union Development Agency, 2021). Yet, a recent report from McKinsey looking only to estimate the economic gains from just generative AI stated that whilst generative AI has the potential to generate $2.6 trillion to $4.4 trillion in value across industries, most of that value will accrue to already highly industrialised nations (Chui et al., 2023). Others cite an optimistic view that Africa has the "potential to build a $1.5 trillion AI economy". There have been some notable African acquisitions, with AI-focused enterprise solutions company InstaDeep being acquired for $682 million in January 2023 (Malik, 2023). Optimism is good, but it is worth reflecting that digital beneficiation is still generally low in Africa. Most African governments remain suspicious of fully leveraging advanced technologies in governance processes, or they tend to adopt them in some sectors more than others, depending on the administration's priority (Onyango, 2023). Also, despite several initiatives to enhance digital opportunities, such as the creation of online jobs, e-commerce and digital financial instruments, few Africans are able to participate actively in the digital economy, given restraints that stem from digital inequalities (Razzano et al., 2020). There are (only) 30 AI developer communities in Africa and around 2400 AI organisations operating across the region (Malik, 2023). Nevertheless, conversations on the governance and regulation of AI are well underway on the continent. African Union policy and strategy documents are already taking proactive positions on regulation:

> It is critical to have policies and regulatory frameworks in place that promotes productive AI harnessing by encouraging innovation and investment. AU should encourage African governments to take a deliberate and proactive approach, to implement supportive regulation, policies, and initiatives. There are several areas relevant to the development of AI-enabled robust digital economies, where policymakers should focus. (African Union Development Agency, 2021)

Internationally, there is movement in both statutory, regulatory and policy interest in AI. The European Union's Parliament has passed an

AI Act, 2021 (EU AI Act, 2023)—though its implementation is still not finalised (Lomas, 2023). The British government in 2023 hosted an "AI Safety Summit", and the US President Biden issued an executive order on "Safe, Secure and Trustworthy Artificial Intelligence" (Amin et al., 2023). Many other activities and reviews are still being conducted across the globe. However, Africa has its own patterns of development and progress in the AI governance area.

The African AI Observatory is mapping progress on AI policy across the region. In so doing, it has catalogued and mapped 489 policy and governance instruments with direct AI references from the continent, as well as 928 instruments with indirect references, which refer to related issues on data governance, with the majority of the direct instruments being passed since 2016. It is worth reflecting on the fact that, whilst 14% of those are on strategy and coordination, a far more significant pool of 40% deal with privacy & security (African AI Observatory, 2024). Whilst on some levels this emphasis may not be surprising—risks and harm are often a significant motivator for the passage of statute and regulation—it must be questioned in the context of the actual state of AI development. As already shown in *this chapter* above, a frequent clarion call is to try and ensure enabling regulation and statute for industry, and given the state of Africa's current digital economy, this must surely be a priority to avoid data extractivism, and digital colonialism (i.e. the decentralised extraction and control of data from citizens, with or without their explicit consent, that is also supported by extracted economic value) (Hicks, 2019).

Thinking about the regulation in context, it is worth noting:

> From certain perspectives, it can be argued that there is a high level of diversity in AI deployment on the African continent. ... [O]ne aspect of diversity is in the types of problems that are being addressed by AI. From financial inclusion to combatting cultural and linguistic marginalisation, AI innovations aim at many aspects of African society, economy, and government. Another form of diversity is in the people implementing AI solutions, and in this regard, women's relatively high level of participation in African entrepreneurship is encouraging. Diversity of location is also noteworthy-whilst AI is clearly developing in countries that are well known as technology hubs (e.g., Kenya, Nigeria, and South Africa), there are also significant AI-focused activities in countries that are less frequently recognised for cutting-edge digital adoption (e.g., Uganda and Ethiopia). In contrast, government policy is an area where there is less diversity, as

> the vast majority of African countries lack a dedicated AI policy instrument. (Gwagwa et al., 2020)

However, an important thing to highlight in the context of calls for regulation is the inherent challenges of both statutory and regulatory processes in the context of technology. This is because law has a 'pacing problem', which refers to the notion that technological innovation is increasingly outpacing the ability of laws and regulations to keep up (Thierer, 2018). As Larry Downes noted: "[T] echnology changes exponentially, but social, economic, and legal systems change incrementally" (Thierer, 2018). The Collingridge Paradox continues these thoughts to explain that efforts of law to influence or control the further development of technology face a "double bind": an information problem (because in emerging technologies, the real impacts can't yet be wholly predicted), and a power problem: because control or change is difficult when the technology has become entrenched before a regulation or law is in place (Petit, 2017). This does not mean AI governance should not be pursued; rather, it is a reality—similar to the reality of the state of AI development in Africa—that should inform strategy.

Civic Tech Lessons for AI Governance

The problem of lagging AI governance needs innovators and policymakers to consider other and more immediate opportunities. Imagining collaborative technology development is an opportunity to rethink the development process and the bureaucratic process as well. Contracts and agreements are an opportunity to advance standards and realities that law and regulation may not yet be able to oblige. When the National Treasury of South Africa circulated its second tender for the Vulekamali platform, following the first phase of development, they expressly required both agile development as the development method and extensive citizen engagement as a part of the essential criteria (National Treasury, 2022). The procurement process—and contractual relationships—are an opportunity to entrench progressive processes and other elements for driving AI ethics, and the experience of collaborative processes in the first phase informed the tender construction of the second, reflecting on learnings. Frequently, policy documents advance recommendations within AI development of privacy and transparency by design (Razzano et al., 2020). Yet, there is seldom any discussion of not just how private companies might build ethics into their products, but also how the public sector might do so as well. The procurement process can potentially be a mechanism for embedding values and standards, even where legal obligations don't yet exist.

As can be seen, entrenching values and ethics is an intrinsic part of civic technology development. This should extend to AI development. Stahl has suggested that, in order to make the entrenchment of ethics possible, the very purpose of AI development should be the pursuit of "human flourishing" (Stahl, 2021). As Dignum notes:

> Responsible Artificial Intelligence is about human responsibility for the development of intelligent systems along fundamental human principles and values, to ensure human flourishing and well-being in a sustainable world. (Stahl, 2021)

Because civic technology is already driven by value-centred development, responsible AI development can be viewed as intrinsic to its pursuits (the practice of this will be expanded upon later). This should not be diminished as a lesson: being clear about the objectives of development is important for establishing shared goals amongst all stakeholders and for establishing from inception the metrics that will be used to define success of these technology projects. In embedding responsible technological development into an organisation, there is a significant governance lesson at the institutional level that can be well-extracted to the national level: That is, sound AI governance relies first and foremost on sound data governance (and governance practice). The priority should be instituting sound data processing governance as a necessary (but not sufficient) regulatory measure for supporting good AI (Razzano, 2021). Many of the traditional risks and harms discussed in relation to AI—such as black box decision-making and bias—are foundationally a data problem. Many of the solutions to AI risks and harms—such as data security and accountability for decisions—rely on sound data practices for their actual implementation. Data cannot be secured if it is not effectively managed.

Civic Tech Lessons for Design Practice

Civic technology entities are already exploring the use of AI to enhance their work and looking to develop their own AI (i.e. having both internal and external AI ambitions) (Civic Tech Innovation Network, 2023b).

AI is seen as an opportunity to amplify outcomes concerning civic technologists' work streams, such as advancing urban planning, enhancing the functioning of different developed applications, or even advancing internal organisational efficiencies. Of particular interest are explorations for using AI to enhance democratic practice and public participation—and the optimistic associations between data-driven technologies and power diffusion (Savaget et al., 2019). What is vital in these accounts is the strongly associated link between advancing technologies coupled with open data and information ambitions for a holistic responsible AI agenda in the civic technology context. Components of civic technology's responsible social technology development history can have a role to play in informing the actual design practice of AI, as well. OpenUp and many other civic technology innovators have acknowledged user-centred design as a gold standard for design processes, particularly given its contribution to advancing the ultimate user experience whilst simultaneously allowing for user participation within the design process itself (Bosman, 2021). Yet, using these methods for social impact technologies requires a degree of adaptation from traditional commercial applications to consider community elements that impact an individual's lived experience (and are thus important for the realities of how a user might engage with technology) (Razzano, 2022). As noted:

> A challenge with an over-emphasis of the individual in a context of social change as an impact is that it too readily presumes total agency in an individual for adjusting behaviour or utilising tools for creating change. There are, of course, structural impediments to taking actions - and those structural impediments can only be understood if we take more of a community focus on the 'agent' as 'user'. (Razzano, 2022)

Once we begin realising that the design process is the implementation mechanism for responsibility and ethics in development, it becomes clear that this process will be central to the future of AI. Those developing AI will need to embed consideration of risk, in particular, into their actual practice (Razzano, 2023). Risk and harm are important aspects of AI governance, as conceptually they place the ultimate potential (negative) impact at the forefront of AI strategies (Frase & Daniels, 2023).

Ideally, consideration of risk will be practically embedded. Development processes can be complex, with multiple actors tasked with differing responsibilities and multi-stakeholder engagement being conducted simultaneously. If there is no process for embedding risk consideration, it is highly naive to expect it to arise organically and then result in changes in practice, even in situations where it might have been raised. When OpenUp began developing Vulekamali, which we implemented through agile methodologies (Beck et al., 2001), user-centred design was not just a process for soliciting design feedback—it also served to improve community engagement and build political buy-in. But user feedback is meaningless if it cannot then be used to alter decisions in d the design process, which is why an iterative process is so central to agile. As can be seen in Fig. 3.1—where the green box highlights specific forms of risk—a staged, iterative approach can also allow for full team reflections on risks at different points. For full incorporation, creating project metrics that include mitigation and prevention of risks will take the practice even further. The evolving nature of AI requires continuous learning and adaptation. Making sure these lessons are captured and shared externally (whilst simultaneously embedded into the development process itself) is crucial for developing adaptable and responsive AI governance frameworks that can evolve with technological advancements and changing societal needs. Civic technology practice is already engaging with complexity and embracing it in practice and development, which is necessary to properly effect responsible AI development.

Civic Tech Lessons for Collaborative Design

The final area of reflection is considering lessons from collaborative design. Collaborative development is not the norm, even within the context of public sector insourcing of development, which is typically created through a client-service provider relationship. Technocratic and centralised practices have often driven the development of public sector technologies in South Africa (Plantinga & Adams, 2019). But this private–public nexus results in a predominance of big tech companies (and solutions), which are also more often than not marred by vendor lock-in (Breckenridge, 2021). And big tech dominance is difficult to compete against:

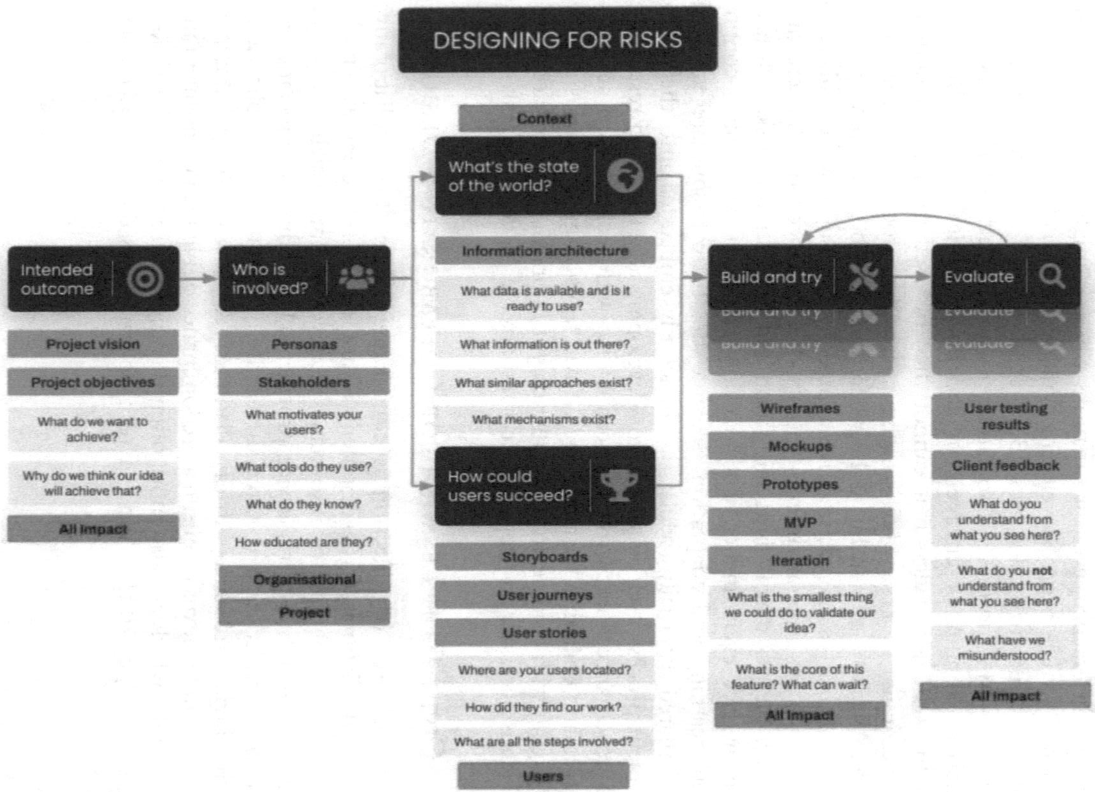

Fig. 3.1 OpenUp's adapted design process, with the green slides indicating the forms of risks considered at different design points (2023)

> The biggest contracts from governments often go to Big Tech, and they sustain their monopolies because of their unassailable scale and scope from having been first to market, compounded by market capitalisation and dominance. Like most business monopolies, this enables them to use their massive profits to consolidate their market position and engage in extensive lobbying and control. (Makumbirofa, 2023)

Nevertheless, there are alternative models. A collaborative design between governments and smaller non-profit or even for-profit technology companies that also intentionally embed civil society engagement, like Vulekamali, offers an alternative path for public sector development projects, which will inevitably include AI. The opportunities are being realised in several different open government project environments:

> In a number of emerging 'open data' projects involving or led by government entities, such as Vulekamali, there are explicit attempts to downplay the role of web portals and externally generated data by redirecting resources towards citizen interactions and supporting the development of local intermediaries and even movements instead of simply building 'solutions'. (Plantinga & Adams, 2019)

This association between civic technology and user-centred design itself acting as a participative mechanism is confirmed in the literature emerging from outside Africa, as well. As Berg et al. note:

> [U]nderstanding the users' needs and wishes will facilitate the quest for citizen involvement [whilst also avoiding] unnecessary and frustrating usability problems once apps are released. (Berg et al., 2021)

This commitment to a form of multi-stakeholderism that included not just the main partners (i.e. National Treasury and Imali Yethu), but broader South African society at large, was evinced through the implementation of engagements that expanded over two years of development in the first phase of the project, conducted over all 9 provinces, and with over 1 100 direct event participants. One can see how this collaborative, participative design process goes way beyond traditional notions of "user-centred" development. This engagement was influential, resulting directly in changes and pursuits of new features, like:

- The inclusion of 'In-Year Monitoring Data'[1];
- The inclusion of downloadable 'Infrastructure Project Data'[2];
- Within the infrastructure project data, providing the ability to be able to filter by sector[3];
- Improvements to the Vulekamali 'Frequently Asked Questions' content;
- Improvements made to the homepage to include interactive treemaps of consolidated budget, national budget, and provincial budget summaries; and
- An emphasis during the latter part of the Community Information Drives on budget literacy training, as requested by civil society organisations during previous events.

The Vulekamali project thus directly demonstrates how increased user participation within the collaborative model not only improved usability (like the content focus, etc.) but also directly led to transparency gains—expanding on the open data originally provided by the National Treasury whilst also providing a form of participative political pressure to do so.

Laying the Foundations for a Positive AI Future

The experiences in the development of *Vulekamali* open up a field of opportunities for the potential of future AI development. However, for this to be facilitated, there are a few essential foundations necessary in domestic contexts. The AU Data Policy Framework emphasises the need for sufficient data and digital infrastructure, as the foundation for developing a data governance agenda (African Union, 2022). This is important for a number of reasons for the ultimate development of responsible AI—and one key reason for this is the role this plays in facilitating local, collaborative technology development. Digital infrastructure is not only a matter of Internet availability but of the affordability of the networks,

[1] You can explore this data here: https://vulekamali.gov.za/datasets/in-year-spending (accessed 22 November 2023).

[2] You can explore this data here: https://vulekamali.gov.za/infrastructure-projects/full/ (accessed 22 November 2023).

[3] You can explore this feature here: https://vulekamali.gov.za/infrastructure-projects/full/ (accessed 22 November 2023).

services and applications as well (Razzano et al., 2020). It is also important for generating sufficient data demand (African Union, 2022). When we look at Vulekamali, the success of the product is in part a result of the Community Information Drives that were able to drum up a community of users around the product itself. This, in turn, spurs use, which helps both politically and economically justify the National Treasury's investment into the existing platform. This is, however, also why such Community Information Drives were later supplemented to include data and digital literacy training—the skills to utilise data and AI products do not necessarily uniformly exist, particularly in African contexts where significant digital inequalities mar the landscape (Gillwald, 2017).

Most importantly, it must be understood that creating conditions that foster both start-ups and civic technology entities is an essential component for creating the landscape for responsible African AI development, and this must be considered within AI governance and policy:

> In order to avoid a repeat of the missed opportunities from the previous industrial revolutions that have left a negative legacy for African countries, governments must create an enabling environment for these AI start-ups to flourish and accelerate the socio-economic development of Africa. [Existing African] AI start-ups have taken the first step to overcome the infrastructure and resource constraints prevalent across Africa to engineer local solutions. (Arakpogun et al., 2021)

If we lay the right foundations, we can only then speculate about the potential opportunities for AI and civic technology's future horizons in Africa converging to contribute to a transformative landscape of social and economic development (particularly as outlined in the Sustainable Development Goals). In a future where AI is integrated with civic technologies (and their practice), innovations can be tailored to African contexts and needs. AI-driven solutions will be collaboratively designed through a broad array of stakeholders, like local communities, government agents, and relevant civil society actors. The focus on ethical and responsible AI that prioritises human flourishing can help address unique African challenges with African development practice. Education and digital literacy will play a critical role in empowering citizens to actively participate in and benefit from AI advancements. Community-driven AI initiatives will flourish, leveraging open data to foster transparency and civic engagement. Governance frameworks will evolve rapidly, adapting to the pace of technological change whilst ensuring responsible and inclusive AI development. This synergy of AI and civic technology will not only bridge digital divides but can also catalyse a new era of participatory democracy and sustainable development on the continent.

Conclusion

Civic technologists will develop AI, but in the immediate term, they also have an immense contribution to make in helping construct a narrative around responsible AI development based on a legacy of experience. Vulekamali provides a useful case study for exploring possible issues—and potential opportunities—for the future of AI, and does this through some key lessons. First and foremost, the development of AI should be led by an agenda: an agenda to further "human flourishing". This agenda needs to be shared by all the stakeholders involved in AI development; and establishing this shared agenda early (immediately) is required if the right metrics are to be established for its development from the outset. The hands-on experience of civic technologists in community-centric projects like Vulekamali has yielded unique insights into both the need for and possible methods for embedding human-centric values in AI. This experience is invaluable in steering AI development towards societal benefits, ensuring that technology advancement aligns with the broader goal of enhancing human welfare.

Second, practice and process matter to outcomes. There is not one way to build technology, but embracing collaborative design methods that centre beneficiaries meaningfully could significantly contribute to the achievement of responsible AI. The participatory nature of civic technology projects offers a blueprint for inclusive AI development. By involving diverse stakeholders in the AI design and decision-making process, we can ensure that AI systems are not only technologically sound but also socially equitable and culturally sensitive. This approach is essential in addressing the diverse needs and contexts of communities, particularly in regions where digital inequalities exist.

Third, the governance and regulation of AI must respond to the realities of not only how AI technology is built, but also the digital, economic, and social realities of the regulatory context. The goal should be efficacy instead of mere intervention. Importantly, the civic technology community has important contributions to make—and it is hoped that these contributions will be directed into regulatory engagements as the role of

Regulators in the field of AI begins to grow. Additionally, where governance lags behind technology development itself, alternative solutions for entrenching responsible AI should be explored—strongly reflective of context. Whilst these general lessons are important, this case study does give insight into some gaps for future research in the AI field, highlighting the importance of research-to-development practice as a missing nexus of work in AI research.

References

African AI Observatory. (2024). *African AI Observatory policy and governance map* [Map]. https://policy.africanobservatory.ai/

African Union. (2022). *AU Data Policy Framework*. https://au.int/en/documents/20220728/au-data-policy-framework

African Union Development Agency. (2021). *AI for Africa: Artificial intelligence for Africa's socio-economic development*. AUDA-NEPAD. https://www.nepad.org/publication/ai-africa-artificial-intelligence-africas-socio-economic-development

Amin, R., Rodgers, D., & Davies, H. (2023, November 14). *A step forward for AI regulation in the US*. Clyde & Co. https://www.clydeco.com:443/insights/2023/11/a-step-forward-for-ai-regulation-in-the-us

Arakpogun, E. O., Elsahn, Z., Olan, F., & Elsahn, F. (2021). Artificial intelligence in Africa: Challenges and opportunities. In *The Fourth Industrial Revolution: Implementation of artificial intelligence for growing business success* (pp. 375–388). Springer.

Ayman, H., & Fakhr, M. W. (2023). Recent computer vision applications for pavement distress and condition assessment. *Automation in Construction, 146*, 104664.

Beck, K., Beedle, M., van Bennekum, A., Cockburn, A., Cunningham, W., Fowler, M., Grenning, J., Highsmith, J., Hunt, A., Jeffries, R., Kern, J., Marick, B., Martin, R., Mellor, S., Schwaber, K., Sutherland, J., & Thomas, D. (2001). *The Agile manifesto principles* [Manifesto for Agile Software Development]. http://agilemanifesto.org/principles.html

Berg, J., Lindholm, J., & Högväg, J. (2021). How do we know that it works? Designing a digital democratic innovation with the help of user-centered design. *Information Polity: THe International Journal of Government & Democracy in the Information Age, 26*(3), 221–235. https://doi.org/10.3233/IP-200282

Bland, J. A. (2024). A Tabu search approach to engineering optimisation. *WIT Transactions on Information and Communication Technologies, 6*, 423–430.

Bosman, J. (2021, September 21). *Human action: The key to good Civic Tech research*. OpenUp Blog. https://openup.org.za/blog/human-action-the-key-to-good-civic-technology-research

Breckenridge, K. (2021). The global ambitions of the biometric anti-bank: Net1, lockin and the technologies of African financialisation. In *Ownership and governance of companies* (pp. 103–128). Routledge.

Chui, M., Hazan, E., Roberts, R., Singla, A., Smaje, K., Sukharevsky, A., Yee, L., & Zemmel, R. (2023). *The economic potential of generative AI: The next productivity frontier*. McKinsey. https://www.mckinsey.com/~/media/mckinsey/featured%20insights/artificial%20intelligence/notes%20from%20the%20frontier%20modeling%20the%20impact%20of%20ai%20on%20the%20world%20economy/mgi-notes-from-the-ai-frontier-modeling-the-impact-of-ai-on-the-world-economy-september-2018.pdf

Civic Tech Innovation Network. (2023a). *The state of Civic Tech research in Africa: An evidence map*. https://civictech.africa/Civicech-EvidenceMap.html

Civic Tech Innovation Network. (2023b, June 12). *Exploring artificial intelligence technologies for enhanced deliberative democracy*. Medium. https://medium.com/civictech/exploring-artificial-intelligence-technologies-for-enhanced-deliberative-democracy-e81a6c27c823

Civic Tech Innovation Network. (n.d.). *Initiatives—CTIN*. https://civictech.africa/initiative/

Eke, D. O., Wakunuma, K., & Akintoye, S. (2023). *Responsible AI in Africa: Challenges and opportunities*. Palgrave Macmillan.

EU AI Act: First regulation on artificial intelligence | News | European Parliament. (2023, June 8). https://www.europarl.europa.eu/news/en/headlines/society/20230601STO93804/eu-ai-act-first-regulation-on-artificial-intelligence

Frase, H., & Daniels, O. (2023, August 11). *Understanding AI harms: An overview*. Center for Security and Emerging Technology. https://cset.georgetown.edu/article/understanding-ai-harms-an-overview/

Gillwald, A. (2017, September 20). *From digital divide to digital inequality: The connectivity paradox*. Law and Development Research Conference, University of Antwerp. https://researchictafrica.net/2017/09/22/from-digital-divide-to-digital-inequality-the-connectivity-paradox/

Gu, X., Han, J., Shen, Q., & Angelov, P. P. (2023). Autonomous learning for fuzzy systems: A review. *Artificial Intelligence Review, 56*(8), 7549–7595.

Gwagwa, A., Kraemer-Mbula, E., Rizk, N., Rutenberg, I., & de Beer, J. (2020). Artificial Intelligence (AI) deployments in Africa: Benefits, challenges and policy dimensions. *The African Journal of Information and Communication, 26*, 1–28. https://doi.org/10.23962/10539/30361

Hicks, J. (2019). *'Digital colonialism': Why some countries want to take control of their people's data from big tech*. The Conversation. https://theconversation.com/digital-colonialism-why-some-countries-want-to-take-control-of-their-peoples-data-from-big-tech-123048

High-Level Expert Group on Artificial Intelligence. (2019). A definition of AI: Main capabilities and scientific disciplines. In *Ethics guidelines for trustworthy AI* (p. 6). European Commission. https://www.aepd.es/sites/default/files/2019-09/ai-definition.pdf

Kasa, M. (2021). *Examining participatory budgeting for stakeholder engagement by the South African National Treasury*. Faculty of Humanities, University of Johannesburg. https://www.proquest.com/openview/2f9462c90b68429cbb653e0d66ad54b2/1?pq-origsite=gscholar&cbl=2026366&diss=y

Liu, Z., Lin, Y., & Sun, M. (2023). *Representation learning for natural language processing* (p. 521). Springer Nature.

Lomas, N. (2023, November 14). *Europe's AI Act talks head for crunch point*. TechCrunch. https://techcrunch.com/2023/11/14/eu-ai-act-trilogue-crunch/

Makumbirofa, S. (2023, March 20). *Regulating big tech: Considerations for the digital single market*. Research ICT Africa. https://researchictafrica.net/2023/03/20/regulating-big-tech-considerations-for-the-digital-single-market/

Malik, S. (2023, August 31). *The future of AI in Africa*. Capacity Media. https://www.capacitymedia.com/article/2c4ohidx4ljizrk7xqcqo/news/the-future-of-ai-in-africa

Matshediso, M. (2020, March). Vulekamali empowers South Africans. *Vuk'uzenzele*. https://www.vukuzenzele.gov.za/vulekamali-empowers-south-africans-0

Mbunge, E., & Batani, J. (2023). Application of deep learning and machine learning models to improve healthcare in sub-Saharan Africa: Emerging opportunities, trends and implications. *Telematics and Informatics Reports, 11*, 100097.

National Treasury. (2022, February 18). *Terms of reference: Phase 2 development of Vulekamali online portal*. https://www.treasury.gov.za/tenderinfo/tenders/NT002-2022%20Bid%20Document.pdf

Neumann, A., Hajji, A., Rekik, M., & Pellerin, R. (2024). Genetic algorithms for planning and scheduling engineer-to-order production: A systematic review. *International Journal of Production Research, 62*(8), 2888–2917.

Onyango, G. (2023). Crafting policy technologies (PolicyTechs): An introduction to policy digitalisation pathways in Africa. In *Public policy and technological transformations in Africa: Nurturing policy entrepreneurship, policy tools and citizen participation* (pp. 1–26). Palgrave Macmillan.

Onyango, G., & Ondiek, J. O. (2022). Open innovation during the COVID-19 pandemic policy responses in South Africa and Kenya. *Politics & Policy, 50*(5), 1008–1031.

OpenUp, & South Africa National Treasury. (2017). Vulekamali. https://vulekamali.gov.za

Peixoto, C. T., Mellon, J., & Sjoberg, F. (2022, October 19). *The haves and have-nots: Who benefits from civic tech?* https://blogs.worldbank.org/en/developmenttalk/haves-and-have-nots-who-benefits-civic-tech, retrieved on 17 October 2024.

Petit, N. (2017). *Law and regulation of artificial intelligence and robots—Conceptual framework and normative implications* (SSRN Scholarly Paper 2931339). https://doi.org/10.2139/ssrn.2931339

Plantinga, P., & Adams, R. (2019). *Open government and innovation for inclusive development: Competing values in policy development, co-creation, brokering and procurement* (SSRN Scholarly Paper 3501484). https://doi.org/10.2139/ssrn.3501484

Razzano, G. (2021). *AI4D—Digital and biometric identity systems*. Research ICT Africa. https://researchictafrica.net/wp/wp-content/uploads/2021/07/Final-FF-Phase-IV-Consolidated-Bio-ID-Thematic.pdf

Razzano, G. (2022, June 13). *Working paper I: HUM-IM centered design?* | OpenUp Blog. https://openup.org.za/blog/working-paper-i-hum-im-centered-design

Razzano, G. (2023, August 10). *Working paper II: Risk and design*. OpenUp Blog. https://openup.org.za/blog/working-paper-ii-risk-and-design

Razzano, G., Gillwald, A., Aguera, P., Ahmed, S., Calandro, E., Rens, A., & van der Spuy, A. (2020). *SADC Parliamentary Forum discussion paper: The digital economy and society*. Research ICT Africa. https://researchictafrica.net/publication/sadc-pf-discussion-paper-the-digital-economy-and-society/

Sartori, L., & Theodorou, A. (2022). A sociotechnical perspective for the future of AI: Narratives, inequalities, and human control. *Ethics and Information Technology, 24*(1), 4. https://doi.org/10.1007/s10676-022-09624-3

Savaget, P., Chiarini, T., & Evans, S. (2019). Empowering political participation through artificial intelligence. *Science and Public Policy, 46*(3), 369–380.

Stahl, B. C. (2021). *Artificial intelligence for a better future: An ecosystem perspective on the ethics of AI and emerging digital technologies*. Springer Nature.

Stempeck, M. (2018). *Civic Tech field guide*. https://civictech.guide/

Thierer, A. (2018, August 16). *The pacing problem, the Collingridge dilemma & technological determinism*. Technology Liberation Front. https://techliberation.com/2018/08/16/the-pacing-problem-the-collingridge-dilemma-technological-determinism/

CHAPTER 4

Designing Ethical AI For Government in Africa

Japheth Otieno Ondiek and Gedion Onyango

Introduction

As governments grapple with and buy into restructuring public services to create automated operations to make governance processes and policy decisions more transparent, efficient, and effective, how can this be leveraged in a manner that central values concerned with equality, representation, responsiveness and accountability of public institutions are not lost or compromised? Are African public bureaucracies mature and ready for such Advanced Technologies, and can these automated processes be

J. O. Ondiek (✉)
University of Nairobi, Nairobi, Kenya
e-mail: japhondiekh@gmail.com

G. Onyango
London School of Economics and Political Science, London, UK

University of Johannesburg, Johannesburg, South Africa

G. Onyango
e-mail: onyangojr@gmail.com

G. Onyango (ed.), *Designing Artificial Intelligence for Public Policy and Governance in Africa*, Studies in National Governance and Emerging Technologies, https://doi.org/10.1007/978-3-031-83445-5_4

trusted to uphold citizens' hard-earned and highly contested political values? How can such automated operations entrench or undermine key principles of administrative law, especially in African contexts where, first, governments are still struggling with realising such values in public affairs and second, citizens have witnessed marginalisation, historical injustice and human rights abuses both locally and internationally? These are some central concerns around Artificial Intelligence (AI) ethics. Undoubtedly, AI technologies are increasingly being integrated into human systems, generally revolutionising how public engagement is managed and organised. This technological phenomenon presents opportunities and challenges, particularly for less developed policy systems in the Global South. AI technologies have significantly disrupted public sector operations by enhancing the service delivery experience (Kulal et al., 2024), improving policy compliance and education policy (Kiemde & Kora, 2022) and increasing efficiency (Chhatre & Singh, 2024a; 2024b). As a result of the disruptions caused by COVID-19, the mobility constraints of public administrators prompted many governments to explore and implement alternative technologically driven solutions to improve service delivery and reduce costs (Onyango & Ondiek, 2022).

Despite the potential for AI to revolutionise public service delivery and accelerate development, many regions are unable to utilise it due to infrastructural and resource limitations (Aderibigbe et al., 2023). According to the 2018 United Nations (UN) E-Government Survey, significant technological advancements in software and hardware have hastened the progress of AI and its potential impact on society. The increased data collection and utilisation enhances machine learning and improves the quality of AI systems, which rely heavily on data. Consequently, AI has the potential to drive rapid development, enabling underdeveloped countries like most of those in Africa to overcome some traditional barriers. However, concerns remain about AI's impact on workforce privacy, the ethical implications of its uses, and the need for capacity-building, which would fundamentally reshape the type of education required for the next generation (Calvo et al., 2023).

While these are global concerns, they pose critical challenges for countries still struggling to establish functional regulatory systems like African countries. According to PriceWater House Coopers (PWC), AI is estimated to contribute USD 1.5 trillion to the African economy, translating to 6% of the continent's GDP. This is due to the increasing number of AI innovations in education, law, health, insurance, and agriculture (OECD,

2021a). This approach emphasises interoperability in AI architecture design, which is crucial for government operations. As the African governments are taking it slow with integrating AI into their operational systems, the private sector is rapidly taking on AI tools to enhance productivity and create more value for customers and shareholders (OECD, 2021a, 2021b). The promise of AI is highly appealing to governments as well. Undoubtedly, AI has great potential to enhance governance processes if adopted seamlessly. It can be a game changer in propelling levels of production and efficiency and government-citizen relations. This potential could transform the public sector from a demand-driven approach to a predictive one while mapping public policy inputs and outcomes and weighing into potential challenges. However, this also carries numerous hazards and blind spots connected with AI, making its use in government extremely difficult and cautious.

First, substantive or procedural policy tools may slow the application of AI to public policies. Difficulties with regulating AI frameworks, for example, may arise. The adverse effects of AI, like prejudice and exclusion, may also be challenging to deal with (Misra et al., 2020). Second, governments are not business entities that could be primarily tied down by pressures to work efficiently and effectively. Instead, they are primarily supposed to deliver democracy (Denhardt & Denhardt, 2015). This means that besides the efficiency and effectiveness values found at the core of AI applications, more critical political values of representation, responsiveness, and accountability may and should be prioritised (Onyango, 2024). This could mean that AI applications in the public sector can be promoted or hindered based on how they promote or threaten these democratic values. Additionally, there are intricacies concerning how these concepts or values are interpreted by different governance actors and evaluated in their implementation. Third, public organisations are yet to master how they can effectively build their institutional capacities, engage in public–private partnerships, and implement customised policy frameworks, which are crucial to closing the gap between digital technologies, especially AI's potential and its actualisation in developing nations (Aderibigbe et al., 2023).

It is within these governance contours that ethical concerns around AI arise. The ethical application of AI in the public sector continues to face significant problems, including safeguarding vulnerable populations and striking a balance between innovation and public benefit. To successfully use AI in the public sector, governments must properly recognise these problems and enforce regulatory public policies to address the probable negative implications of AI (Misra et al., 2020). Even though there is AI development traction in some African governments today, the main challenges arising from adoption include poor quality of data, low access to AI technology, poor digital infrastructure, lack of digital skills, and lack of legal and policy frameworks for AI implementation.

Notably, the legislative framework for privacy and data protection designs has yet to progress or define what AI means for many governments, especially in the global South (Wong et al., 2022). These aspects create a need for immediate formulation of clear policies to guide the integration and adoption of AI in the public sector amid the growth of automated services that could improve citizen engagement, service delivery, and cost-saving measures. For example, according to OECD (2021a), in Africa, AI analytics and decision-making tools for financial institutions and regulators have been used to track and flag illicit financial flows totalling USD 80 billion. In Brazil, an AI fraud detector was used to detect and flag 500 civil servants doing business with governments and winning or supervising contracts. In contrast, in the UK, a robotic automated AI was used to process 30,000 pension claims in 2 weeks, a task that would have taken thousands of human hours of manual work. These examples indicate a deliberate need for policies in the public sector (OECD, 2021a). As elaborated by the preceding chapters in this volume, gender parity, cultural diversity, and changes in the labour market are important issues to address (also see Gwagwa et al., 2020).

Generally, the global environment of AI ethics is fast changing, with a focus on five fundamental principles: transparency, openness, fairness, non-maleficence, accountability, and privacy (Jobin et al., 2019). However, there is significant variation in the interpretation and application of these principles across different contexts and cultures (Daly et al., 2019; Jobin et al., 2019). As AI gets more interwoven into numerous industries, it exacerbates current ethical difficulties and adds new challenges, particularly in copyright, individual autonomy, and our understanding of authenticity and creativity (Floridi, 2024). The global scope of AI's influence in the public sector needs international collaboration and culturally specific ethical rules to address issues such as prejudice, accountability, and societal ramifications. Continuous critical vigilance in public sector implementation, inventive conceptual design, and collaborative efforts among different stakeholders are vital for creating an enduring and socially acceptable future for AI, that is, if AI is to impact public sector organisations positively (Floridi, 2024).

While some rules are based on international human rights law, others use a weaker ethical framework with no enforceable norms or accountability measures, significantly impacting rolling AI systems in government frameworks. While there is an increasing understanding of the need for explicit ethical rules to handle issues like privacy violations and AI responsibility, it is anticipated that international and continental organisations will be essential in developing moral guidelines for the application of AI, weighing its advantages against the defence of human rights and dignity. This aspect at the continental level is now driven by the African Union's *Continental Artificial Intelligence Strategy 2024* to present African countries with a blueprint for harnessing AI technologies. Such frameworks should create thorough and useful AI ethics rules; governments, businesses, and civic society must continue their research and work together (Rawat et al., 2024).

The ethical consideration for AI systems is that they must be transparent and explainable to ensure public confidence and accountability. According to the African Union's Continental Artificial Intelligence Strategy 2024, AI ethical considerations should respect human rights and dignity within regional and international human rights law, diversity, inclusivity and African culture and values. Another ethical aspect is the protection of children to ensure the responsible and unbiased use of AI, respecting intellectual property rights and addressing potential societal and legal implications forming part of algorithmic bias.

According to a recent study, algorithmic decision-making systems must have functional transparency for stakeholders to assess the systems' fairness (Hosain et al., 2023). It has been suggested that AI explainability be approached from a principles-based perspective, emphasising impact reflection, meaningful explanations, transparency, and clarity (Leslie, 2020). Designing transparent AI systems with stakeholders in mind is advised to ensure regulatory compliance (Bell et al., 2023). This entails considering the requirements of diverse stakeholders, particularly marginalised groups, when putting transparency measures into practice. According to Leslie (2020), offering justification, accountability, data, fairness, safety and performance, and impact explanations are essential to explainable AI. These initiatives aim to increase the accessibility and comprehension of AI systems for all parties involved, fostering confidence and reducing the possibility of biases in AI-assisted decision-making processes. To understand the topic of discussion, this chapter primarily highlights three objectives as elements looking into ethical AI design and impacts approach for human rights, vulnerable groups and marginalised groups, and the public sector regulatory approach to AI misinformation. It then recommends a consolidated AI design framework for public sector institutions. The rest of the section discusses methodology, findings, and policy propositions. The last section highlights the conclusion based on the review of the study. In doing so, the chapter is anchored on a thorough review of existing literature and AI policy frameworks already designed for African public sector institutions.

Methodology

The review focused on three main areas: the impact of the AI design framework, the AI design approach to misinformation in the public sector, and the public sector's regulatory approach to human rights and marginalised groups. We applied a qualitative and secondary search of existing information on AI design and ethical frameworks approach, organising the data into a question-and-answer format database to guide the outcomes and findings based on the areas explored. Qualitative data sources included government AI frameworks, webpages of multilateral bodies and organisations dealing with AI governance, existing AI journals and article databases, and government policy papers on AI ethical frameworks. Since there was limited specific data for Global South, the analysis also included information from Global North. We carried out an iterative qualitative process to extract data and create a consistent narrative from the themes, followed by pattern-matching analysis to consistently analyse the narrative and findings. These were then categorised and thematically analysed findings from the articles and retrieved literature based on multiple categories to build explanations, create an AI framework approach, and develop conclusive findings. The next section of the chapter discusses the synthesis of the findings.

Discussions and Synthesis: Designing Ethical AI for African Public Service

The use of AI in decision-making within the public sector raises important concerns about transparency and accountability. AI systems, especially those that use complex machine learning models, often operate as "black boxes," making it difficult to understand their decision-making processes, even for sophisticated governance systems. This lack of transparency may impede effective oversight and accountability, potentially endangering basic human rights (Webb, 2019). Public servants and contractors from OECD countries have expressed differing views on transparency in relation to trust, decision-making, and preventing manipulation (OECD, 2021b; Veale, 2017). Relying solely on human oversight of automated systems is insufficient; addressing transparency and accountability during the integration of AI is crucial (Goldenfein, 2019). However, achieving transparency, fairness, and explainability in machine learning systems has limitations and risks (Goldenfein, 2019). To ensure accountability, both direct public transparency and indirect disclosure to auditors are beneficial and may be necessary for democratic self-governance (Loi & Spielkamp, 2021).

The growing use of AI in public institutions has raised concerns about bias and justice, particularly in predictive policing, where algorithms may disproportionately target specific communities (Sreerama & Krishnamoorthy, 2022). AI systems trained on biased datasets can perpetuate historical disparities and cultural biases, leading to unfair treatment and a loss of public trust (Leavy et al., 2020). To address these concerns, researchers have developed tools such as Aequitas, which allow users to assess models for bias and fairness across different population segments (Saleiro et al., 2018). Approaches to data preparation, algorithmic transparency, and diverse representation in training datasets are all examples of strategies to mitigate bias (Sreerama & Krishnamoorthy, 2022). Additionally, understanding the types and causes of data bias and implementing de-biasing approaches throughout the model's lifespan is crucial for creating fair AI systems (Zhou et al., 2021). Continuous efforts are necessary to build trustworthy and equitable AI technologies prioritising fairness.

Privacy concerns in the public sector AI systems are a serious ethical issue because these systems frequently rely on sensitive personal data to function properly (Leslie, 2019). Despite universal privacy concerns, citizens may be less likely to share personal information than predicted, resulting in a "privacy paradox" (Willems et al., 2022). To overcome these problems, ethical guidelines for public sector AI should emphasise fairness, non-discrimination, transparency, accountability, safety, and privacy. Implementing privacy-preserving technologies like differential privacy, homomorphic encryption, and federated learning can assist in safeguarding individuals' privacy while maintaining AI utility (Radanliev et al., 2024). Furthermore, responsible AI application in the public sector requires effective communication, evidence-based reasoning, and moral justification (Leslie, 2019). To fully realise the potential of AI while protecting individual privacy, a holistic approach is required to integrate technological innovation with ethical and legislative initiatives.

Therefore, the ethical use of AI in the public sector is critical to sustaining public trust. Fairness, openness, accountability, privacy, and safety are all important factors that must be integrated into public sector processes. The public's distrust of AI originates from the lack of a robust regulatory framework that ensures AI trustworthiness. To overcome this, a framework for ethical AI in government should attempt to gain public trust, comply with administrative law requirements, and assure good societal impact (Andrews et al., 2022). This includes creating externally auditable AI documentation and providing clear rules and enforcement procedures (Knowles & Richards, 2021). An integrated strategy is required to implement ethical AI ideas, including high-level principles, trust/trustworthiness notions, and product/process support (Zhu et al., 2021). Adhering to these ethical principles and guidelines allows public institutions to improve service delivery while demonstrating their commitment to fairness and transparency, ultimately increasing public trust in AI-driven government systems.

Policy and Regulatory Designs

Globally, governments face challenges in developing AI policies and regulatory frameworks. There is a need to strike a balance between innovation, morality, and legal responsibilities. While some African countries, like Kenya and South Africa, have proposed comprehensive AI policies, others still need the necessary AI legal framework and legislation (Chhatre & Singh, 2024a; 2024b). Implementing AI in the public sector in Africa presents specific difficulties that necessitate explicit legislative measures to minimise negative effects, such as exclusion and bias (Misra et al., 2020). The current AI policy designs are rarely tailored to fit the local context, making AI implementation difficult. Adopting AI legislative and framework templates from successful drafters like the EU may make it difficult for African governments to customise local AI implementation that aligns with citizens' needs. Regional differences in global AI governance approaches can be observed in the US, EU, Asia, Africa, and the Americas, where different approaches are taken (Walter, 2024).

The responsible development and application of artificial intelligence (AI) in the public sector requires a human-centred, context-sensitive strategy that prioritises communication, evidence-based reasoning, and moral justifiability (Leslie, 2019). Public institutions must prioritise these principles to guarantee that AI systems designs and regulatory frameworks cater to improving public benefit without endangering people. Public sector institutions must ideally encourage moral AI systems in the design processes that advance justice and defend human rights by implementing extensive data protection and laws and regulations. In doing this, there has to be harmonious governments, businesses, and civil society must work together to achieve this as proposed (Rawat et al., 2024). Public sector organisations should reform and restructure their systems to allow AI laws and regulations to be integrated from the onset to foster responsible innovation and governance procedures that support moral and secure AI systems to reduce potential risks. The design of the AI-supported results should also be comprehensible and interpreted for decision subjects and users.

Incorporating AI into public governance creates potential and obstacles to AI design. The obstacles to designing AI systems start at the legislative level, where the legislatures and multinationals deliberately push for their interests. While multinationals may always be keen on the design and protection of some of the underlying principles that may hurt, the businesses and legislatures, in most circumstances, tend to fall for this interference without interrogating the potential outcomes and harm to the citizens. In most instances, this has led to the passage of a draconian set of legislative pieces and laws that hamper the progress of AI implementation and legislation in the African context. While the emphasis is that the design of AI can improve public services, automate decision-making, and increase security, its implementation poses questions regarding transparency, accountability, fairness, and individual rights. Therefore, governments should create strong regulatory frameworks and governance procedures to solve these concerns, starting with legislation. The key issues for consideration should include assuring accuracy, minimising bias and discrimination, maintaining legal compliance, and protecting administrative fairness. In addition, transparency and explainability of AI systems are critical for building public trust and facilitating inspection. This should be embedded with aligning public sector needs with a citizen-centred AI approach to accountability and justice in algorithmic decision-making (Henman, 2020; Mehrabi et al., 2021; Veale et al., 2018).

Emerging literature also shows that global regulation of artificial intelligence (AI) is complicated. For example, a precedent for organised regulation has been established by the European Union's AI Act, which classifies AI systems according to risk levels (Kretschmer et al., 2023). Although this risk-based strategy seeks to avoid negative consequences, its execution could be better, mainly related to human oversight and the quality of the data (Kretschmer et al., 2023). Walter (2024) highlights the importance of adaptable legislation to keep up with technological changes and data patterns. To this aim, a collaborative network that combines industry expertise with political power is suggested. Although risk regulation is a popular strategy, it has drawbacks of its own, such as being difficult to measure damage that cannot be quantified and having few avenues for citizen-led public participation (Kaminski, 2022). Integrative risk-based models are becoming more and more necessary to direct legislation and guarantee compliance across borders as international efforts to standardise AI regulation, as demonstrated by the Bletchley Declaration (Weismann, 2024).

At the AI design level, AI technologies' ethical and responsible regulation and application present substantial issues for public sector organisations. Fairness, accountability, openness, privacy, and human rights are important issues (Bîgu & Georgescu, 2024; OECD, 2021b). Governments must set precise rules for AI deployment, purchase, and monitoring in public administration to address these problems (Hickok, 2022). Two examples are creating frameworks for ongoing auditing to detect and address biases and formulating criteria for choosing AI systems that follow moral guidelines (Bîgu & Georgescu, 2024; OECD, 2021a). It is recommended that public entities prioritise the documentation of AI decision-making processes, publicising them, and putting strong data protection mechanisms in place (Goldenfein, 2019). Furthermore, given that present deployment frequently lacks thorough due diligence and transparency, AI-specific procurement norms are desperately needed to safeguard fundamental rights and due process (Hickok, 2022). Maintaining moral principles and public confidence depends on proactive regulation and governance of AI in the public sector.

A Human Rights-Centred AI Strategy and Marginalised Groups

A human rights-centred strategy is necessary for the ethical use of AI in the public sector to safeguard marginalised groups and maintain inclusion. Scholars propose that ethical considerations should be combined with international human rights frameworks to form the basis of AI governance (Pizzi et al., 2020; Yeung et al., 2019). It has been emphasised that impact analyses, stakeholder consultations, and affected communities' involvement in AI development and implementation are all part of this strategy (Thinyane & Sassetti, 2020). AI systems should be developed from a human rights perspective, considering approaches like *value-sensitive design and participatory design* to address potential biases and inequities (Aizenberg & van den Hoven, 2020). To ensure AI systems don't perpetuate pre-existing prejudices or exclude specific groups from using services, regular audits and supervision methods must be implemented as part of the legislative framework. By using these approaches, public sector AI can promote inclusivity while avoiding worsening inequities, helping accomplish sustainable development goals (Pizzi et al., 2020).

A recent study emphasises matching AI systems with human values and ethical norms in public-sector settings. Dignum (2017) suggests accountability, responsibility, and openness as important design principles for value-sensitive AI development. A human rights-based framework for responsible AI is proposed, focusing on possible harm to people rather than machine prejudices (Prabhakaran et al., 2022). To promote ethical AI development and deployment, public administrations should employ inclusive policy-making techniques and transition away from top-down governance (Sigfrids et al., 2022). Global convergence revolves around five ethical principles: openness, justice and fairness, non-maleficence, responsibility, and privacy (Jobin et al., 2019). However, there is tremendous variation in the understanding and application of these ideas. These findings highlight the necessity of comprehensive governance frameworks that include ethical analysis, stakeholder involvement, and workable implementation methodologies to enable responsible AI development and deployment in the public sector.

One viable benchmark for moral AI systems is a human rights-centred design. According to the literature, governance should shift from top-down to more inclusive and include stakeholders in decision-making (Sigfrids et al., 2022). The papers under evaluation underscore the significance of ethical regulation of AI in the public domain. A focus on inclusive policymaking and the preservation of human rights informs their frameworks for responsible AI development and use. Some of the main recommendations are to create specialised governance committees, create metrics to track policy efficacy and carry out frequent evaluations to guarantee relevance (Sigfrids et al., 2022). Leslie (2019) emphasises the significance of interpretability and transparency in AI-supported outcomes and the necessity of communicating these conclusions to decide subjects clearly and understandably. The chapter generally emphasises that thorough, institutionalised, and executable governance structures are necessary to guarantee responsible AI use in the public sector.

The concept of meaningful human control over AI systems in the public sector is critical for maintaining accountability, responsibility, and transparency (Methnani et al, 2021). To do this, AI systems should be built with flexible autonomy, allowing for human intervention and decision-making in key instances. Human oversight is critical but must go beyond mere presence to be effective. Decision-makers must have adequate authority to control AI systems and handle unintended consequences (Mitrou et al., 2021). However, more than human oversight may be required to preserve fundamental rights (Koulu, 2020). To achieve meaningful human control, four actionable properties have been proposed: defining a domain of morally loaded situations, ensuring compatible representations between humans and AI, aligning responsibility with control ability, and explicitly linking AI actions to human moral responsibility. These methods can help to preserve human judgment and discretion in AI-powered decision-making processes.

Public Sector Regulatory Approach to AI Misinformation

It is well understood that AI presents difficulties for public sector administration and regulation since it is a major factor in disseminating and eradicating disinformation. AI systems can amplify disinformation campaigns that erode public confidence in democratic institutions (Mega, 2023). For example, the harm caused by Big Tech manifests on various levels. At the individual level, users often face privacy violations, misinformation, and exploitation of personal data using manipulated algorithmic codes (Humprecht et al., 2020). For instance, in 2017, the social media analytics company Cambridge Analytica was cited for intentionally using AI tactics that influenced the presidential election outcome in Kenya, using millions of Kenyans' big data based on microbehavioural targeting. This polarisation of democratic society's influences voters' patterns through profiling campaigns targeted based on ethnic hate, fear, mis and disinformation, and population manipulation (Wangari, 2017). The asymmetrical influence and power of Big Tech on the harm space relies on the policing of the internet through several layers of algorithm detection of harmful content, policy-based guidelines restricting certain contents and paid content moderators flagging content that violates platform policies.

This problem is worsened by how online platforms make money through advertising (Bontridder & Poullet, 2021). Governments need to create legal frameworks that guarantee responsibility, openness, and human rights protection in the governance of AI to allay these worries (OECD, 2021a). This entails defining distinct lines of accountability, establishing strong data protection procedures, and opening the criteria used to make decisions for the general public (OECD, 2021b). Artificial intelligence (AI) systems can help combat the manipulation of the digital environment, even though they might not be the best choice for monitoring or identifying misinformation content (Bontridder & Poullet, 2021). Ultimately, it is imperative to prioritise the battle against misinformation to protect democratic processes and promote informed citizens (Mega, 2023).

Mitigating bias and ensuring justice in AI systems is essential to prevent misinformation, especially in public sector applications. Thorough fairness audits are necessary to detect and reduce prejudices that can result in unfair outcomes through misinformation (Gupta, 2023). According to Saleiro et al. (2018), the Aequitas toolkit provides a user-friendly method for assessing several bias metrics across different population subsets. It is essential to establish explicit training data rules to maintain variety and avoid reinforcing already existing disparities. Equitable results can be attained by implementing bias mitigation tactics, such as algorithmic modifications and sophisticated methods like demographic inclusion, to avoid misleading content and misinformation in the public sector. Establishing avenues for input from impacted people and communities permits continuous assessment and enhancement of equity metrics (Gupta, 2023).

Public sector organisations and the government must work with tech developers to create policies that support inclusive AI development.

AI Ethical Principles and Governance Frameworks

Using AI in public administration creates serious privacy and data protection problems. While the General Data Protection Regulation (GDPR) seeks to protect personal data in the EU and other emerging policies, its applicability to AI systems is still being determined, potentially impeding innovation (Tupay et al., 2021). To develop confidence, public sector institutions must implement tough data protection rules, strong encryption, and openness. However, research shows a privacy paradox: despite broad privacy concerns, citizens are unaffected by the amount of personal information necessary when dealing with AI-powered public services (Willems et al., 2022). To solve these difficulties, governments must create comprehensive legal frameworks that combine innovation with ethical ideals such as justice, accountability, and openness in AI-powered decision-making processes (Bernardes et al., 2020).

These are critical dimensions when undertaking algorithmic Impact Assessments. In public service delivery, algorithmic impact evaluations are critical for identifying and minimising potential biases and harms, especially for the public sector in Kenya and South Africa cases (Joshua & Daniel, 2018). However, to effectively reflect the implications of algorithms, these assessments should be prepared with the input of affected groups and professionals in public administrations (Metcalf et al., 2021). This is especially relevant in sensitive sectors, especially for social policies and child welfare services, where algorithmic decision-making can aggravate pre-existing scepticism (Brown et al., 2019). As a result, a collaborative approach to algorithmic impact evaluations, including a variety of stakeholders, is required for successful public sector accountability (Metcalf et al., 2021).

Algorithmic impact assessments for AI systems in public service delivery need in the countries of the case study require a thorough examination of the system's architectural design, data sources, and intended use, with the goal of uncovering any algorithmic biases that may disproportionately harm demographic groups. Analysing the effects on various demographics, such as race, gender, age, and socioeconomic position, is critical for identifying any discrepancies or biases in the system's functionality (Castets-Renard, 2021). These evaluations seek to identify biases within algorithms, datasets, or decision-making processes that may result in discriminatory outcomes, demanding mitigation techniques such as algorithm changes or procedural protections. Furthermore, these assessments must be reviewed and updated on a regular basis in order to adapt to changing AI systems and assure continuous relevance and efficacy (Shefeh & Marco, 2022).

To prevent harm and safeguard vulnerable populations, the safety and security of AI systems in public sector applications are crucial considerations that necessitate stringent testing, validation, and risk management techniques (Leslie, 2019). Dobbe (2022) highlights that end-to-end hazard analysis and design that considers the context of use and impacted stakeholders are essential components of a socio-technical approach to AI safety. Holzinger et al. (2021) draw attention to the possible risks associated with using AI, highlighting how crucial it is to provide traceability, transparency, and explainability in AI applications. Public sector organisations need to set up governance procedures that enable moral, just, and secure AI systems to meet these problems. Hickok (2022) contends that as the existing deployment frequently lacks thorough due diligence and monitoring, AI-specific procurement criteria are necessary to safeguard fundamental rights and due process. These steps are necessary to reduce risks and guarantee the responsible application of AI in vital public services. (Leavy et al., 2020; Leslie, 2019).

Preventing bias and discrimination in AI systems is essential, especially regarding high-stakes public sector decisions (Veale et al., 2018). According to Son (2023), fairness in AI refers to treating all users equally and without prejudice based on characteristics like gender, race, or socioeconomic background. Measures such as using a variety of datasets, examining algorithms, creating rules, taking development ethics into account, and putting feedback systems in place are necessary to achieve fairness (Son, 2023). Nonetheless, there is frequently a gap between the state of research on useable, transparent, and discrimination-aware machine learning and organisational realities (Veale et al., 2018). Scholars have distinguished between several types of bias in AI systems and have created taxonomies for notions of fairness. According to Pessach and Shmueli (2023), there are three types of fairness-enhancing mechanisms: pre-process, in-process, and post-process. These mechanisms are appropriate for different situations. According to Son (2023), addressing justice in AI is crucial for fostering trust and avoiding the escalation of social inequality.

Recent studies have shown that implementing AI in the public sector requires professional responsibility and human control. According to Fjeld et al. (2020), key ethical criteria for AI are professional accountability and human control over technology. Bîgu and Georgescu (2024) emphasise fairness, openness, and safety as essential moral principles for public sector AI. To guarantee that AI advances rather than compromises human interests in humanitarian situations, Pizzi et al. (2020) emphasise the necessity of a framework based on human rights. As demonstrated by Kawakami et al., the adoption of AI in public organisations is influenced by power dynamics (2024), who also point out obstacles to stakeholder involvement. These studies emphasise how important it is to have human oversight, moral standards, and inclusive decision-making procedures when using AI in the public sector to ensure it serves the public interest. They also stress the significance of accountability frameworks, training initiatives, and collaborative methods for addressing potential prejudices and moral dilemmas in applying AI in the public sector.

Human values and ethical norms must be carefully considered while integrating AI into the public sector. Chen et al. emphasise the significance of stakeholder participation and openness in AI governance. (2023). "Social value alignment" is necessary, according to Gabriel and Ghazavi (2021), to guarantee that AI systems consider a variety of societal values. Dignum (2017) suggests using the ART (accountability, responsibility, and transparency) design principles for creating AI systems sensitive to value, especially considering how they may affect the labour market. By conceptualising AI systems as socio-technical systems made up of technological artefacts, human agents, institutions, and artificial agents, Van de Poel (2020) provides a paradigm for integrating values into AI systems. These articles emphasise how important it is to match AI with human values like justice, fairness, and inclusivity, particularly when using it in settings where people's lives are at stake. To guarantee that AI fosters human flourishing and social good, they support the creation of governance frameworks, diversified community interaction, and ethical design processes (Araujo, 2019; Chhatre & Singh, 2024b; George Manias, 2023; Golpayegani et al., 2023; Susar & Aquaro, 2019).

Policy Propositions

Broadly, policy propositions for public sector institutions should strive towards promoting human-centric AI based on ethical principles, respect for human rights, operational frameworks and institutional arrangements. Public sector institutions can establish AI policy design based on risk management associated with AI biases that could undermine core government responsibilities. Specifically, the designs must be iterated with frameworks that guide unintended consequences, algorithmic biases, privacy, and security. More sustainably, there is a need for public sector institutions to realise that AI complexities override the skills and expertise of the constituted public sector employees. Therefore, there is a need for public sector institutions to promote innovative hubs that pool skilled digital public administrators and partnerships with AI research institutes, academia and the private sector to drive digital skills centred on research (Onyango & Ondiek, 2021). Similarly, promoting digital skills and Science, Technology, Engineering and Mathematics (STEM) based education, especially targeting the global south, can tilt the scale of misrepresentation on unskilled and disadvantaged groups to harness emerging AI potential. Public sector institutions should strengthen regulatory and governance frameworks to manage cybercrimes, privacy, and misinformation. Moreover, embedding algorithmic codes for citizens requires public administrators to participate in understanding and facing codes that predominantly discriminate against citizens and public servants based on race, colour, gender, and political alienation. Legislators need to be informed about AI values, taking into account issues such as human rights context, AI bias, and misinformation laced with a citizen-centred approach. The legislation should be guided by experts who understand the ideal framework of AI implementation.

Hence, governments can enhance their influence and role in global AI governance. Notably, strengthening data protection frameworks, privacy policies, and monitoring of AI compliances are essential settings that can strengthen the transparency framework for AI implementations. Also, governments should channel investments that address education, digital skills developments, STEM education, and research with emphasis on disadvantaged populations like minorities, women, and those at risk. To spur growth at the public sector level, governments should create innovation hubs that attract the best talents in AI designs and algorithm impact assessment frameworks.

Conclusions and Way Forward

The discussions in this chapter outline a clear potential for ethical AI for Government in the public sector if implemented responsibly with appropriate frameworks and policy guidelines. In this discussion, there is a growing understanding of the eminent and potential risks associated with using AI in public sector institutions. There is homogenous agreement that governments are taking raft measures by integrating new institutional frameworks and compelling policy propositions for responsible AI use and implementation. The chapter notes the potential need for establishing consistent ethical frameworks as critical tools for deploying AI operations across public sector institutions. Governments need to consider establishing alternative AI policy options that create systems for trust and privacy in using AI in the public sector. The discussions suggest a common approach towards AI integration, framing, and engagement of policy measures. Promoting and trustworthy use of AI requires collective efforts from multi-stakeholder engagements beyond national governments to jointly explore emerging challenges and opportunities in AI implementations.

It is also shown that AI dependency on high-quality data requires established and robust data governance to drive ethical and trustworthy AI strategies. The primary algorithmic accountability and open registry standards for public transparency of algorithms, traceability, accountability, and expansibility are required. The chapter highlights that many governments have made similar efforts towards the ethical design of AI. However, there is a need for robust analysis and institutional structures for effective accountability and implementation of AI systems in each setting of the public administrative context. This includes looking at the enablers that drive AI accountability and deployment and legislation and guidelines. Overall, a coherent and trustworthy AI design that secures oversight for misinformation and human rights abuses requires a whole government approach and participatory mechanisms with engagements of stakeholders in the development, design, and deployment of AI in the public sector. To ensure the reliability of AI systems, the right metrics and tools must be scrutinised and integrated fairly to ensure safeguards that rectify biases in gender, race, and misleading algorithmic models for misinformation are included in the design.

References

Aderibigbe, A., Ohenhen, P., Nwaobia, N., Gidiagba, J., & Ani, E. (2023). Artificial intelligence in developing countries: Bridging the gap between potential and implementation. *Computer Science & IT Research Journal, 4*, 185–199. https://doi.org/10.51594/csitrj.v4i3.629

Andrews, P., de Sousa, T., & Haefele, B. (2022). *A trust framework for government use of artificial intelligence and automated decision making*. https://doi.org/10.48550/arXiv.2208.10087

Araujo, R. (2019). *Data protection in the era of artificial intelligence. Trends, existing solutions and recommendations for privacy-preserving technologies*. Retrieved from https://www.semanticscholar.org/paper/Data-protection-in-the-era-of-artificial-Trends%2C-Araujo/bbbbcb1cb0f25918c4883491f71451141c842ff0

Aizenberg, E. & van den hoven, J. (2020). Designing for human rights in AI. https://doi.org/10.48550/arXiv.2005.04949

Bell, A., Nov, O., & Stoyanovich, J. (2023). Think about the stakeholders first! Toward an algorithmic transparency playbook for regulatory compliance. *Data & Policy, 5*. https://doi.org/10.1017/dap.2023.8

Bernardes, M. B., de Andrade, F. P., & Novais, P. (2020). Data protection in public sector: Normative analysis of Portuguese and Brazilian legal orders. In Á. Rocha, H. Adeli, L. P. Reis, S. Costanzo, I. Orovic, & F. Moreira (Eds.), *WorldCIST* (2) (pp. 807–817), : Springer. ISBN: 978-3-030-45691-7.

Bîgu, D., & Georgescu, D.-S. (2024). *Ethical standards for public sector digitalization*. Proceedings of the International Management Conference. https://doi.org/10.24818/imc/2023/05.03

Bontridder, N., & Poullet, Y. (2021). The role of artificial intelligence in disinformation. *Data & Policy, 3*. https://doi.org/10.1017/dap.2021.20

Brown, C., Story, G., Mourão-Miranda, J., & Baker, J. (2019). Will artificial intelligence eventually replace psychiatrists? *The British Journal of Psychiatry, 218*. 1–4. https://doi.org/10.1192/bjp.2019.245

Castets-Renard, C. (2021). Human rights and algorithmic impact assessment for predictive policing. In H.-W. Micklitz, O. Pollicino, A. Reichman, A. Simoncini, G. Sartor, & G. de Gregorio (Eds.), *Constitutional Challenges in the Algorithmic Society*. Cambridge University Press. https://doi.org/10.1017/9781108914857

Calvo, A., Ortiz, N., Espinosa, A., Dimitrievikj, A., Oliva, I., Guijarro, J., & Sidiqqi, S. (2023). *Safe AI: Ensuring safe and responsible artificial intelligence* (pp. 1–4). https://doi.org/10.23919/JNIC58574.2023.10205749

Chen, Y.-C., Ahn, M. J., & Wang, Y.-F. (2023). Artificial intelligence and public values: Value impacts and governance in the public sector. *Sustainability, 15*(6), 4796. https://doi.org/10.3390/su15064796

Chhatre, R., & Singh, S. (2024a). Policy and regulatory frameworks for artificial intelligence. *Harbin Gongcheng Daxue Xuebao/Journal of Harbin Engineering University, 45*, 443. https://doi.org/10.2139/ssrn.4848705

Chhatre, R., & Singh, S. (2024b). The AI jungle book! *International Journal of Innovative Science and Research Technology, 9*, 3132. https://doi.org/10.38124/ijisrt/IJISRT24MAY2051

Daly, A., Hagendorff, T., Li, H., Mann, M., Marda, V., Wagner, B., Wang, W., & Witteborn, S. (2019). Artificial intelligence, governance and ethics: Global perspectives. *SSRN Electronic Journal*. https://doi.org/10.2139/ssrn.3414805

Denhardt, J. V., & Denhardt, R. B. (2015). *The new public service: Serving, not steering*. Routledge.

Dignum, V. (2017). *Responsible artificial intelligence: Designing AI for human values*. Retrieved from https://www.itu.int/dms_pub/itu-s/opb/journal/S-JOURNAL-ICTF.VOL1-2018-1-P01-PDF-E.pdf

Dobbe, R. (2022). *System safety and artificial intelligence*. Conference on Fairness, Accountability and Transparency. https://doi.org/10.1145/3531146.3533215

Fjeld, J., Achten, N., Hilligoss, H., Nagy, A., & Srikumar, M. (2020). Principled artificial intelligence: Mapping consensus in ethical and rights-based approaches to principles for AI. *SSRN Electronic Journal*. https://doi.org/10.2139/ssrn.3518482

Floridi, L. (2024). The ethics of artificial intelligence: Exacerbated problems, renewed problems, unprecedented problems—Introduction to the Special Issue of the American Philosophical Quarterly dedicated to The Ethics of AI. *SSRN Electronic Journal*. https://doi.org/10.2139/ssrn.4801799

George Manias, D. A. (2023). *AI4Gov: Trusted AI for transparent public governance fostering democratic values*. 2023 19th International Conference on Distributed Computing in Smart Systems and the Internet of Things (DCOSS-IoT). https://doi.org/10.1109/DCOSS-IoT58021.2023.00090

Goldenfein, J. (2019). *Algorithmic transparency and decision-making accountability: Thoughts for buying machine learning algorithms*. Retrieved from https://www.semanticscholar.org/paper/Algorithmic-Transparency-and-Decision-Making-for-Goldenfein/f6182f378b464cb3c1a18b567875fa746c950201

Golpayegani, D., Pandit, H. J., & Lewis, D. (2023). *To be high-risk, or not to be—Semantic specifications and implications of the AI Act's high-risk AI applications and harmonised standards*. Proceedings of the 2023 ACM Conference on Fairness, Accountability, and Transparency (FAccT '23). Association for Computing Machinery, New York, NY, USA, pp. 905–915. https://doi.org/10.1145/3593013.3594050

Gupta, P. (2023). *Addressing bias and fairness issues in artificial intelligence*. https://ijsdr.org/papers/IJSDR2309008.pdf

Gwagwa, A., Kraemer-Mbula, E., Rizk, N., Rutenberg, I., & De Beer, J. (2020). Artificial Intelligence (AI) deployments in Africa: Benefits, challenges and policy dimensions. *The African Journal of Information and Communication, 26*, 3–30. https://doi.org/10.23962/10539/30361

Henman, P. (2020). *Improving public services using artificial intelligence: Possibilities, pitfalls, governance*. https://doi.org/10.1080/23276665.2020.1816188

Hickok, M. (2022). Public procurement of artificial intelligence systems: New risks and future proofing. *AI & Society*. https://doi.org/10.1007/s00146-022-01572-2

Holzinger, A., Weippl, E., Tjoa, A. M., & Kieseberg, P. (2021). Digital transformation for sustainable development goals (SDGs)—A security. *Safety and Privacy Perspective on AI*. https://doi.org/10.1007/978-3-030-84060-0_1

Hosain, Md. T., Anik, M. H., Rafi, S., Tabassum, R., Insia, K., & Siddiky, Md. (2023). Path to gain functional transparency in artificial intelligence with meaningful explainability. *Journal of Metaverse, 3*, 166–180. https://doi.org/10.57019/jmv.1306685

Humprecht, E., Esser, F., & Van Aelst, P. (2020). Resilience to online disinformation: A framework for cross-national comparative research. *The International Journal of Press/Politics, 25*(3), 493–516. https://doi.org/10.1177/1940161219900126

Jobin, A., Ienca, M., & Vayena, E. (2019). The global landscape of AI ethics guidelines. *Nature Machine Intelligence, 1*. https://doi.org/10.1038/s42256-019-0088-2

Kaminski, M. (2022). Regulating the risks of AI. *SSRN Electronic Journal*. https://doi.org/10.2139/ssrn.4195066

Kawakami, A., Coston, A., Heidari, H., Holstein, K., & Zhu, H. (2024). Studying up public sector AI: How networks of power relations shape agency decisions around AI design and use. *Proceedings of the ACM on Human-Computer Interaction*. https://doi.org/10.48550/arXiv.2405.12458

Kiemde, S. M. A., & Kora, A. D. (2022). Towards an ethics of AI in Africa: Rule of education. *AI and Ethics, 2*(1), 35–40.

Knowles, B., & Richards, J. T. (2021). *The sanction of authority: promoting public trust in AI*. Proceedings of the 2021 ACM Conference on Fairness, Accountability, and Transparency (FAccT '21). Association for Computing Machinery, New York, NY, USA, pp. 262–271. https://doi.org/10.1145/3442188.3445890

Koulu, R. (2020). Proceduralizing control and discretion: Human oversight in Artificial intelligence policy. *Maastricht Journal of European and Comparative Law*. https://doi.org/10.1177/1023263X20978649

Kulal, A., Rahiman, H. U., Suvarna, H., Abhishek, N., & Dinesh, S. (2024). Enhancing public service delivery efficiency: Exploring the impact of AI. *Journal of Open Innovation: Technology, Market, and Complexity, 10*(3), 100329.

Kretschmer, M., Kretschmer, T., Peukert, A., & Peukert, C. (2023). The risks of risk-based AI regulation: Taking liability seriously. *SSRN Electronic Journal*. https://doi.org/10.2139/ssrn.4622405

Leavy, S., O'Sullivan, B., & Siapera, E. (2020). *Data, power and bias in artificial intelligence*. https://doi.org/10.48550/arXiv.2008.07341

Leslie, D. (2019). Understanding artificial intelligence ethics and safety. *Social Science Research Network*. https://doi.org/10.5281/zenodo.3240529

Leslie, D. (2020). Explaining decisions made with AI. https://doi.org/10.2139/ssrn.4033308

Loi, M., & Spielkamp, M. (2021). *Towards accountability in the use of artificial intelligence for public administrations* (pp. 757–766). https://doi.org/10.1145/3461702.3462631

Mega, R. A. (2023). Countering democratic disruption amid the disinformation phenomenon through artificial intelligence (AI) in public sector. *Jurnal Manajemen Pelayanan Publik, 7*, 49. https://doi.org/10.24198/jmpp.v7i1.48125

Methnani, L., Aler Tubella, A., Dignum, V., & Theodorou, A. (2021). Let me take over: Variable autonomy for meaningful human control. *Frontiers in Artificial Intelligence, 4*. https://doi.org/10.3389/frai.2021.737072

Metcalf, J., Moss, E., Watkins, E.., Singh, R., & Elish, M. (2021). Algorithmic impact assessments and accountability: The co-construction of impacts. 735–746. https://doi.org/10.1145/3442188.3445935

Misra, S. K., Das, S., Gupta, S., & Sharma, S. K. (2020). Public policy and regulatory challenges of artificial intelligence (AI). In S. K. Sharma, Y. K. Dwivedi, B. Metri, & N. P. Rana (Eds.), *Re-imagining diffusion and adoption of information technology and systems: A continuing conversation*. TDIT 2020. IFIP Advances in Information and Communication Technology, Vol. 617. Springer. https://doi.org/10.1007/978-3-030-64849-7_10

Mitrou, L., Janssen, M., & Loukis, E. (2021). *Human control and discretion in AI-driven decision-making in government* (pp. 10–16). https://doi.org/10.1145/3494193.3494195

Mehrabi, N., Morstatter, F., Saxena, N., Lerman, K., & Galstyan, A. (2021). A survey on bias and fairness in machine learning. *ACM Computing Survey, 54*(6), Article 115 (July 2022), 35 pp. https://doi.org/10.1145/3457607

OECD. (2021a). *The OECD framework for digital talent and skills in the public sector* (OECD Working Papers on Public Governance, No. 45). OECD Publishing. https://doi.org/10.1787/4e7c3f58-en

OECD. (2021b). *Tools for trustworthy AI: A framework to compare implementation tools for trustworthy AI systems* (OECD Digital Economy Papers, No. 312). OECD Publishing. https://doi.org/10.1787/008232ec-en

Onyango, G. (2024). DHR-PA—Democracy and human rights in public administration in Africa. *Politics & Policy, 52*(2), 426–449.

Onyango, G., & Ondiek, J. O. (2021). Digitalization and integration of sustainable development goals (SGDs) in public organizations in Kenya. *Public Organization Review, 21*, 511–526. https://doi.org/10.1007/s11115-020-00504-2

Onyango, G., & Ondiek, J. O. (2022). Open innovation during the COVID-19 pandemic policy responses in South Africa and Kenya. *Politics & Policy, 50*(5), 1008–1031. https://doi.org/10.1111/polp.12490

Pessach, D., & Shmueli, E. (2023). Algorithmic fairness. In *Machine learning for data science handbook: Data mining and knowledge discovery handbook*. Springer. https://doi.org/10.1007/978-3-031-24628-9_37

Pizzi, M., Romanoff, M., & Engelhardt, T. (2020). AI for humanitarian action: Human rights and ethics. *International Review of the Red Cross, 102*, 145–180. https://doi.org/10.1017/S1816383121000011

Prabhakaran, V., Mitchell, M., Gebru, T., & Gabriel, I. (2022). *A human rights-based approach to responsible AI*. https://doi.org/10.48550/arXiv.2210.02667

Radanliev, P., Santos, O., Brandon-Jones, A., & Joinson, A. (2024). Ethics and responsible AI deployment. *Frontiers in Artificial Intelligence, 7*, 1377011. https://doi.org/10.3389/frai.2024.1377011

Rawat, D., Rawat, A., Pandey, A., Chauhan, G., & Aluvala, S. (2024). *Ethics in the era of Intelligent Machines: Legal perspective and regulatory implications* (pp. 1–7). https://doi.org/10.1109/KHI-HTC60760.2024.10481959

Saleiro, P., Kuester, B., Stevens, A., Anisfeld, A., Hinkson, L., London, J., & Ghani, R. (2018). *Aequitas: A bias and fairness audit toolkit*. https://doi.org/10.48550/arXiv.1811.05577

Shefeh, P. M., & Marco, O. (2022). Algorithmic impact assessment for an ehical use of AI in SMEs. https://doi.org/10.14236/ewic/HCI2022.34

Sigfrids, A., Nieminen, M. P., Leikas, J., & Pikkuaho, P. (2022). How should public administrations foster the ethical development and use of artificial intelligence? A review of proposals for developing governance of AI. *Frontiers in Human Dynamics*. https://doi.org/10.3389/fhumd.2022.858108

Son, Y.-H. (2023). *Research on AI fairness—Achieving an AI-inclusive society without discrimination*. https://doi.org/10.35227/hylr.2023.8.34.3.275

Sreerama, J., & Krishnamoorthy, G. (2022). Ethical considerations in AI addressing bias and fairness in machine learning models. *Journal of Knowledge Learning and Science Technology, 1*, 130–138. ISSN: 2959-6386 (online). https://doi.org/10.60087/jklst.vol1.n1.p138

Susar, D., & Aquaro, V. (2019). *Artificial intelligence: Opportunities and challenges for the public sector*. In Proceedings of the 12th International Conference on Theory and Practice of Electronic Governance (ICEGOV '19). Association for Computing Machinery, New York, NY, USA, pp. 418–426. https://doi.org/10.1145/3326365.3326420

Thinyane, H., & Sassetti, F. (2020). *Towards a human rights-based approach to AI: Case study of apprise*. https://doi.org/10.1007/978-3-030-52014-4_3

Tupay, P., Ebers, M., Juksaar, J., Kohv, K. (2021). Is European data protection toxic for innovative AI? An Estonian perspective. *Juridica International, 30*, 99–110. https://doi.org/10.12697/JI.2021.30.12

van de Poel, I. (2020). Embedding values in artificial intelligence (AI) systems. *Minds & Machines, 30*, 385–409. https://doi.org/10.1007/s11023-020-09537-4

Veale, M. (2017). *Logics and practices of transparency and opacity in real-world applications of public sector machine learning*. ArXiv, https://arxiv.org/abs/1706.09249

Veale, M., Van Kleek, M., & Binns, R. (2018). *Fairness and accountability design needs for algorithmic support in high-stakes public sector decision-making*. International Conference on Human Factors in Computing Systems. https://doi.org/10.1145/3173574.3174014

Walter, Y. (2024). Managing the race to the moon: Global policy and governance in Artificial Intelligence regulation—A contemporary overview and an analysis of socioeconomic consequences. *Discover Artificial Intelligence*. https://doi.org/10.1007/s44163-024-00109-4

Wangari, N. (2017). *Data and democracy: What role did Cambridge analytica play in Kenya's elections?* Retrieved from https://advox.globalvoices.org/2017/11/03/data-and-democracy-what-role-did-cambridge-analytica-play-in-kenyas-elections/. Accessed on 17th September 2024.

Webb, H. (2019). *A governance framework for algorithmic accountability and transparency*. https://doi.org/10.2861/59990

Weismann, M. F. (2024). *Artificial intelligence regulatory models: Advances in the European Union and recommendations for the United States and evolving global markets*. https://doi.org/10.46697/001c.120396

Willems, J., Schmid, M. J., Vanderelst, D., Vogel, D., & Ebinger, F. (2022). AI-driven public services and the privacy paradox: Do citizens really care about their privacy? *Public Management Review, 25*(11), 2116–2134. https://doi.org/10.1080/14719037.2022.2063934

Wong, J., Morgan, D., Straub, V. J., Hashem, Y., Bright, J. (2022). *Key challenges for the participatory governance of AI in public administration*. SocArXiv, https://doi.org/10.31219/OSF.IO/PDCRM

Yeung, K., Howes, A., & Pogrebna, G. (2019). AI governance by human rights-centred design, deliberation and oversight: An end to ethics washing. *SSRN Electronic Journal*. https://doi.org/10.2139/ssrn.3435011

Zhou, N., Zhang, Z., Nair, V., Singhal, H., Chen, J., & Sudjianto, A. (2021). *Bias, fairness, and accountability with AI and ML algorithms*. https://doi.org/10.48550/arXiv.2105.06558

Zhu, L., Xu, X., Lu, Q., Governatori, G., & Whittle, J. (2021). *AI and ethics—Operationalising responsible AI*. https://doi.org/10.48550/arXiv.2105.08867

Webpages Searched

EU: Shaping Europe's digital future: https://digital-strategy.ec.europa.eu/en/policies/regulatory-framework-ai

EU: European Centre for Algorithmic Transparency: https://algorithmic-transparency.ec.europa.eu/index_en

AU: Continental AI Strategy: https://au.int/sites/default/files/documents/44004-doc-EN-_Continental_AI_Strategy_July_2024.pdf

CHAPTER 5

Feminist Artificial Intelligence (AI) Approaches for Civic Governance in Africa

Mardiya Siba Yahaya and Zanele Sokatsha

Introduction

On a day in September, a friend and I (Mardiya) decided to go on an impromptu trip to Europe. As we booked our accommodation for the said trip, we got an error message stating that the booking site only accepted credit cards. At first, this strange occurrence made us wonder whether this was an issue with our debit cards. However, we also questioned why an institution would not accept a debit card in the first place. After several alternate tries, I asked my friend to change her nationality from Nigerian to British and try again. This time, the same debit card initially denied was accepted, making us realise that it was yet another case of *automated bias and aggression*. The scenario is not isolated, as I

M. S. Yahaya (✉)
Johannesburg, South Africa
e-mail: mardiyasiba@gmail.com

Z. Sokatsha
Gender Rights In Tech (GRIT), Johannesburg, South Africa

G. Onyango (ed.), *Designing Artificial Intelligence for Public Policy and Governance in Africa*, Studies in National Governance and Emerging Technologies, https://doi.org/10.1007/978-3-031-83445-5_5

have had to deal with false fraud alerts by retailers who would cancel an order because my (Mardiya) debit card and billing address were registered in Ghana. These form part of the many events where automated systems have been designed and trained in ways that reproduce frustrations, exclusions, and burdens against Africans. Such automated systems and existing data usually go along to inform AI models that are tested and deployed at scale. Some of these cost money reinforce racial narratives in the case of the Sudanese Artificial Intelligence (AI) generated Barbie (Lynch, 2023), and other times; it costs lives when critical life-altering decision-making is outsourced to an automated system.

As AI tools and systems gain momentum among governments while being hailed as a pathway to more efficient civic governance globally and as an opportunity for Africa to *leapfrog* into the technological revolution, we need to interrogate the implications of embedding these systems actively and strategically in everyday lives. Current approaches and use cases of AI technologies and powered services tend to centre hegemonic views and practices that harm minoritised communities at gendered, racial, class, ethnic and religious margins within matrices of domination (Costanza-Chock, 2020). We argue that for AI to be remotely ethical and safe, design justice and feminist AI principles need to be centred from the research and design to the deployment phases of the technology and its uses. Part of this requires us to create a baseline understanding of the dynamics and experiences technologies dubbed as AI create and reinforce within the lives of Africans and who creates and enforces these technologies, all while answering whether policy can help address the effects of AI technologies on the lives of Africans. All while trying to point out that "African" is not monolithic, thus throughout the essay, contextualising through location, gender, ethnicity and nationality in the cases we use. We situate these arguments and discussions using cases of predatory ride-hailing algorithmic systems, the associated gendered violence, inequalites and the layers of human exploitation platforms and companies use to create, deploy, and derive the benefits from technologies.

This chapter does not seek to contribute to the many works that tout how AI could be used to solve challenges in the world faster and better. We, however, invite readers to carefully consider the limitations of the technology by detailing some of the existing threats while operationalising Claudia Aradau's (2023) and Francis Hunger's (2023) recommendations that to "unhyped AI" we need to start from "mundane socio-technical practices from the data that needs to run the algorithms, and the processing required by whom and which platform". Hence, we begin our chapter with a story of a rather simple engagement with an automated payment system that produces inequalities for two individuals from Ghana and Nigeria. The chapter concludes by expanding an existing work proposing how the African Union (AU) Information and Communication Technology (ICT) policy framework can include a gender mainstreaming approach to AI (Chabikwa, 2023).

As already indicated by some contributors to this volume, we recommend community-led and design justice practices that enable community ownership, and accountability as AI technologies, policies and frameworks are being created and deployed in Africans' lives. Participatory action and design justice often require designers, be it technology or policy, to work with communities, including ones of practice and take contextualised pathways to design. While automated systems, models, or technologies may be seemingly neutral, Nanjala Nyabola (2022) reminds us that "one cannot understand how technology will affect a society unless they understand the society in question". In other words, for policymakers and designers to understand how their framings and designs will affect a specific group of people, they have to contend with the dynamics and implications of how different technologies organises and facilitates the livelihoods of individuals and communities in a manner that is non-exploitative. Participatory Action (PAR) and Design Justice pathways, when rightfully implemented, also move designers and policymakers to integrate the multiple marginalities of harm and power that are encoded in the lives of certain communities. Finally, feminist approaches, which, in our view, pull together the above frameworks of PAR and Design Justice, community ownership, and accountability, allow policymakers to learn from digital justice communities of practice that continuously work and advocate for public interest technologies that do not reproduce and reconfigure violations against people, restrict their desires, and exploit their lands.

Whose Existence Is in Crisis Now?

A 2021 African sci-fi musical film, Neptune Frost, set in Burundi, attempted to address the power dynamics between people whose labour and resources make our technology realities and devices possible. The film focuses on showing that people who, through the labour of their hands, body, and resources, truly control technology and metaphorically demonstrate how they intervene in our Internet use. A practice they detail using a form of metaphysical hacking, where the world's Internet is labelled "Netupe", without traces of where the invasion originated. Neptune Frost uses symbolism to manoeuvre between labour and resource exploitation, speaking to powers that control technology and how the people at the production level are often exploited and disadvantaged by said 'innovation' that supposedly advance the world. By situating the symbolic representation the film attempts to communicate, we also come to understand the role of AI in the everyday lives of Africans. Thus far, most of the conversations on AI in Africa have revolved around border management and civic governance. Databases built from biometric identification systems are used in AI models that facilitate the "filtering and fracturing" (Aradau, 2023) of people on the move where border management and surveillance are concerned. However, the connection between labour exploitation, predatory algorithms, ethnic, locational, gendered, and racial dynamics provides additional perspectives on unequal burdens of AI technologies . Sometime between 2021 and 2022, many black people in South Africa discovered that when they changed their names on Uber to a white/non-black or ethnic presenting name, the prices of their trips significantly reduced for the same destination. This inspired more people to change their names on Uber, and in other locations within the global minority, i.e., North, changing your name to a white/non-black or ethnic presenting one often meant being able to get a ride faster.

The predatory algorithm of Uber goes beyond race and ethnicity but also shows up differently in various locations and genders. For instance, in some locations, Uber drivers were provided with estimated cost of a trip, which allowed drivers to make informed decisions. However, in most other African locations such as Ghana, Kenya, and Uganda, at the time, the worker was not informed of these estimations and can only find out by engaging with the customer or at the end of the trip. Sometimes, these workers were also women who had to navigate gendered threats where male customers may refuse to pay them or experience sexual violence and violations, which are often ignored by the platform when they report such incidents (Fairwork, 2023). Similarly, price surges due to lower battery charges are exploitative but often mean that a woman or queer person at risk and in need of critical transportation at a certain moment may experience harm due to Uber's predatory algorithm. There have also been reports of Uber's identification algorithm failing to verify

Nigerian workers who are also asked to submit new photos regularly (Barry, 2021).

In each of these instances, the worker experiences significant exploitation and discrimination. As a customer who often relies on ride-hailing apps like Uber also has to navigate the discriminatory effects such algorithmic systems. Transportation is fundamental to movement within and between locations. Meanwhile, with the emergence of Uber and other platforms, traditional taxi industries have been widely known to be disrupted (Mourdoukoutas, 2017), making some of these platforms monopolise transportation with no other practical and safe alternative. Opaque algorithmic management systems, often termed algorithmic black boxes, have significantly shaped people's lives, livelihoods, and income. These happen in various ways at borders, through civic technologies and systems, AI surveillance pipelines (Kalluri et al., 2023), and transportation, to name a few. The models used to frame and design the technologies have been demonstrated to be biased in a manner that either overly or underrepresent marginalised groups towards reproducing harm and various documented violations (Bender et al., 2021). The language used to describe products often dubbed as AI, frames them as exceptional with extraordinary abilities to perform tasks and *decision making*, as though the decisions being outsourced to some of these systems and models are not incredibly complex and require decision makers' ability to derive contextual meaning, which AI systems have been pointed out by researchers not to have (Bender et al., 2021).

The examples of how technology companies have become significant mediators of transportation, employment and leisure enable us to shift "from the exceptional black-boxed and the spectacular to the ordinary, the dispersed and every day, [where] we can understand how these technologies work, for whom and what they do when they do not work" (Aradau, 2023). Black South Africans realised that Uber's dynamic pricing works best for white customers, so they changed their names to access reasonable prices. My friend and I (Mardiya) realised that our African nationalities could not afford a leisure trip without navigating the aggressions implemented by biased payment management systems. Once we strip all these messages of exceptional AI, the Uber and hotel management scenarios help us see how such technologies organise the lives of different Africans.

We are also presented with a clear case of an exploitative production lifeline where workers who actively contribute to building technology companies and train their algorithmic systems are underpaid, overworked and invisibilised (Perrigo, 2023). The violence that is constructed and enforced at the production level is experienced by end users and supposed beneficiaries in aggressive and micro-aggressive ways. For instance, female customers have continuously shared life-threatening cases of drivers taking wrong turns with an excuse that the final price would increase. Others have also detailed stories of physical and verbal assault when prices are lower than expected at the end of the trip (Idris, 2022). Women platform workers also shared that the risks of working with the platform outweigh the benefits because the "onus of safety is solely on the workers", and the platforms facilitate violence through their design decisions and governing policies (Fairwork, 2023).

AI harms, risks, and inequalities exist at borders, within regimes and practices of control, labour, and human desire. Collectively demonstrating that movement, that is, the filtering and fracturing of certain people to enable convenience, cause delays (Aradau, 2023), and restrictions are not reserved for people at borders but show up in our everyday lives as AI systems are being deployed and tested in African. These issues have physical, financial, and practical implications, making us realise that our visions for a system that mediates civic services, delivery, and engagements in ways that benefit minoritised groups at the margins of gender, race, class, location, sexuality, and ethnicity might be aspirational. The aspiration of where we would like to be, however, requires us to fundamentally shift our conceptualisation, approach, policy, and design of AI systems from the constant disregard for marginalised people, or the idea that for a technological revolution to happen, it has to cost human lives and livelihoods.

In Chabikwa's (2023) work on AI, Gender, and Development in Africa, she highlights that "the absence of any clear definition and framing of [multiple] ICT policy documents in Africa affects policymaking, and in turn, affects the implementation of such technologies". Beyond the need for such clear definitions in policy documents, we also need to actively trace and document how technologies dubbed as AI, including existing automated and algorithmic systems, are reconfiguring social, economic and political experiences. First, lets collectively map out how marginalised groups are experiencing these technologies now and today. And to borrow from Professor Pumla Dineo Gqola (2007), the aspirations of these policy documents, framings, convenings, and hype cannot be crafted around "silences and gaps on the gendered, capitalist, ethnic and racial dimensions of our pasts" and presents (Gqola, 2007).

African Feminist Approaches to AI

The question then becomes, can we imagine and create AI with non-exploitative production lifelines, that is in tune with the realities of people at the margins and thus is created within the margins themselves? While we interact with AI as a technology of exclusion and regurgitated social harms, an African Feminist approach may necessitate us to redefine and reframe AI as technology that mainly and solely interacts with groups we consider to be marginalised by virtue of its active exclusion and harm that it inflicts on minoritised groups in practice. In this sense, at the very core of its fabric, AI is borne from the violence of racial, gendered, cultural, and economic minorities, and not despite them. Thus, innovations and developments that seek to create along with the AI hype do not do so from innocent, imaginative play but from the lived realities of those it actively marginalises. The underlying privilege hazard is so prominent that it underscores that all AI innovation has to have implications for how we define AI. A definition for AI that does not acknowledge this overarching tendency/dynamic is disingenuous.

Yet, we also caution that the work of African feminist-informed AI ought to move beyond a place of centring otherness. As Minna Salami (2020) puts it in Sensuous Knowledge, "to rethink ideas that are central to the human mind with an Africa-centred black feminist sensibility is not to essentialise the ways that African, black, or female identities have been "othered" by a Europatriarchal value system", as this further reinforces europatriachal ideals, and stunts imagination for and of African people outside of these confines. Instead, we are called to draw inspiration from our subjectivities in their cultural and spiritual fullness.

We adopt Design Justice and Participatory Action AI research principles to build an understanding of what is required for an African feminist approach to AI. We find these frameworks and consequential principles fit for such an endeavour as they are founded upon the concern of the violence and aggressions experienced by minoritised groups and further place the onus of safety and regard of people's dignity on the designers and creators of technological and AI tools. Design Justice's first principle of practice can be used to define the "why" of such an approach: "We use design to sustain, heal, and empower our communities, as well as to seek liberation from exploitative and oppressive systems", encompassing both the venture to remedy ill AI, and provisions for creative design that affirms people's dignity, spirituality, intentions for their world.

We turn to efforts around the globe that have championed basic principles and values that contribute to an African Feminist approach to AI. What is required in an African feminist approach to AI centres *on the experiences of those pushed to the margins by our capitalist europatriachal realities*? These are principles that are valued:

Community Engagement and Bidirectional Participation

To be attuned to the needs of those at the margins is intentionally creating space that allows these communities to engage as experts of their own experiences. At the same time, designers interact as facilitators whose work is instructional and informed by the community. This often turns into forms of extractivism, or recommendation that requires the process to engage so that the community continues to be custodians and owners and shape the accountability process of the technology's design, interpretations of the problem, and governance. This offers a sense of agency to the community in shaping the design process and technology in ways consistent with their cultural and spiritual values. We see this in the functioning and values of a South African-based grassroots organisation, Masakhane NLP, that strives to promote linguistic diversity and inclusion in natural language processing (NLP) and machine translation (MT). Masakhane adopts a participatory design and research approach that involves end users and researchers in every stage of the design and research process. Providing an analysis of their inner working Birhane et al. (2022) explain that

> [...] there were no prerequisites placed on participation or fixed roles assigned to participants, but rather the roles emerged organically, and participatory input was sought at every level of the process from language speaking to model building, and participants moved fluidly between different roles. The research process was defined collaboratively and iteratively, and meeting agendas were public and democratically voted on. Language data was crowd-sourced, annotated, evaluated, analysed and interpreted by participants (from participants).

Accountability After and During Participation

What foregrounds Masakhane's objective of purposeful engagement is a clear value and prioritisation of accountability and transparency at every stage of the design process. Understanding that the architecture of a tool (not its use) has meaning and consequences for the well-being of those it not only creates for but actively excludes, compels facilitators to be accountable to said well-being and thus accountable to the owners of the well-being. An AI tool that seeks to centre marginalised communities must start by recognising that the individuals within the community are humans with dignity and the right to respect, not personified end-users. These are communities who, after participation and extraction, may wonder how their mental, physical, cultural, and spiritual properties and energies may have gone and how they are being used within a technological framework that initially sought to misrepresent them and disregard their humanity. Thus, accountability calls for more than participation and feedback; it ensures that the extraction is comparable to the tool's benefits. The effort of disseminating one's experiences, ideas, goals, and cultural philosophies to a facilitator is reflected within the design process and the tool itself. In practice, this is something along the lines of Masakhane's adoption of a value system that reflects the participant's philosophy of what language is to the community, a point of understanding and connectivity, which is reflected in one of their core values *umntu ngumntu ngabantu,* that is, "a person is a person through other people".

Transparency (Sharing Design Knowledge and Tools)

While transparency is often dangerously connotated to accountability, it takes on a different function in practice. Transparency is not only a means to offer the community access to the inner world of the design process, but it also shares tools and knowledge that allow the community to interact with this process in ways that ensure an informed and empowered engagement. Does the design and participation process offer training, workshops, etc., to enrich the community with knowledge that allows them to understand the mechanisms involved in solving their issues? Do they understand the technology that is being employed? Such knowledge allows the community to ensure that the design and other processes used to create the tool align with their values and cultural and philosophical principles. Does the community know how much energy, water, and biometric surveilling is involved in making the tool as is? Has the participation process provided the community with alternatives to such processes, thus allowing an informed engagement and contribution that does not force misalignment and abandonment of one's driving values in the face of addressing need? Such knowledge sharing is what Sasha Costanza-Chock (2020) explains as "reasoning through design is a mode of knowledge production".

Intentional Consideration of the Design/ Technology's Impact on the Recipient Community

Going into the heart of ethical and technological development, intentional consideration of a design or technology's impact on the community it serves becomes an ethical imperative, resonating with the principles of justice and equity that underscore responsible innovation and development. In this regard, technology is not a detached entity but an active participant in social dynamics, and its deployment must be characterised by a meticulous understanding of the nuanced needs and challenges of the community that interacts with it. This intentional approach is crucial in avoiding the unintentional reinforcement of existing inequalities and harm and ensuring that technology contributes positively to the community's well-being.

The pursuit of designing technology with intentional consideration of its impact on the community necessitates specific questions that must guide the process to ensure a nuanced and equitable outcome. Who within the community stands to benefit most from this technology, and conversely, who might be disproportionately burdened or excluded (D'Ignazio & Klein, 2020)? This allows us to scrutinise potential disparities along lines of gender, race, or socioeconomic. Costanza-Chock (2020) *discourages designers from reinventing the wheel*, as this often displaces existing knowledge, practices, and efforts to solve problems that the community has likely been navigating for a substantial amount of time. Recognising the community's inherent dignity and respect involves amplifying this existing knowledge by involving the community's organisations and projects and creating from where the community currently is. This prevents facilitators from designing from the point of assumption and imposing their ideals on the community, further infantilising them and stripping them of their dignity and agency, much like the relationship that one has with their coloniser.

Conclusion

Community by design, accountability, learning, and governance have become our recommended approaches to building, framing, and governing AI tools and technologies in everyday life. Our aspirations towards building and advocating technologies dubbed AI must begin with an understanding and framing how AI reorganises and configures lives in various African contexts. A community-by-design approach to designing, framing and governing technologies also requires investment in localised and transnational communities of practice across various African contexts, cultures, and lives. The communities of practice can provide nuanced perspectives towards creating policies and frameworks on AI within the parameters necessary for many Africans. This could be achieved by learning with and supporting community-based organisations and digital justice practitioners actively advocating and working on public interest technologies. Most of these practices might also require fundamental social issues such as movement, labour, gender and sexual violence, and racial aggression, which are complicated through digital societies, to be understood and addressed as they are without taking a solutionist approach. There might be a higher chance that acknowledging and addressing some of these issues may not require technology in the first place. However, in the space where states deem it important to mediate civic engagements and lives through technology, centring a community-based approach to technology design might be a first start to demonstrating that they are listening and engaging with the people of their communities in ways that are needed to rebuild trust, and create shared aspirations, imaginations and visions of a flourishing public space, and life for minoritised people.

References

Aradau, C. (2023). Borders have always been artificial: Migration, data and AI. *International Migration, 61*(5), 303–306. https://doi.org/10.1111/imig.13186

Barry, E. (2021). Uber drivers say a 'racist' algorithm is putting them out of work. *Time*. Available at: https://time.com/6104844/uber-facial-recognition-racist/

Bender, E., Mcmillan-Major, A., Shmitchell, S., Gebru, T., & Shmitchell, S.-G. (2021). *On the dangers of stochastic parrots: Can language models be too big?* FAccT '21: Proceedings of the 2021 ACM Conference on Fairness, Accountability, and Transparency. https://doi.org/10.1145/3442188.3445922

Birhane, A., et al. (2022). *Power to the people? Opportunities and challenges for participatory AI*. Equity and Access in Algorithms, Mechanisms, and Optimization (EAAMO'22), 8 pp. https://doi.org/10.1145/3551624.3555290

Chabikwa, R. (2023). *AI, gender and development in Africa: Feminist policy considerations*.

Costanza-Chock, S. (2020). *Design justice: Community-led practices to build the worlds we need*. MIT Press.

D'Ignazio, C., & Klein, L. F. (2020). *Data feminism*. MIT Press.

Fairwork. (2023). *Gender and platform work: Fairwork gender report 2023*. Fairwork Project, University of Oxford & WZB Berlin Social Science Center. https://fair.work/wpcontent/uploads/sites/17/2023/07/Fairwork-Gender-Report-2023-FINAL-red.pdf

Gqola, P. D. (2007). How the 'cult of femininity' and violent masculinities support endemic gender based violence in contemporary South Africa. *African Identities, 5*(1), 111–124. https://doi.org/10.1080/14725840701253894

Hunger, F. (2023, April). Unhype artificial "intelligence"! A proposal to replace the deceiving terminology of AI. *Training the Archive Working Paper No. 6*, Ludwig Forum Aachen. Available at: https://trainingthearchive.ludwigforum.de/en/working-paper-6-en

Idris, A. (2022). *Bolt drivers in Nigeria are illicitly selling their accounts, putting passengers at risk*. Rest of World. Available at: https://restofworld.org/2022/bolt-drivers-in-nigeria-are-illicitly-selling-their-accounts-putting-passengers-at-risk/ [Accessed 2 December 2023].

Kalluri, P. R., Agnew, W. S., Cheng, M., Owens, K., Soldaini, L., & Birhane, A. (2023). *The surveillance AI pipeline*. arXiv (Cornell University), 1. https://doi.org/10.48550/arxiv.2309.15084

Lynch, S. (2023). *AI gave Sudanese Barbie a gun, beware the bias*. The Drum. Available at: https://www.thedrum.com/opinion/2023/08/30/ai-gave-sudanese-barbie-gun-beware-the-bias [Accessed 2 December 2023].

Mourdoukoutas, E. (2017). Africa's app-based taxis battle Uber over market share. *Africa Renewal*. Un.org. Available at: https://www.un.org/africarenewal/magazine/august-november-2017/africa%E2%80%99s-app-based-taxis-battle-uber-over-market-share

Nyabola, N. (2022). *Vertical Atlas*. verticalatlas.net. Available at: https://verticalatlas.net/#the-phone-changed-everything [Accessed 2 December 2023].

Perrigo, B. (2023). Exclusive: The $2 per hour workers who made ChatGPT safer. *Time*. Available at: https://time.com/6247678/openai-chatgpt-kenya-workers/

Salami, M. (2020). *Sensuous knowledge: A black feminist approach for everyone*. Zed Books Ltd.

PART II

Implementing AI in African Policy Sectors

SECTION OVERVIEW

This section contains chapters presenting various case studies showcasing implementation experiences of AI in selected policy sectors and governance processes. Each chapter examines the role of AI in driving socio-economic and political transformations. The focus is on areas that include challenges and opportunities that can characterise leveraging AI to achieve such transformations, economic growth, ensuring public accountability, security and crime, electoral processes, and enhancing peacebuilding efforts in conflict zones in Africa.

Highlights for practitioners and researchers

- Effective leveraging AI needs capacity building and skills training of policymakers and all other actors involved

- There is a need for a more localised digital maturity index, specifically for the public sector in Africa

- Sector-to-sector evaluation of AI readiness of public organisations and governance sectors

- Consideration of deep-seated challenges like organisational culture and historical inequality

- AI optimisation should go beyond infrastructural investment to address the inconsistencies of the state's approach levels of digital transformation

- Learning from the experiences of benchmark countries while developing an AI strategy. This could help with building a robust and sustainable impact

- Robust monitoring and evaluation mechanisms will ensure sustainable adaptation of AI strategies

- AI regulation must also regulate private entities using AI tools, ensuring effective checks and balances.

- Public investment in AI and human capital produces increased value in all sectors

- Engaging stakeholders and fostering cooperation are crucial for leveraging AI to reduce conflict and promote peace.

CHAPTER 6

Digital Maturity as AI Governance Pathways: Public Sector Challenges and Opportunities in South Africa

Odilile Ayodele, Petronella Saal, Tahiya Moosa, Krish Chetty, Emmanuel Fundisi, and Nondumiso Masuku

Introduction

In the three decades since the dawn of inclusive democracy, the South African government has grappled with how to transform the country economically and societally. The long history of Apartheid has meant that the country's developmental trajectory has been lopsided, contributing to a growing bureaucratic stagnation that has hampered the efficiency of the public service. Implementing advanced technologies has been suggested as a viable way to address the problems of insufficient service delivery

O. Ayodele (✉) · P. Saal · T. Moosa · K. Chetty · E. Fundisi · N. Masuku
Human Sciences Research Council (HSRC), Pretoria, South Africa
e-mail: oayodele@hsrc.ac.za

O. Ayodele
Department of Politics and International Relations, University of Johannesburg, Johannesburg, South Africa

G. Onyango (ed.), *Designing Artificial Intelligence for Public Policy and Governance in Africa*, Studies in National Governance and Emerging Technologies, https://doi.org/10.1007/978-3-031-83445-5_6

and inefficiencies in the public sector (Manda & Backhouse, 2018). This chapter examines how South Africa can advance along a digital maturity index to effectively leverage artificial intelligence (AI) for improved public sector governance while addressing unique contextual challenges such as the unequal distribution of resources, including the absence of hard and soft infrastructure. South Africa's Department of Science, Technology and Innovation's Research, Development and Innovation Roadmap emphasises that the pursuit of a National Artificial Intelligence (AI) Strategy should be anchored on AI infrastructure to bolster economic competitiveness and socioeconomic impact. The roadmap outlines a strategy to integrate AI into public services such as healthcare, education, and government operations, aiming to enhance efficiency and address local needs. Despite the enabling AI policy frameworks, South Africa struggles to harness AI fully for effective e-government initiatives. This chapter argues that AI governance involves optimisation of the digitalisation of public sector processes. Doing so details an examination of South Africa's digital maturity and how they could position strategies for implementing AI solutions and governance environment by creating an effective regulatory framework.

A digital maturity pathway could assist in identifying specific implementation AI strategies that government agencies can adopt to enhance public service efficiency and address socioeconomic disparities. This chapter shows that a lack of a dedicated digital maturity index undermines the creation of AI systems and governance, specifically for the public sector in African countries. To address this gap, this chapter leans on the Global Index on Responsible AI to assess the progress in leveraging AI for the public sector in South Africa. This framework allows for a nuanced evaluation of AI readiness in the public sector context. It is important to note that there is not yet a dedicated digital maturity index specifically designed for the public sector in South Africa. A focus on digital maturity assists in acknowledging the fundamental constraints of digital transformation in a digitally unequal society like those in Africa, and the potential advantages of technology integration in public service are crucial (Onyango, 2023). Information and communication technologies (ICTs) are the bedrock of service delivery; government-to-citizen (G2C) relations and the overall transformation and optimisation of government services have become commonplace in the twenty-first century. Terms like electronic government (e-government) and digital government have become part of the lexicon. Although these words are sometimes used interchangeably, they are not synonymous. E-government can be described as using ICTs to enhance government operations, thereby improving the efficiency, transparency, and accessibility of services provided to citizens (Rakhmanov, 2009). Digital transformation can fundamentally alter the dynamics of G2C and Government-to-business (G2B) interactions. Meanwhile, the concept of digital government extends beyond e-government. Digital government, an evolution of e-government, leverages digital technologies to refine governmental operations, bolster citizen engagement and participation, and foster transparency and collaboration.

It incorporates frontier technologies such as mobile platforms, data analytics, cloud computing, and AI to revolutionise the delivery of government services and interactions with citizens (Sullivan et al., 2022). In other words, it represents a more comprehensive approach to digitalising governance. In a developing country like South Africa, the digital transformation of governance promises to fundamentally transform public service. However, the promise of increased service delivery has yet to be realised outside of the absence of infrastructure and the existing digital divide (Nel-Sanders & Malomane, 2022, p. 9). The problem goes beyond material infrastructure and speaks to the inconsistency of the state's approach (at both local and national levels) to digital transformation. For instance, Wikus Visser and Hosanna Twinomurinzi (2008) reveal that various government departments and agencies are embarking on e-government initiatives. However, there is a need for more overarching management for these projects (Visser & Twinomurinzi, 2008). These findings align with studies conducted by Fanie Cloete (2012) and the collaborative study by Keneilwe Maremi et al. (2022).

Despite its challenges, South Africa has a policy framework, the *National e-government Strategy and Roadmap* (DTPS, 2017), which supports e-government. The South African Department of Communications and Digital Technologies (DCDT) has drafted a strategy around AI—*South Africa National Artificial Intelligence Policy Framework, 2024*. This is one of the first concrete steps towards developing a national policy—various government agencies, including the National Advisory Council on Innovation (NACI), are drafting policy instruments and recommendations. This draft AI National Policy framework provides a structured approach to AI adoption and offers clear guidance to all stakeholders in the public sector. However, like in the case of most advanced technologies, it faces significant challenges, such as the need for more communication, sensitisation, and integration between different government systems, social barriers and low digital and basic literacy levels (Manda, 2017). While research on AI applications in the public sector is expanding (Chen et al., 2023; de Sousa et al., 2019; Zuiderwijk et al., 2021), few empirical studies and systematic reviews look specifically at how African countries fare in public sector governance along AI maturity indices; a notable exception is the World Bank GovTech Maturity Index (GTMI) and a recent volume *Digitalisation and Public Policy in Africa: GovTech and CivicTech Innovations* (Onyango & Karuri-Sebina, 2025). Additionally, there still needs to be more knowledge about the specific contextual difficulties African nations confront in utilising AI to enhance public services. This gap is especially noticeable in South Africa, which is considered one of the continent's most robust economies. However, more needs to be understood about how the South African public sector can successfully promote the adoption of AI while tackling the country's deep-seated challenges related to governance and socioeconomic inequality. Some studies suggest the main issues are problems with leadership and governance, while others argue it is more about infrastructure and resource limitations (Chilunjika et al., 2022; Manda, 2021).

Though these viewpoints have merit, this chapter proposes that South Africa's challenges with achieving digital transformation stem from issues across government, as the country's overall digital maturity still needs to be advanced enough to enable successful large-scale transformation that would usher AI realisation in public policy. There is a need for a coordinated effort from all levels of government to improve its digital readiness and enable digital transformation in the public sector. The research question guiding this is: *What AI implementation strategies can government agencies adopt to advance along AI maturity indices while enhancing public service efficiency and addressing socioeconomic disparities?* This chapter's analysis draws on a review of scholarly literature and government reports. The proceeding sections are structured as follows: First, the chapter begins with an overview of digitalisation and its impact on the public sector in South Africa. It adopts Janowski's (2015) definition of digitalisation, which "entails the integration of digital technologies into everyday processes and government operations". While acknowledging other interpretations, this conceptualisation aligns closely with our focus on digitally transforming government services and operations. Doing so also provides background on South Africa's e-government strategy. Third, the digital maturity framework that underlies this analysis. Fourth, the discussion links the digital maturity framework with the AI framework, drawing lessons for South Africa. Fifth, the chapter concludes by synthesising the key issues, suggesting areas for further discussion and research, and providing recommendations.

Digitalisation in the South African Public Sector

The historical context of digitalisation in South Africa's public sector reveals a strategic evolution towards utilising ICTs for enhanced governance and service delivery. The journey began in 1995 with the release of the White Paper on transforming public service, advocating for structural reforms such as the Presidential Review Commission (PRC) (DPSA, 1995). Following this initial step, in 1997, the Batho Pele White Paper introduced a framework prioritising citizen-centred service delivery, emphasising the principles of transparency and efficiency (DPSA, 1997). In the late 1990s, significant advancements were made in 1999 by establishing the Thuso Service Centre program to extend government services to underserved areas (GCIS, 1998). Entering the early 2000s, the public sector saw the introduction of the *Electronic Government: The Digital Future—A Public Service IT Policy Framework* (DPSA, 2001), which set technical guidelines for ICT systems across the public sector.

In addition to these developments, 2002 marked a significant year with enacting the Electronic Communications and Transactions Act (ECTA), further solidifying the legislative framework for digital transactions (Republic of South Africa, 2002). By 2011, the National Development Plan (NDP) emphasised the widespread diffusion of ICTs across all societal facets (DTPS, 2017). The subsequent years saw further institutional developments. For instance, the establishment of the Department of Telecommunications and Postal Services in 2014 and the formulation of provincial e-government strategies by Gauteng and Western Cape in 2015 underscored the ongoing efforts to enhance digital governance (DTPS, 2017). Finally, the approval of the National ICT Integrated Policy White Paper in 2016 highlighted a renewed commitment to a comprehensive digital transformation in public service, culminating in the development of a national e-government Strategy and Roadmap (DTPS, 2017).

However, recent studies show that the digital transformation of the South African government faces numerous challenges and barriers, impeding its progress and efficiency. One significant issue is the lack of synchronisation and integration among government departments, leading to fragmented e-government initiatives (DTPS, 2017; Maremi et al., 2022). This fragmentation results from diverse applications, platforms, software, and databases not designed to share information across departments (DTPS, 2017). Furthermore, these systems lack interoperability with e-government systems, further complicating the seamless exchange of data and services (CSIR, 2020). Moreover, financial constraints are another critical challenge, with no dedicated budget allocation for the specific implementation of e-government projects (DTPS, 2017). Insufficient funding and high operational costs hinder progress, exacerbated by austerity measures and the return of unused funds to the treasury (Maremi et al., 2022; Shibambu, 2024). In addition, leadership and management issues also need to be addressed. The lack of direction and collaborative management leads to overlapping roles and responsibilities, resulting in limited accountability (DTPS, 2017). Poor leadership, lack of top-down support, and inadequate participation of ICT heads in executive committees further undermine the implementation of e-government services (CSIR, 2020; Shibambu, 2024).

Meanwhile, civil servants and senior officials accustomed to old organisational cultures resist change, slowing the adoption of digital transformation (Shibambu, 2024). Additionally, the continuing digital divide means that specific subsets of society need more access to ICTs, limiting the reach and effectiveness of digital services (CSIR, 2020). Furthermore, technological challenges are prevalent, including lagging technological uptake, connectivity issues, and frequent rolling blackouts that hinder IT system readiness (Chilunjika et al., 2022). The public sector also needs more skilled personnel to run IT systems effectively (Shibambu, 2024). Beyond these issues, societal and structural challenges, such as persistent poverty, crime, corruption, inequality, and service delivery protests, add another layer of complexity to the digital transformation efforts (Coetzer, 2022; Mhlanga, 2020). These issues are compounded by inadequate communication between the government and communities, leading to impatience and protests when services are delayed (Coetzer, 2022). Significantly, strategic and operational issues, such as implementing e-government initiatives without adequate e-readiness and the influence of external, primarily Western, agencies, also pose challenges (CSIR, 2020). The underestimation of digitalisation's impact and the reliance on outdated communication tools further impede progress (Shibambu,

2024). Finally, cybersecurity concerns related to officials' cloud-based emails highlight the need for more robust security measures (Shibambu, 2024).

The Digitalisation Policy

Emerging trends have significantly transformed the governance and public sector landscape in recent years, and South Africa has not been left behind. AI is a key driver, revolutionising government operations by automating administrative processes, enhancing decision-making through predictive analytics, and improving citizen engagement via chatbots and virtual assistants. Other smart technologies, like blockchain technology, are gaining traction for their secure and transparent nature, utilised for secure document management and supply (Champlain College Online, 2024). Moreover, e-government portals and mobile applications enhance civic engagement by offering seamless service access, thus reducing bureaucratic hurdles. In cybersecurity, governments are adopting AI-powered threat detection to protect sensitive data and infrastructure from sophisticated cyber threats (Yigitcanlar et al., 2024). Furthermore, open data initiatives promote transparency and foster innovation, enabling more innovative policymaking through data-sharing collaborations (OECD, 2023). Additionally, advancements in IoT, augmented reality (AR), virtual reality (VR), and quantum computing are enhancing connectivity and problem-solving capabilities within public administrations (Kelly, 2024). These technological advancements improve efficiency and foster a more interactive and transparent relationship between governments and citizens. As these trends continue to evolve, they hold the potential to revolutionise public sector operations further, making governance more effective and citizen-centric.

Digitalisation can improve the management of public resources through better data collection and analysis (Onyango, 2023). Nižetić et al. (2019) noted that smart city technologies can optimise the use of various utilities, including water and electricity, leading to cost savings and more sustainable resource use. Through online consultations and digital forums, citizens can quickly provide policy input and hold the government accountable. It should be noted that South Africa has recognised the potential of digitalisation and has undertaken various initiatives to integrate digital technologies into the public sector. For instance, the

NDP 2030 is South Africa's comprehensive strategic framework to eliminate poverty and reduce inequality by 2030. Launched in 2012, the NDP and purpose outlined a multi-faceted approach to e-commerce development, emphasising inclusive economic growth, enhanced education and healthcare, and improved infrastructure (NPC, 2012). Some key goals include reducing unemployment, ensuring all South African citizens have equal access to quality services, and fostering a capable state to drive and foster development (Matyana & Thusi, 2023). Most importantly, the NDP seeks to address historical inequalities and create a more just and prosperous society through sustainable and inclusive development.

In line with the NDP, South Africa's e-government strategy aims to harness the power of digital technology to enhance the efficiency, accessibility, and transparency of government services. Equally important, by leveraging ICT, the strategy seeks to create a more responsive and capable government that can serve the citizens better, affording them access to the latest technologies. The strategy's crucial components include digitising public services, establishing a centralised digital platform for citizen interaction, and promoting digital literacy among government employees and the public. This approach aims to modernise administrative processes and foster engagement and participation in governance (Matyana & Thusi, 2023). The e-government strategy is also earmarked to bridge the digital divide and ensure that all South African citizens, irrespective of their socioeconomic status or geographical location, can at least have access to government services. Such services rendered by the initiative focus on expanding internet connectivity, particularly in under-serviced areas, and providing digital tools and resources to use capable online services effectively. The e-Government Strategy also focuses on cybersecurity to protect sensitive information and ensure the integrity of digital transactions across the country (Nižetić et al., 2019). By implementing these measures, South Africa hopes to achieve and build a more inclusive and efficient public sector, ultimately contributing to the broader objectives of the NDP.

Challenges to Fully Harness Digitalisation in South Africa

Despite the progress made thus far, South Africa still needs to overcome multiple significant challenges in fully harnessing digitalisation, which could stand in the way of realising AI systems. Several factors have hindered the effective implementation of digital initiatives. Many South Africans lack access to digital infrastructure and skills (Aruleba & Jere, 2022). Rural areas and low-income communities are particularly affected, limiting their ability to benefit from digital services. The digital divide exacerbates existing inequalities, making it essential for the government to address this issue through targeted investments in digital infrastructure and education (Mhlanga, 2020). South Africa's digital infrastructure, including broadband coverage and internet connectivity, is inadequate, especially in remote and underserved areas (Mhlanga, 2020). The high cost of data and limited access to high-speed internet further hinder digital adoption (Aruleba & Jere, 2022).

To overcome these challenges, the government should invest in expanding and upgrading digital infrastructure, ensuring affordable and reliable connectivity for all citizens. An awareness of digital opportunities is crucial but often needs to be improved, given the public sector's shortage of digital skills. This shortage impedes the effective implementation and management of digital initiatives (Mhlanga, 2020). Training and capacity-building programs are essential to equip public sector individuals with the skill set to leverage such technological developments. Additionally, promoting digital literacy among the general population is crucial to ensure the widespread adoption and utilisation of digital services. Resistance to change within the public sector can also negatively affect and impede digital transformation efforts (Atwah Al-ma'aitah, 2022). Moreover, a lack of political will and concerns about job displacement can also slow the adoption of digital technologies (Aruleba & Jere, 2022). Thus, overcoming this resistance requires strong leadership, clear communication of the benefits of digitalisation, and efforts to involve public servants in the transformation process.

On the contrary, heavy and increased reliance on digital technologies exposes the public sector to cybersecurity threats (Sule et al., 2021). Ensuring the security and privacy of citizens' data is of paramount importance. Thus, there is a need for robust cybersecurity measures. The government must invest in cybersecurity infrastructure, conduct regular audits, and raise awareness about cyber threats. Poor coordination among government departments and agencies can lead to fragmented and ineffective digital initiatives (Atwah Al-ma'aitah, 2022). Harnessing digitalisation offers South Africa significant opportunities to enhance public sector efficiency, transparency, and service delivery. However, challenges such as the digital divide, infrastructure deficiencies, skills gaps, resistance to change, cybersecurity risks, coordination issues, and limited financial resources must be addressed (Sule et al., 2021). Through the public sector digitalisation initiative, South Africa's government can fully leverage digitalisation to achieve its development goals and improve people's livelihoods.

While South Africa works on a National AI Strategy, the Department of Science, Technology and Innovation's Research, Development and Innovation Roadmap emphasises adopting AI infrastructure to bolster economic competitiveness and socioeconomic impact. The roadmap outlines a strategy to integrate AI into public services such as healthcare, education, and government operations, aiming to enhance efficiency and address local needs. The focus is on creating a sustainable innovation ecosystem through public–private partnerships, fostering human capital development, and leveraging AI for broader socioeconomic benefits, including poverty reduction and job creation. The goal is to position South Africa as a significant player in the global ICT arena.

Digital Maturity Framework and Digital Maturity Assessment

Digitalisation considers the social, technical, and economic aspects that affect the deployment and utilisation of digital technologies within governmental structures. Regular evaluations of any organisation's digital maturity, including the public sector, can offer insights into its changing relationship with new technologies and whether its mandate is being fulfilled. In essence, digital maturity refers to the extent of integration and effectiveness of the adopted and implemented digital technologies (Eggers & Bellman, 2015). Digital maturity assessment models are management tools which assess the status quo and evaluate which areas could be optimised for efficiency. However, as Kim Viborg Andersen and Helle Zinner Henriksen (2006) argue, maturity models should focus more than just technical integration and operations. Instead, these models should prioritise strategic ambitions for how governments can leverage information technology (Andersen & Henriksen, 2006, p. 237). In other words, these models should speak to the state's values and vision. In the public sector, assessment models are essential because they provide a structured framework for evaluating the progress and effectiveness of digital transformation initiatives. They help identify gaps and weaknesses, highlight best practices, and guide strategic planning and resource allocation. Building on this framework, digital maturity encompasses strategy, organisation, people, technologies, and data. A successful digital transformation strategy should integrate seamlessly with existing organisational goals, enhancing them with necessary changes and resources (Andersen & Henriksen, 2006, p. 237). Organisational readiness involves management's ability to adapt to cultural shifts and process restructuring. Employee engagement, motivation, and digital competence are critical for implementing strategic changes. Lastly, effective data management ensures consistent and reliable information underpinning the digitalisation process.

This index emphasises not only technical integration but also the strategic ambitions of the government to create public value, reflecting the need for tailored governance frameworks that address unique challenges in the African context (Noymanee et al., 2022). Ultimately, the Digital Maturity Index can guide South Africa and other African nations in identifying areas for improvement, fostering a more inclusive public sector that effectively serves its citizens while addressing infrastructure and digital literacy issues. Figure 6.1 depicts six of twelve key principles for digital government produced by the Organization for Economic Cooperation and Development (OECD):

openness, transparency, and inclusiveness;
engagement and participation in policymaking and service delivery;
effective organisational and governance frameworks;
protecting privacy and ensuring security;
leadership and political commitment;
and coherent use of digital technology across policy areas.

These principles emphasise the importance of open access to government data, inclusive participation from diverse stakeholders, robust organisational and governance frameworks, and the need to safeguard user data and digital services. Digital maturity assessments (DMAs) evaluate technological infrastructure, governance, policy, and operational frameworks supporting digital initiatives. They consider stakeholder inclusion, leadership evaluation, security and privacy measures, and integration and coherence. The figure emphasises that successful digital government is not solely about technology but its integration into governance and policy frameworks, engagement with citizens, and alignment with broader

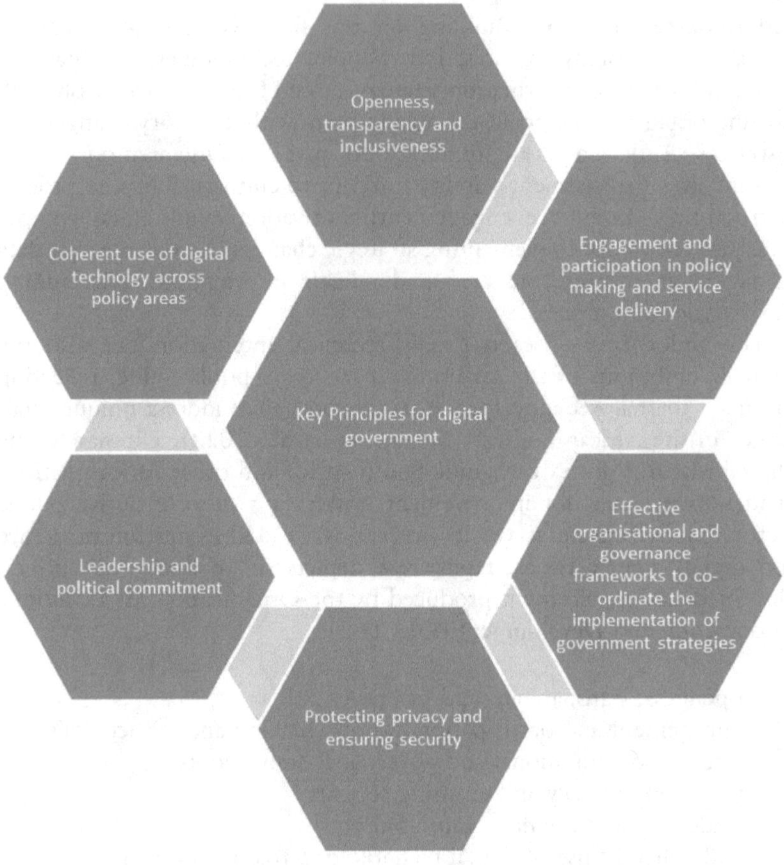

Fig. 6.1 6 of the 12 OECD principles of digital government (*Source* Adapted from OECD, Digital Government Toolkit [n.d.])

administrative principles. To effectively implement these principles and identify areas for improvement, DMAs are crucial.

DMA evaluates an organisation's, which in our case, the South African government's digital capability. It needs to know whether it is using its technology effectively, whether it has the appropriate infrastructure, and whether the appropriate technology is in place. In the context of developing states, it is important to know whether the data being collected or managed improves its decision-making and service delivery. As discussed in Table 6.1, Tristan Thordsen, Matthias Murawski, and Markus Bick critically analyse 17 existing private sector digital maturity models, and they note that existing models have several shortcomings in testing their validity. Moreover, they point out that a significant shortcoming is the need for precise terminology. They suggest a research agenda that leans towards a clear definition and measurement supported by empirical data (Thordsen et al., 2020, pp. 365–367).

Even though DMAs are a growing area of interest, the discourse mostly centres around private organisations, and there needs to be more focus on the public sector. Digital governance themes for both private and public sectors emphasise regular monitoring, data analytics, culture shift, digital literacy, and clear leadership, emphasising the importance of digital literacy (Jonathan, 2020). Johan Magnusson and Andreas Nilsson contend that there needs to be three assumptions underlying the design of digital maturity models for the public sector:

> Digital capability is a dynamic capability.
> Digital maturity is dependent on existing information infrastructure.
> Digital maturity requires the ambidextrous balancing of activities related to both exploration (innovation) and exploitation (efficiency). (Magnusson & Nilsson, 2020, p. 3)

Table 6.1 Thordsen, Murawski & Bick's suggested research agenda

Category	*Selected research problems/questions*	*Proposed research strategies/methods*
Definition and measurement	How is DM defined? How is the measurement defined	Conceptual research Validity checks Construct development
Theoretical framework	Link to DMM to existing theory? Develop a new theory—what would the contours of such a theory look like?	Conceptual research Theory development
Empirical aspects	Generalisability? Evolution of DM	Multiple case study design Longitudinal design

Source Adapted from Thordsen et al. (2020, p. 366)

As nations advance their digital capabilities, the GTMI is crucial for assessing government technology initiatives, focusing on core systems, service delivery, citizen engagement, and enabling factors (World Bank, 2022). For South Africa, the GTMI highlights the need for a DMA to improve digital capabilities while addressing the challenges identified by the GTMI (World Bank, 2022). While DMAs have traditionally focused on organisations, applying them to government is essential. For South Africa, key digital transformation themes include monitoring progress, fostering cultural shifts, enhancing digital literacy, and ensuring strong leadership (Magnusson & Nilsson, 2020). Ultimately, a DMA supports the GTMI's objectives by promoting GovTech initiatives that help improve public sector outcomes in South Africa, such as more efficient service delivery, increased transparency, and greater citizen engagement. This alignment can bridge existing gaps, enhance resource allocation, and drive socioeconomic development through informed decision-making and innovative solutions (Magnusson & Nilsson, 2020).

Global Index on Responsible AI (GIRAI) and Lessons for Its Application in South Africa

Understanding the Digital Maturity indices is crucial as South Africa develops a National AI strategy. These indices assess public sector readiness to leverage technology effectively, ensuring that AI implementation enhances efficiency while creating public value (Pooe & Munyanyi, 2022). This alignment is vital in countries like South Africa, where fostering inclusivity and addressing historical inequalities are essential for effective governance (Visser & Twinomurinzi, 2008). As Moore (1995) articulates, Public Value Theory offers an incisive lens through which to understand and guide the implementation of AI in the South African public sector while fostering inclusivity. Public value is "the value created by the government through services, laws, regulations and other actions" (Kelly et al., 2002, p. 4).

In this chapter, we are not evaluating current AI policies, as in South Africa, AI policy development is still embryonic. The Global Center on AI Governance developed the first index on responsible AI, the GIRAI, quantifying the extent to which AI systems are designed and implemented according to responsible AI standards. It is a comprehensive framework that evaluates AI ecosystems based on three primary pillars: Government Frameworks, Government Actions, and Non-State Actors. These pillars are assessed in 19 thematic areas grouped into three dimensions: *Responsible AI Governance*, *Responsible AI Capacities*, and Human Rights and AI.

The index combines scores from primary data collected in these regions. It modifies them using secondary data to account for national context factors, including regulatory quality, rule of law, and freedom of expression. It is essential to consider the GIRAI as a framework for evaluating public value creation. The GIRAI provides a comprehensive measure of how effectively public services meet the needs of citizens, emphasising the importance of accountability and transparency in governance. By integrating the principles of public value theory with the GIRAI, public sector organisations can better assess the impact of AI initiatives on service delivery and citizen satisfaction. This approach aligns with the *Batho Pele* principles and encourages a participatory governance model where citizens are actively involved in shaping AI policies and practices. As AI technologies evolve, continuous evaluation through such metrics will be crucial in addressing the challenges identified by Chen et al. (2023) and ensuring that AI is a tool for enhancing public value rather than undermining it.

As illustrated in Table 6.2, South Africa's scoring on the GIRAI, an aggregate score of 27.61 out of 100, indicates a significant discrepancy between various aspects of responsible AI implementation. The private sector, academia, and civil society organisations have played an important role, as non-state actors have a relatively high score of 68.53. Conversely, the Framework pillar's score of 3.26 is alarmingly low, suggesting a critical absence of established guidelines and regulations. The government's action scored moderately at 31.50, implying some effort, with significant room for improvement. Responsible AI capacities score 32.40 among the dimensions, suggesting that there has been some progress in developing the requisite skills and resources- but more investment is needed. Government action must be more proactive to encourage responsible AI practices. The high score of non-state actors suggests collaboration opportunities with private corporations, academic institutions, and civil society organisations. However, Chen et al. (2023, pp. 7–17) identify key obstacles to AI implementation in the public sector. These challenges encompass transparency, the erosion of human judgment, algorithmic bias, privacy and safety risks, equity issues, accountability deficits, and the potential for misuse. Public value theory serves as a lens through which to

Table 6.2 South Africa's GIRAI scores

Index score	*Pillar score*			*Dimension score*		
27.61	Framework	Government action	Non-state actors	Human rights and AI	Responsible AI capacities	Responsible AI governance
	3.26	31.50	68.53	28.93	32.40	24.99

Source The Global Index on Responsible AI. https://global-index.ai/Region-Africa (Accessed: August 7, 2024)

examine and a mechanism to ensure the proper implementation of *Batho Pele* in the public sector.

Application of AI in South Africa

The South African government is gradually adopting AI across various domains. For example, the South African Revenue Service (SARS) uses AI and machine learning to improve compliance and revenue collection. SARS can significantly boost revenue by identifying and reducing criminal activity and non-compliance (Mzekandaba, 2024). AI is also being used in the healthcare sector. Innovative AI-powered systems predict disease likelihoods, such as tuberculosis, based on patient symptoms and medical records, improving early diagnosis and treatment (ITWeb, 2024). Telemedicine solutions and remote monitoring applications, like the University of Johannesburg's '*e-mutakalo*' device, also facilitate real-time patient monitoring and emergency alerts, particularly benefiting rural areas with limited healthcare access (ITWeb, 2024). Considering the above-mentioned government operations, there are opportunities related to greater digitalisation within the public sector space in South Africa. This can be particularly beneficial where geographical and infrastructural barriers impede service access.

Designing AI implementation strategies to advance along the maturity index while enhancing public service delivery and bridging societal gaps in South Africa necessitates a comprehensive and context-sensitive approach. Firstly, to align with the Batho Pele principles, South Africa needs to create robust AI governance frameworks that incorporate actionable principles of responsible AI to ensure the protection of human rights and the integration of ethical considerations into AI policies and regulations. As already suggested in Chapter 3 of this volume, policymakers in South Africa could learn from successful AI framework drafters in strengthening their national AI strategy. This can, for example, borrow some aspects similar to Croatia's amendment to its Labor Law, which addresses algorithmic decision-making and fosters transparency and accountability (Parliament of Croatia, 2022). Rwanda, Senegal, Benin, and Nigeria have recently formulated national AI strategies, becoming the first in mainland Sub-Saharan Africa to do so and ending Mauritius's five-year status as the region's sole AI strategy holder (Adams et al., 2024). This trend diverges from other regions where the most developed or largest economies typically lead in creating national AI strategies. The recently drafted AI policy framework in South Africa has much to borrow from how these countries have implemented these policies.

Moreover, as shown in *Chapter 5* above, modernising public procurement processes is essential for acquiring practical and ethical AI systems (WEF, 2020). This entails creating regulatory frameworks and training public officials to enhance the efficiency and effectiveness of AI procurement, drawing valuable lessons from Chile's National AI Policy (Ministry of Science, Technology, Knowledge, and Innovation, 2024). In addition to procurement, focusing on inclusion and equality in AI deployment is crucial (WEF, 2020). By integrating gender equality, labour protections, and cultural and linguistic diversity into AI strategies, South Africa can ensure that AI benefits all segments of society. Universities and civil society organisations can play an essential role in promoting these values, as evidenced by initiatives in South America that emphasise gender equality and cultural diversity in AI (Adams et al., 2024).

Furthermore, tackling the digital divide issue is vital to guarantee that underprivileged communities have access to technology and internet connectivity and can take advantage of breakthroughs in artificial intelligence (WEF, 2020). South Africa could also utilise UNESCO's Recommendation on the Ethics of AI to build capacity and support AI ethics and responsible AI development (UNESCO, 2021). Adopting international best practices and keeping up with AI advances could also be facilitated by South Africa's participation in multilateral projects and collaboration with foreign organisations (Adams et al., 2024). In addition, starting with pilot projects in key sectors like healthcare, education, and social services can effectively demonstrate AI's potential and scalability (Lopez-Molina, 2024). Implementing robust monitoring and evaluation mechanisms will ensure continuous improvement and adaptation of AI strategies. The progression along the maturity index for South Africa involves a strategic blend of establishing robust governance frameworks, modernising procurement processes, promoting inclusion and equality, utilising international cooperation, and initiating pilot projects. Through these integrated efforts, South Africa could ensure that AI development aligns with the goals of societal equity and improved public service delivery.

Conclusion and Recommendations

Digital maturity presents a more consolidated transformation for realising AI systems in the public sector, as shown in this chapter concerning South Africa. The chapter's findings imply that the persistent gap between the privileged and underprivileged in South Africa requires further efforts to ensure that digital technologies, particularly frontier technologies such as AI, are accessible and beneficial to all citizens. Results of the GTMI 2022 suggest that South Africa reached moderate digital maturity, particularly regarding introducing e-government services. This suggests that the country has a digitalisation infrastructure but needs to address the gaps and enhance its digital services and literacy rates. South Africa is reasonably positioned to leverage AI to further enhance its public service delivery. According to the Oxford Insights Government AI Readiness Index (2023, p. 26), South Africa leads the region in the Data, Infrastructure, and Technology Sector pillars. It is the only Sub-Saharan African country to surpass the AI average for the Technology Sector pillar. As much as AI could enhance public policy process, infrastructural gaps, ethics, and data availability must be addressed.

Three major intersecting patterns emerge by drawing on the GIRAI utilising the Public Value theory lens to assess South Africa's AI progress—first, aligning AI to South Africa's national priorities to achieve the NDP's goals, particularly around service delivery and fostering economic growth. Second is the potential of AI to enhance transparency and accountability. Trust in the state and state institutions in South Africa has fluctuated downwards in the thirty years since the advent of inclusive democracy (Human Sciences Research Council, 2020; Lefko-Evertt, 2023, pp. 8–15, 33). Some of the decline in trust relates to corruption and poor accountability. Effective, transparent, and ethical applications of AI can improve trust in the state and the public sector (Madan &

Ashok, 2022; Ringson & Matshabaphala, 2024). Third is improving citizen engagement- particularly at the local government level.

As the results indicate, alignment with the NDP (which necessitates a whole-of-government approach) is needed to elevate South Africa's digital maturity and create an environment conducive to public sector digital transformation, resulting in more effective AI systems. While South Africa is not representative of the entire African continent or the Global South, its experiences can provide them with valuable insights. Implementing AI in the South African public sector requires a comprehensive approach to addressing various challenges and obstacles. First, the government must enhance interoperability by developing a unified framework with common data standards and investing in integrated digital platforms for better data sharing. Securing dedicated funding with specific budgets for AI and digital transformation and fostering public–private partnerships is also crucial. Strong leadership and governance are essential to advancing the AI agenda within the public sector, promoting collaborative management practices, and clearly defining roles and responsibilities. Building capacity is vital, including comprehensive training programs and competitive opportunities to equip civil servants with digital literacy and AI skills. Specifically, Public Sector staff need to build their skills and awareness of digitalisation/AI opportunities.

The government must implement change management strategies to address resistance to change, ensure regular communication and stakeholder engagement, and encourage a culture of innovation and continuous learning. Bridging the digital divide is necessary to ensure equitable access to ICTs. Strengthen IT infrastructure, ensure stable internet, invest in data centres, and implement backup systems to enhance technological readiness. There is a need for policymakers to stay updated with advancements and incorporate emerging technologies in addressing societal challenges by establishing strong community communication, engaging local leaders in AI planning, and implementing social programs to tackle poverty, crime, and inequality. Lastly, cybersecurity must be ensured with stringent measures, secure communication, regular audits, staff training, and compliance with data protection regulations. By addressing these critical areas, African governments can successfully implement AI in the public sector, enhancing service delivery and improving efficiency.

References

Adams, R., Adeleke, F., Florido, A., de Magalhães Santos, L. G., Grossman, N., Junck, L., & Stone, K. (2024). *Global Index on Responsible AI 2024* (1st ed.). Global Center on AI Governance.

Andersen, K. V., & Henriksen, H. Z. (2006). E-government maturity models: Extension of the Layne and Lee model. *Government Information Quarterly, 23*(2), 236–248.

Aruleba, K., & Jere, N. (2022). Exploring digital transforming challenges in rural areas of South Africa through a systematic review of empirical studies. *Scientific African, 16*, e01190.

Atwah Al-ma'aitah, M. (2022). Employees' resistance to change impacts e-government innovation and value creation. *International Journal of eBusiness and e-Government Studies, 14*(2), 166–198.

Baker, J. B. (2019). *The antitrust paradigm: Restoring a competitive economy*. Harvard University Press.

Barnard, L. (2024). *AI could create a turning point for financial inclusion in Africa*. https://www.retailbankerinternational.com/comment/ai-could-create-a-turning-point-for-financial-inclusion-in-africa/?cf-view

Champlain College Online. (2024). *Types of emerging technologies transforming public administration*. https://online.champlain.edu/blog/emerging-technologies-public-administration

Chen, Y., Ahn, M., & Wang, Y. (2023). Artificial intelligence and public values: Value impacts and governance in the public sector. *Sustainability*. https://doi.org/10.3390/su15064796

Chilunjika, A., Intauno, K., & Chilunjika, S. R. (2022). Artificial intelligence and public sector human resource management in South Africa: Opportunities, challenges and prospects. *SA Journal of Human Resource Management, 20*, 12.

Cloete, F. (2012). e-Government Lessons from South Africa 2001–2011: Institutions, State of Progress and Measurement. *The African Journal of Information and Communication (AJIC)* [Preprint], (12). https://doi.org/10.23962/10539/19712.

Coetzer, S.-G. (2022). *A comparative study of the e-Government services of South Africa, Brazil, and Estonia* (PhD diss.). Stellenbosch University, Stellenbosch.

Council for Scientific and Industrial Research (CSIR). (2020). *Evaluation of the e-Government strategy and roadmap of South Africa* (Unpublished report).

Das, A., Malaviya, S., & Singh, M. (2023). The impact of AI-driven personalization on learners' performance. *International Journal of Computer Sciences and Engineering, 11*(8), 15–22. https://doi.org/10.26438/ijcse/v11i8.1522

Davenport, T., & Kalakota, R. (2019). The potential for artificial intelligence in healthcare. *Future Healthcare Journal, 6*(2), 94–98. https://doi.org/10.7861/futurehosp.6-2-94

Deming, W. E. (2018). *The new economics for industry, government, education*. MIT Press.

Department of Public Services and Administration (DPSA). (1995). *White Paper on the Transformation of the Public Service*. Notice 1227 OF 1995. https://www.gov.za/sites/default/files/gcis_document/201409/168380.pdf.

Department of Public Services and Administration (DPSA). (1997). *Batho Pele—"People First" White Paper on transforming public service delivery*. https://www.dpsa.gov.za/dpsa2g/documents/acts&regulations/frameworks/white-papers/transform.pdf

Department of Public Services and Administration (DPSA). (2001). *Electronic government: The digital future a public service IT policy framework*. https://www.gov.za/sites/default/files/gcis_document/201409/it0.pdf

Department of Public Services and Administration (DPSA). (2007). *Minimum Interoperability Standards (MIOS) for information systems in government*. https://www.dpsa.gov.za/dpsa2g/documents/egov/MIOSVer4_1_2007.pdf

Department of Telecommunications and Postal Services. (DTPS). (2017, November 10). Electronic Communications and Transactions Act: National e-government strategy and roadmap (Government Gazette No. 41241 General Notice 886). Government of South Africa. Retrieved from https://www.gov.za/sites/default/files/gcis_document/201711/41241gen886.pdf

de Sousa, W. G., de Melo, E. R. P., Bermejo, P. H. D. S., Farias, R. A. S., & Gomes, A. O. (2019). How and where is artificial intelligence in the public sector going? A literature review and research agenda. *Government Information Quarterly, 36*, 101392.

Eggers, W. D., & Bellman, J. (2015). *The journey to government's digital transformation*. Deloitte University Press. https://www2.deloitte.com/content/dam/insights/us/articles/digital-transformation-in-government/DUP_1081_Journey-to-govt-digital-future_MASTER.pdf

Forestier, O., & Kim, R. E. (2020). Cherry-picking the sustainable development goals: Goal prioritisation by national governments and implications for global governance. *Sustainable Development, 28*(5), 1269–1278.

González-Zapata, F., & Piccinin-Barbieri, M. (2021). Making the leap from e-government to digital government. In *Development cooperation report 2021: Shaping a just digital transformation*. OECD Publishing.

Government Communications and Information Systems (GCIS). (1998). *Background on Thusong service centres*. https://www.gcis.gov.za/sites/default/files/docs/resourcecentre/multimedia/thusong-brochure.pdf

Human Sciences Research Council. (2020). *South African Social Attitudes Survey (SASAS) 2020: Questionnaire 1—All provinces*. SASAS 2020 Q1. Version 1. Human Sciences Research Council [producer], Human Sciences Research Council [distributor], 2024. https://doi.org/10.14749/1704913130

ITWeb. (2024). *UJ Develops E-Device to Monitor Health Conditions*. ITWeb. https://www.itweb.co.za/article/uj-develops-e-device-to-monitor-health-conditions/Kjlyr7w1yQBqk6am. (Accessed: June 24, 2024).

Janowski, T. (2015). Digital government evolution: From transformation to contextualisation. *Government Information Quarterly, 32*(3), 221–236.

Javaid, M., Haleem, A., Khan, I. H., & Suman, R. (2023). Understanding the potential applications of artificial intelligence in the agriculture sector. *Advanced Agrochem, 2*(1), 15–30. https://doi.org/10.1016/j.aac.2022.10.001

Jonathan, G. M. (2020). *Digital transformation in the public sector: Identifying critical success factors*. In Information Systems: 16th European, Mediterranean, and Middle Eastern Conference, EMCIS 2019, Dubai, United Arab Emirates, December 9–10, 2019, Proceedings 16 (pp. 223–235). Springer.

Joshi, P. R., & Islam, S. (2018). E-government maturity model for sustainable e-government services from the perspective of developing countries. *Sustainability, 10*(6), 1882.

Kahn, T., Baron, A., & Vieyra, J. C. (2018). *Digital technologies for transparency in public investment: New tools to empower citizens and governments*.

Kariyanna, B., & Sowjanya, M. (2024). Unravelling the use of artificial intelligence in the management of insect pests. *Smart Agricultural Technology*, 100517. https://doi.org/10.1016/j.atech.2024.100517

Kelly, G., Mulgan, G., & Muers, S. (2002). *Creating public value*. Cabinet Office.

Kelly, P. (2024). *7 emerging public sector technology trends*. https://blog.govnet.co.uk/technology/emerging-technology-trends-in-the-public-sector (Accessed: August 7, 2024).

Lefko-Everett, K. (2023). *SA Reconciliation Barometer 2023 report*. https://www.ijr.org.za/home/wp-content/uploads/2023/12/SA-Reconciliation-Barometer-2023_Final.pdf (Accessed: August 2, 2024).

Lindgren, I., & van Veenstra, A. F. (2018). *Digital government transformation: A case illustrating public e-service development as part of public sector transformation*. Proceedings of the 19th Annual International Conference on Digital Government Research: Governance in the Data Age. https://doi.org/10.1145/3209281.3209302

Lopez-Molina, A. I. (2024). *Digital transformation in healthcare: AI pilot projects that are revolutionising the industry*. https://www.linkedin.com/pulse/digital-transformation-healthcare-ai-pilot-projects-lopez-molina-emi2e

Madan, R., & Ashok, M. (2022). *A public values perspective on the application of artificial intelligence in government practices: A synthesis of case studies* (pp. 162–189). https://doi.org/10.4018/978-1-7998-9609-8.ch010

Magnusson, J., & Nilsson, A. (2020). *Digital maturity in the public sector: Design and evaluation of a new model*. https://gup.ub.gu.se/file/208009 (Accessed: November 3, 2023).

Manda, M. I. (2017). Towards "smart governance" through a multidisciplinary approach to E-government integration, interoperability and information sharing: A case of the LMIP project in South Africa. In M. Janssen et al., *Electronic government. EGOV 2017. Lecture Notes in Computer Science* (Vol. 10428). Springer.

Manda, M. I. (2021). Power, politics, and the institutionalisation of information systems for promoting digital transformation in the public sector: A case of the South African's government digital transformation journey. *Information Polity, 27*, 311–329.

Manda, M. I., & Backhouse, J. (2018). Smart governance for inclusive socioeconomic transformation in South Africa: Are we there yet? In *E-participation in smart cities: Technologies and models of governance for citizen engagement*. Public Administration and Information Technology. Springer.

Maremi, K., Thulare, T., & Herselman, M. (2022). *The benefits of digital transformation addressing the hindrances and challenges of e-government services in South Africa: A scoping review*. In 2022 IST-Africa Conference (IST-Africa) (pp. 1–8). IEEE.

Matyana, M., & Thusi, X. (2023), Unemployment and poverty in South Africa: Assessing the National Development Plan 2030 predictions. *International Journal of Development and Sustainability, 12*(6), 212–226.

McNulty, N. (2024). *How AI tutors could save the South African education system*. https://medium.com/@niall.mcnulty/how-ai-tutors-could-save-the-south-african-education-system-ad9291d09a1a

Mhlanga, D. (2020). Industry 4.0: The challenges associated with the digital transformation of education in South Africa. *The Impacts of Digital Transformation, 13*(51), 13–26.

Ministry of Science, Technology, Knowledge, and Innovation. (2024). *National policy on artificial intelligence*. Government of Chile. https://www.minciencia.gob.cl/uploads/filer_public/bc/38/bc389daf-4514-4306-867c-760ae7686e2c/documento_politica_ia_digital_.pdf

Moore, M. H. (1995). *Creating public value: Strategic management in government*. Harvard University Press.

Mzekandaba, S. (2024). *SITA to Ramp Up Access to Digitised Govt Services*. ITWeb. https://www.itweb.co.za/article/sita-to-ramp-up-access-to-digitised-govt-services/j5alr7QAN157pYQk. (Accessed: February 16, 2024).

National Planning Commission (NPC). (2012). *National Development Plan 2030*. Government Print.

Nel-Sanders, D., & Aaron P. M. (2022). Challenges and best practices for e-municipalities. *Africa's Public Service Delivery and Performance Review, 10*(1), 646.

Nižetić, S., Djilali, N., Papadopoulos, A., & Rodrigues, J. J. (2019). Smart technologies for promotion of energy efficiency, utilization of sustainable resources and waste management. *Journal of Cleaner Production, 231*, 565–591.

Noymanee, J., Iewwongcharoen, B., & Theeramunkong, T. (2022). *Artificial intelligence maturity model for government administration and service.* International Conference on Digital Government Technology and Innovation (DGTi-CON). https://doi.org/10.1109/dgti-con53875.2022.9849184.

OECD. (2023). *Global trends in government innovation 2023.* https://www.oecd-ilibrary.org/sites/0655b570-en/1/3/2/index.html?itemId=/content/publication/0655b570-en&_csp_=81514dda47e6d6cb4cb62f97e5c3e4e4&itemIGO=oecd&itemContentType=book.

OECD. (n.d.) *Digital government toolkit.* https://www.oecd.org/governance/digital-government/toolkit/ (Accessed: November 1, 2023).

Oxford Insights. (2023). *Government AI readiness index 2023.* https://oxfordinsights.com/wp-content/uploads/2023/12/2023-Government-AI-Readiness-Index-2.pdf (Accessed: August 7, 2024).

Onyango, G. (Ed.). (2023). *Public policy and technological transformations in Africa: Nurturing policy entrepreneurship, policy tools and citizen participation.* Palgrave Macmillan.

Onyango, G., & Karuri-Sebina, G. (2025). *Digitalisation and public policy in Africa: GovTech and CivicTech innovations.* Palgrave Macmillan.

Parliament of Croatia. (2022). *Act on Amendments to the Labour Act.* https://narodne-novine.nn.hr/clanci/sluzbeni/2022_12_151_2343.html (Accessed: August 7 2024).

Plantinga, P., Dlamini, N., & Gordon, T. (2023, March 18). *Implementing e-participation in Africa: What roles should public officials play?* https://doi.org/10.31235/osf.io/cbwx5

Pooe, D., & Munyanyi, W. (2022). Delivering public value by selected government departments in South Africa—Perceptions of senior managers. *South African Journal of Economic and Management Sciences, 25*(1), 3791.

Pooe, D., & Pearce, P. (2023). Public service delivery and the impact of artificial intelligence and digitisation on performance. In *Perspectives on volunteering: Voices from the South.* Springer.

PricewaterhouseCoopers. (2018). *E-government and the digital citizen.* https://www.pwc.com/mt/en/publications/egovernment-digital-citizen.html (Accessed: November 1, 2023).

PWC. (2020). *The potential impact of artificial intelligence on the South African economy.* https://www.pwc.co.za/en/publications/the-potential-impact-of-ai-on-the-sa-economy.html

PWC. (2024). *AI readiness assessment: Rethinking digital transformation for AI*. PricewaterhouseCoopers. https://www.pwc.com/us/en/tech-effect/ai-analysis.html

Raj, V. (2024). *How AI can help educators create engaging and effective lessons*. https://www.linkedin.com/pulse/how-ai-can-help-educators-create-engaging-effective-lessons-ved-raj-ygf5c#:~:text=Automated%20Planning%3A%20AI%20tools%20can,enhancing%20the%20overall%20learning%20experience (Accessed: August 7, 2024).

Rakhmanov, E. (2009, November). The barriers affecting E-government development in Uzbekistan. In *2009 Fourth International Conference on Computer Sciences and Convergence Information Technology* (pp. 1474–1480). IEEE.

Republic of South Africa. (2002). Electronic Communications and Transactions Act, No. 25 of 2002. *Government Gazette, 446*, (August 2), 23708.

Republic of South Africa (RSA). (2005). *Social Assistance Act 13 of 2004*.

Ringson, J., & Matshabaphala, M. D. J. (2024, March). Agility in South African public service leadership. *Journal of Public Administration and Development Alternatives, 9*(1.1), 127–143. https://doi.org/JPADA.2024.307

Rumbold, J., & Pierscionek, B. (2018). AI ethics: A matter of design. *AI & Society, 33*(4), 499–507.

Seneviratne, R. (2023). Revolutionizing government service delivery: Unveiling the future of customer experience. *American Journal of Industrial and Business Management, 13*(2), 56–71.

Shibambu, A. (2024). Transformation of digital government services in the public sector in South Africa. *Africa's Public Service Delivery & Performance Review, 12*(1), 7.

Sibanda, M., & Manda, A. (2016). The state of E-government implementation in Zimbabwe: A comparison with South Africa, South Korea, and Estonia. *Information Development, 32*(4), 845–860.

Sule, M-.J., Marco Z., & Godwin, T. (2021). Cybersecurity through the lens of digital identity and data protection: Issues and trends. *Technology in Society, 67*(2021), 101734.

Sullivan, M., Joel, B., Jamie, S., & Joe, M. (2022). Accelerated digital government. Deloitte Insights. *Deloitte*. https://www2.deloitte.com/us/en/insights/industry/public-sector/g2021/digital-government-transformation-trends-covid-19.html. (Accessed: April 15, 2022).

Swanepoel, E., & Vyas-Doorgapersad, P. (2020). Examining e-government in the context of e-participation in South Africa. *African Renaissance, 17*(1), 73–90.

The World Bank. (2016). *South Africa economic update: Promoting faster growth and poverty alleviation through competition*. http://hdl.handle.net/10986/25514

Thomas, C., & Manda, M. (2023). Digital transformation in the South African government: Experiences from the National Department of Health. *The Electronic Journal of Information Systems in Developing Countries, 89*(3), e12311.

Thordsen, T., Murawski, M., & Bick, M. (2020). How to measure digitalization? A critical evaluation of digital maturity models. In M. Hattingh, M. Matthee, H. Smuts, I. Pappas, Y. K. Dwivedi & M. Mäntymäki (Eds.), *Responsible Design, Implementation and use of Information and Communication Technology*. Springer International Publishing.

UCLA Luskin Center for Innovation. (2020). *Evaluation of the digital inclusion pilot projects*. University of California, Los Angeles. https://innovation.luskin.ucla.edu/wp-content/uploads/2020/11/Evaluation-of-the-Digital-Inclusion-Pilot-Projects.pdf

UNESCO. (2021). *Recommendation on the ethics of artificial intelligence*. https://unesdoc.unesco.org/ark:/48223/pf0000380455

Van Zyl, C., Sibanda, S., Reichelt, C., & Meyer, N. (2017). *Evaluation of the e-government strategy and roadmap of South Africa* (Unpublished report). CSIR.

Veljković, N., & Budimac, Z. (2021). Framework for evaluating digital maturity: A case study in the public sector. *Journal of Organizational and End User Computing, 33*(3), 43–63.

Visser, W., & Twinomurinzi, H. (2008). E-government & public service delivery: Enabling ICT to put People First—A case study from South Africa. In *IMSCI 2008—2nd International Multi-Conference on Society, Cybernetics and Informatics, Proceedings* (Vol. 3, pp. 81–86). International Institute of Informatics and Systemics, IIIS.

Wen, L., Manda, M., & Maharaj, M. (2022). Interorganizational information sharing and interoperability for public service delivery: A stakeholder perspective from South Africa. *Journal of African Public Administration and Management, 34*(4), 123–146.

Wilson, D. (2024). *AI is transforming financial services*. https://it-online.co.za/2024/07/30/ai-is-transforming-financial-services/

World Bank. (2022). *GovTech Maturity Index 2022 update: Trends in public sector digital transformation*. https://www.worldbank.org/

World Economic Forum (WEF). (2020). *AI procurement in a box: AI government procurement guidelines*. https://www3.weforum.org/docs/WEF_AI_Procurement_in_a_Box_AI_Government_Procurement_Guidelines_2020.pdf

Xu, X., Wang, J., & Zhang, S. (2021). A study on the digital transformation and sustainable development of China's public sector: The role of digital government. *Sustainability, 13*(12), 6703.

Yang, T.-C., & Shih, D.-H. (2020). Development of a digital maturity model for government agencies: A case study of a government-owned research institute. *Information Technology & People, 33*(5), 1533–1551.

Yigitcanlar, T., Senadheera, S., Marasinghe, R., Bibri, S. E., Sanchez, T., Cugurullo, F., & Sieber, R. (2024). Artificial intelligence and the local government: A five-decade scientometric analysis on the evolution, state-of-the-art, and emerging trends. *Cities, 152*, 105151. https://doi.org/10.1016/j.cities.2024.105151

Zuiderwijk, A., Chen, Y. C., & Salem, F. (2021). Implications of the use of artificial intelligence in public governance: A systematic literature review and a research agenda. *Government Information Quarterly, 38*(3), 101577. https://doi.org/10.1016/J.GIQ.2021.101577

CHAPTER 7

Simulation of the Impact of Artificial Intelligence on Economic Growth, the Labour Market and Well-Being in Senegal

François Joseph Cabral, Adama Sow Badji, Ben Omar Ndiaye, and Souleymane Ndao

Introduction

With nearly \$40 billion in private investment in 2019, a fourfold increase in five years, Artificial Intelligence (AI) is attracting a growing share of global capital flows, led by the USA, China and Canada. In Africa, countries like Mauritius, Tunisia, South Africa and Rwanda are at the forefront of AI initiatives, with strategies and policies already in place. Despite the reliance on wealthy countries, leading to potential sustainability issues for investments in innovative technologies, there has been a noticeable surge in AI interest across Africa in recent years (Chen

F. J. Cabral (✉) · A. S. Badji · B. O. Ndiaye · S. Ndao
Université Cheikh Anta Diop de Dakar (UCAD), Dakar, Senegal
e-mail: joecabral7@gmail.com

G. Onyango (ed.), *Designing Artificial Intelligence for Public Policy and Governance in Africa*, Studies in National Governance and Emerging Technologies, https://doi.org/10.1007/978-3-031-83445-5_7

et al., 2021; Hanson, 2023). The development of artificial intelligence (AI) is expected to have several positive impacts. Firstly, AI can enhance overall factor productivity by automating production tasks and expanding the economy's production capabilities. Additionally, in fields such as healthcare, AI can increase healthcare capacity by filling gaps in human expertise or errors of omission. Put differently, Artificial intelligence can be deployed to produce goods and services, potentially affecting growth and income. However, AI can also change the process of creating new ideas and technologies, helping solve complex problems and offering opportunities to scale up creative efforts. In extreme versions, some observers have argued that AI can become rapidly self-improving, leading to "singularities" that characterise unlimited artificial intelligence and/or economic growth.

Furthermore, AI could revolutionise educational offerings by developing intelligent tutoring systems, as well as other sectors, as covered by other chapters in this volume. However, the development of AI in Africa faces various limitations, such as the absence of a governance framework, human and financial resource constraints and infrastructure challenges. The African Union has highlighted in its *Digital Transformation Strategy for Africa* that these significant challenges need to be addressed by member countries to formulate effective strategies for sustainable growth and development. Therefore, for a country like Senegal, it would be crucial to learn from the experiences of benchmark countries in developing an AI strategy capable of driving a robust and sustainable growth trajectory. There is no doubt that AI technologies are structurally transforming economies that invest in this emerging sector (Ondiek & Onyango, 2024). AI systems are often associated with improved efficiency and productivity because they enable routine tasks to be performed quickly, activities carried out on a larger scale and services made accessible to more people (Etscheid, 2019).

It has also been established that developing an Artificial Intelligence system increases productivity in the long term (Hanson, 2023; Lu, 2021). Barro (1990) proposes that economic growth stems from investment in public infrastructure, while Lucas (1988) states that human capital drives economic growth. In his 1950 article *Computing Machinery and Intelligence*, Alan Mathison Turing proposed a test of artificial intelligence known as the "Turing test", based on a machine's ability to imitate human conversation. The test consists of putting a human in a blind verbal confrontation with a computer and another human. If the person engaging in the conversation is unable to tell which of his or her interlocutors is a computer, the computer can be considered to have passed the test. Turing's test was initially designed to answer an existential question: "Can a machine think?" The aim was to see if a computer could reach a level of human intelligence. The same year, Claude Shannon (1950) proposed the creation of a machine that could be taught to play chess. While AI research has progressed steadily since then or over the past 60 years, the promises made by its precursors proved too optimistic at the time. In the 1970s, AI reached a standstill (known as the "AI winter"), marked by a drop in funding and interest in research in this field.

The 1990s saw a revival on both fronts, thanks to advances in computing power. In 1995, AI took a decisive step forward with Richard Wallace's development of A.L.I.C.E. (Artificial Linguistic Internet Computer Entity), a program capable of holding a basic conversation. Also, in the 90s, IBM developed a computer called Deep Blue, which used a brute-force approach to take on world chess champion Gary Kasparov. Deep Blue can anticipate six or more moves and calculate 330 million positions per second. In 1996, Deep Blue lost to Kasparov before winning the rematch a year later. After two periods of expansion between 1940 and 1960 and again between 1980 and 1990, AI experienced a new boom in 2010, thanks to so-called machine learning algorithms.

Two factors are at the root of this new craze between researchers and the information technology (IT) industry: access to massive volumes of data *and* the discovery that processors on simple computer graphics cards are highly efficient in accelerating the computation of learning algorithms. It is worth noting that some of the most interesting developments in AI are occurring not in IT but in fields such as health, medicine, biology and finance. In many ways, the transition to AI resembles the process of computer diffusion, which, after being the preserve of a few specialised companies, spread throughout the economy and society in the 90s. Nor is it, unlike the expansion of Internet access from multinational companies to most of the population in many countries in the 2000s. Economies will increasingly need people with dual specialities, i.e., expertise in a discipline such as economics, biology or law and skills in AI techniques such as machine learning.

According to Aghion et al. (2019), artificial intelligence (AI) can be defined as "the ability of a machine to mimic human behaviour" or "the ability of an agent to achieve goals in a wide range of environments". These definitions raise fundamental economic questions. For example, what happens if AI enables an ever-increasing number of tasks previously carried out by humans to become automated? From one perspective, Yu-Hsien Chu et al. (2020) were able to show that with the rapid development of digital computing capabilities, the emergence of the Internet of Things (IoT), cloud analytics and big data, artificial intelligence (AI) has become an important innovative tool for digital transformation and technological modernisation on a global production scale. Using a dynamic computable general equilibrium (CGE) model based on Taiwan's input–output tables to capture supply chain interdependence and resource constraints, Yu-Hsien Chu et al. (2020) assess the impact of government policies and private company investments in smart manufacturing on Taiwanese semiconductor production and employment and the ICT industry. Their simulations show that, under the effect of increased investment in AI, semiconductor production would be 10.34% above the reference value and employment demand 24.61% below the reference in 2025.

The result is also similar in the information and communications technology (ICT) industry. The development of intelligent manufacturing is thus an adaptation strategy by private companies to cope with the falling birth rate, a source of labour shortage. At the same time, unemployment and unequal income distribution may be unintended consequences of AI development. Consequently, it is suggested that in addition to focusing on cultivating AI talent and developing supporting infrastructures, policymakers could adopt fiscal policies and measures to improve income distribution and enhance labour transfer.

This chapter aims to simulate the impact of artificial intelligence on the Senegalese economy. Specifically, the aim is to (i) quantify the impact of an artificial intelligence policy on economic growth, (ii) measure its sectoral impact and identify the most reactive branches of the economy, (iii) assess the impact of this policy on the labour market; (iv) evaluate its effect on household well-being. In what follows, we first analyse a few stylised facts. We then describe the methodology and present the simulation results. Finally, we draw some policy lessons.

Some AI Experiences Around the World and in Africa

In addition to being pioneers, the USA, Canada and China are among the most successful countries in AI. In Africa, Mauritius is a forerunner. Canada launched its "pan-Canadian" Artificial Intelligence Strategy in March 2017, led by the Canadian Institute for Advanced Research (CIFAR). Four key objectives back the Pan-Canadian Artificial Intelligence Strategy: (i) to increase the number of qualified artificial intelligence researchers and graduates in Canada; (ii) to establish interconnected centres of scientific excellence in Canada's three major artificial intelligence institutes, located in Edmonton (Alberta Machine Intelligence Institute, Amii), Montreal (Montreal Institute for Learning Algorithms, MILA) and Toronto (Vector Institute for Artificial Intelligence); (iii) develop a global program on artificial intelligence in society, and lead international reflection on the economic, social, ethical, political and legal implications of advances in artificial intelligence; (iv) support a national artificial intelligence research community. To achieve its goals, CIFAR has received public funding of CAD 125 million (USD 100 million) over five years to develop human capital, support AI research in Canada, and work to ensure that AI research leads to applications for the public and private sectors. A more sustained budgetary effort is planned in several key areas, such as data analytics, AI and design, cybersecurity, Canada's aboriginal languages, support for federal "superclusters" and collaborative centres with Canadian universities, and strategic partnerships with international players. Canada also participates in the International Group of Experts on Artificial Intelligence (G2IA), whose mission is to lead initiatives in the field of AI. This group's mission is to support and guide the responsible adoption of AI, centred on people and focused on human rights, inclusion, diversity, innovation and economic growth.

As for China, the three-year National Plan for AI adopted there in 2016 was drawn up jointly by the National Development and Reform Commission, the Ministry of Science and Technology, the Ministry of Industry and Information Technology and the Cyberspace Administration of China. The Internet Plus initiative, launched in 2015 as a national strategy to boost economic growth through innovative Internet-related technologies, encompasses AI. This initiative focuses mainly on (i) strengthening AI hardware capabilities, (ii) consolidating network platform ecosystems, (iii) AI applications in necessary socio-economic fields, and (iv) the impact of AI on society. As part of this, the Chinese government forecast the creation of a 15 billion USD R&D market for the AI sector in China in 2018. In mid-2017, policymakers revised their ambitions upwards to (i) achieve AI-driven economic growth by 2020, (ii) make major advances in fundamental theories and the development of an intelligent society by 2025, and (iii) make the country a global AI innovation hub by 2030 and build an AI industry worth CNY 1 trillion, or USD 150 billion (China, 2017). The targets are set to call for "next-generation information technologies" to account, as a strategic sector, for 15% of the gross domestic product by 2020.

In sub-Saharan Africa, Mauritius is the only country to have adopted a proactive approach to AI backed by a clear strategy, and other countries are following suit. In April 2024, Kenya launched its National AI Strategy Development Process. In August 2024, South Africa also published its National Artificial Intelligence Policy Framework. These policies lay out broader regulatory measures to govern the adoption and adaptation of AI in public policy and production processes. In its Government AI Readiness Index 2020 report, Oxford Insights ranks Mauritius as the leading nation out of 41 sub-Saharan African countries regarding artificial intelligence (45th globally out of 172 countries). The strategy dated 2018 refers to the use of AI as a key option to support the ocean economy, which accounts for more than 10% of Mauritian GDP. Thus, the state wants to invest in the maritime Internet of Things, blue biotechnology, the development of smart ports and other areas. In addition, Mauritius wants to use AI to transform public services. To encourage R&D collaboration between academia and the private sector, the Mauritius Research and Innovation Council runs a program offering grants to small and medium enterprises (SMEs) to collaborate with local academic and research institutions.

Regarding developing digital skills within the workforce, the Human Resources Development Council (HRDC) has initiated a program to support the development of AI skills. The strategy reinforced the policy of granting an eight-year tax exemption to companies involved in innovation-driven activities for intellectual property assets developed in Mauritius. It also established a council to guide the government in supporting the AI ecosystem. These plans are supported by a "Digital Mauritius 2030" strategy, which aims to strengthen the country's position as a regional ICT leader. The latter focuses on digital government, cybersecurity and data protection, all areas favourable to the development of AI.

Senegal does not yet have an AI strategy. Nevertheless, private-sector-led AI experiments are being implemented in fields as varied as financial technology (fintech), telemedicine and biotechnology. These experiments, essentially driven by the private sector, are still in their infancy, so an ex-ante impact assessment exercise would be useful to assess the scope of an AI policy for the Senegalese economy and draw lessons for economic policies.

Methodology

Computable general equilibrium models have been widely used in many countries to analyse the impact of economic policies and external shocks (Burfisher, 2021). Because of the interdependence of sectors and economic agents and the significant feedback effects linked to the impact of AI on the economy, a general equilibrium analysis is more appropriate, as it has the advantage of presenting an overview of the economy and the channels through which shocks are transmitted to microeconomic agents while considering the macroeconomic constraints within which they operate. In the past, several general equilibrium models have been developed and applied in Senegal to analyse a wide range of policies (Boccanfuso et al., 2007; Cabral et al., 2009, 2012, 2013; Cissé & Fofana, 2015; Diagne et al., 2008). The basic model structure used is PEP 1-t, developed by Decaluwé et al. (2013).

However, a set of features has been added, namely the inclusion of public capital and transmission channels for the impact of public investment, the inclusion of human capital, research and development (excluding artificial intelligence), Artificial Intelligence (AI), infrastructure approximated by physical investment and public capital externalities in the specification of market sector production functions through the introduction of a total factor productivity (TFP) function. Consequently, the total public capital stock creates a positive externality for each activity, affecting this sector's productivity. TFP is also affected by the distribution of public investment between human capital, R&D (excluding AI), AI and infrastructure. The trade-off in the allocation of public investment between these factors depends on the rationality of policymakers. Thus, TFP is determined endogenously and is assumed to be a function of human capital (KH), non-AI research and development (RDhia), AI, infrastructure (IP) and the ratio of total public capital to sectoral private capital (KDpubG/KDpriv), a proxy for public capital externalities to the private sector.

In addition, we precede the extensive segmentation of the labour market with a specification of the labour market marked by the introduction of a wage curve. Similarly, in modelling foreign trade, we consider the existence of a finite export demand. The model is dynamically recursive, meaning that it is solved as a sequence of static equilibria linked in time through capital accumulation, labour force growth and behavioural equations. One of the advantages of a dynamic model specification is the ability to generate a medium to long-term path. In addition, structural changes can be analysed over time. The model applies to a small economy for which world prices are given. The 2020 social accounting matrix is used as the model's accounting framework. It considers 33 categories of institutions: the 10 categories of households in Dakar, other urban centres and rural areas, classified by gender and middle-class status, businesses, the State and the rest of the world. It incorporates two types of capital factors (private and public). On the labour market, we distinguish between four qualification levels ("bac + 4 et over"[1], "bac + 2 and/or + 3"[2] and "bac",[3] "BFEM/BEP"[4] and "CFEE"[5] and the uneducated and/or those who have not completed primary school), divided by gender, for eight types of labour input. The model includes 25 sectors of activity and 25 products/services.

Production Block Structure

Production technology is described as a multi-level process. First, the sector's output is expressed by a Leontief-type function combining fixed shares of value added and intermediate consumption. Total intermediate consumption is a fixed share of production. Each product represents a fixed share of the sector's total intermediate consumption. Value added is formulated differently for each sector. In the non-market sector,

[1] Master, engineers, Doctorate and more.

[2] Higher National Diploma, Bachelor's degree.

[3] Diploma of Secondary Education.

[4] Certificate of Completion of Basic Studies/*Certificate of Professional Studies.*

[5] Primary school certificate.

value added is a function with constant elasticity of substitution (CES), combining composite labour and public capital. On the other hand, value added is a CES function combining composite labour and capital in the market sectors. Composite labour is a CES function combining the 24 different labour categories. The first-order condition of profit maximisation determines the demand for labour in each industry. Composite capital is represented as a CES function combining private and public capital. The first-order profit-maximisation condition determines the demand for industry-specific capital. Total factor productivity (TFP) is endogenous. It is a function of human capital, research and development, physical investment, the ratio between the rate of accumulation of public and private capital in the sector and the elasticity of TFP to these different arguments.

Modelling the Labour Market

The labour market segments considered in this study are those related to qualification and gender. The heterogeneity observed in the skilled labour market has led us to make distinctions according to gender and qualification level. In this model, one of the features of the labour market is, on the one hand, the segmentation into four categories of qualification ("bac + 4 and over", "bac + 2 and/or +3" and "bac", "BFEM/BEP" and "CFEE" and the uneducated and/or those who have not completed primary school) and, on the other, the taking into account of gender and age heterogeneities. As a result, we distinguish eight labour market segments. On the other hand, we take account of the rigid character of the different segments of the skilled labour market by introducing unemployment endogenously. Workers are assumed to be mobile within the different labour market segments. However, there is no labour mobility between different labour market segments.

The wage curve approach, developed by Blanchflower and Oswald (1994), is used to model the labour market, where we assume the existence of unemployment in the skilled labour segments. Workers in this market segment are mainly employed in the modern or formal sector, where we assume relative rigidity in wage setting. The wage rate evolves according to the situation in the labour market, which is in line with the situation described by the wage curve. This describes a negative relationship between unemployment levels and wages. It reflects that areas and sectors with high unemployment rates are associated with low wages, while high wage levels mark those with low unemployment rates. The wage rate is assumed to be determined by the confrontation of labour supply and demand. Thus, in this market, the equilibrium resulting from equality between the sum of supply and demand for unskilled labour determines the equilibrium wage rate.

Foreign Trade

To account for Senegalese exporters' constraints on the external market, we introduce an export demand function into the model. This function has a finite elasticity and is a function of the ratio between the world and fob prices. Indeed, local producers are obliged to reduce their export prices to increase their market share abroad. Notably, in Senegal, agri-food products and those of other industries are particularly subject to strong competition in foreign markets.

Equilibrium Process

The savings-investment equilibrium is achieved by introducing an endogenous indirect tax that enables the State to collect the additional resources needed for investment purposes. The savings rate of other institutions is fixed. Public spending is assumed to be fixed in real terms in the first period. However, it increases at the same rate as the population. The same applies to budget savings, transfers and labour supply, all increasing at the same rate as the population.

Model Dynamics

Economic dynamics are driven by capital accumulation and population growth. Capital growth through investment is the main source of economic growth. Investment covers capital depreciation and contributes to its accumulation from one period to the next. The private capital accumulation rule is determined as follows: the sectoral private capital accumulation rate is assumed to be an increasing function of the capital cost–benefit ratio, the latter evolving at a decreasing rate. Public investment flows are linked to private investment flows, reflecting the relative complementarity between these two market sector investments. In the non-market sector, public investment flows depend on government disposable income. While the above rationality guides capital accumulation, the supply of labour increases at the rate of population growth and is, therefore, exogenous. Public consumption is, therefore, assumed to increase at the same rate as population growth. This assumption also applies to inter-household transfers, public transfers to households, private and public transfers from the rest of the world to resident institutions and vice versa, and minimum private consumption.

Parameters and Specification of Model Functional Forms

Calibration of the CGE requires an appropriate accounting framework (SAM) and consistent elasticities. The specification of production, household consumption and import/export demand functions require the following parameters: income elasticity of product demand, the Frisch parameter, the elasticity of substitution between capital and labour, the elasticity of substitution between imported and local products, the elasticity of transformation between foreign and local sales, and elasticity of foreign demand. Without a long series, these parameters have not been estimated using Senegalese data. Instead, they were borrowed from the CGE literature and empirical studies in other developing economies like Senegal (also see Annabi et al. [2004] for details of the parameters in MEGC). The elasticities associated with the total factor productivity function are borrowed from R. Bronzini and Piselli (2009). All other model parameters were calibrated using SAM data to ensure consistency with base-year data.

The model's accounting framework is provided by the social accounting matrix for the Senegalese economy in 2020, constructed by Institutions and Growth Research Laboratory (*Laboratory de Recherche sur la croissance et les Institutions*-LINC) from the National Agency of Statistics and Demography of Senegal (ANSD) data. We have further disaggregated the sectoral workforce into four types of qualification by gender for 8 types of labour input. We distinguish the private segment of the capital market from the public segment. The SAM integrates 15 categories of institutions, including households in Dakar, other urban centres and rural areas, classified according to their position in relation to the middle class, firms, the state and the rest of the world. The disaggregation of the workforce is carried out using data from the 2018 Senegal Poverty Monitoring Survey (ESPS) and the Labour Market Survey (ENES).

Simulation and Results

Justification

In this simulation, we analyse the consequences of a change in the weight of endogenous growth instruments in the allocation of public investment: human capital, physical investment and research & development, conceived as a continuum running from the production of new ideas in the laboratory to the inventions and innovations to which they give rise. R&D is sequenced into R&D (excluding AI) and AI. The simulation consisted of introducing AI into the model, then increasing its weight and that of R&D (excluding AI) and human capital in the order of priorities of decision-makers across the economy, the latter being raised to the detriment of infrastructure investment, on which they focused during the 2000, 2010 and 2020 decades. We draw inspiration from a country at the frontier of knowledge in this field—Canada—and assume that AI's share of public investment rises from a weight of 0.1–0.4%, a variation of 300% over five years (2023–2027). The latter is justified by the period of use chosen in Senegal's reference document, the *Plan d'actions prioritaires ajusté et accéléré* (PAP2A) of the *Plan Sénégal Emergent*. This change in the composition of public investment, shown in Table 7.1, is accompanied by an increase in the latter, in proportion to the growth recorded in the telecommunications sector, which is an estimated increase of 32%, on average, over the 2023–2027 period.

Table 7.1 Change in the weight of human capital, physical investment and research & development in public investment for each sector

Growth instruments	*Reference*	*Sim 1*	
	Weight	*Weight*	*Change in % (with respect to the reference)*
Human capital	0.35	0.5	43
R&D (excluding IA)	0.029	0.187	545
IA	0.001	0.004	300
Infrastructure	0.62	0.309	−50
Total	1	1	–

Source Calculations of the authors

Simulation Results

We will analyse the sectoral effects following an analysis of the shock's impact on GDP due to the increased weight in public investment of AI combined with human capital. Consequently, shocks are analysed with reference to the growth path followed by the economy in the absence of any shock (baseline or business as usual).

Impact on GDP

When the priority is raised for AI, R&D (non-AI) and human capital, GDP increases by 7.02 and 2.92 percentage points from 2023 to 2027[6] (Fig. 7.1). The reallocation of public investment from the infrastructure sector to AI, R&D, and human capital results in a leverage effect on the stock of public capital reallocated to these priority areas and, in turn, on the private capital that this reallocation induces. Due to the strong inter-branch links between the AI destination sector (ICT) and the rest of the Senegalese economy (other sectors, households, the State, businesses), the leverage effect on the capital stock allocated to these areas translates into a significant leap in GDP. This suggests that combining AI, lab-based research (non-AI R&D), and human capital may offer a good option for wealth creation within the Senegalese economy. However, this effect fades over the rest of the period as the initial capital stock is amortised. For North America, particularly Canada, GDP will be 14.5% higher in 2030, as suggested by the results obtained through the Spatial Computable General Equilibrium (S-CGE) model that has been used to estimate the net global impact of AI on the economy until 2030. Global GDP on a global scale could be up to 14% higher than this figure in 2030 because of AI. Economic gains from AI will be experienced by all sectors of the economy, with each industry expected to see a gain in GDP of at least approximately 10% by 2030 (Gillham et al., 2018).

Sector Impact

An analysis of factor intensity by sector shows that the agricultural and service sectors are relatively more labour-intensive, particularly in

[6] As the reference SAM is that of 2020, the simulation is conducted over the five-year period 2023–2027.

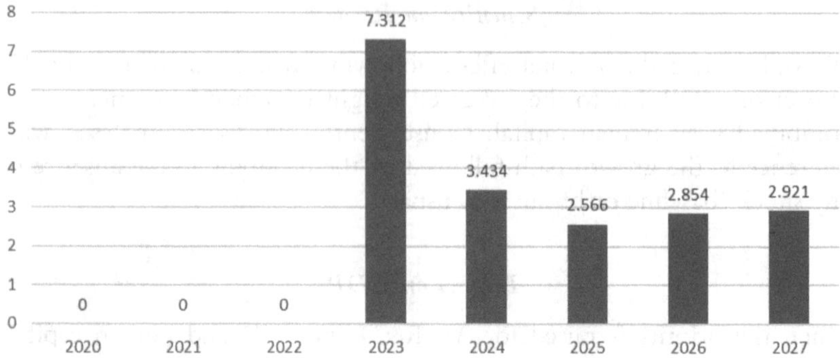

Fig. 7.1 Change in GDP (in percentage points relative to the BAU[7] scenario), 2020–2027 (*Source* Authors)

unskilled and low-skilled labour. The industrial sector, on the other hand, is relatively more capital-intensive. Based on this factor intensity structure, we trace the impact of increased sectoral public investment in AI, R&D (non-AI)[8] and human capital on sectors and the labour market through the model, bearing in mind that all variables interact and are determined simultaneously in a computable general equilibrium model. An increase in public investment in AI, R&D (excluding AI) and human capital translates into increased value added in all sectors by 2027.

In the simulation, where the relative weights of AI, R&D (excluding AI) and human capital are taken into account, the biggest increases in value added are recorded in the sectors of fatty foodstuffs manufacturing, mining, other non-food industries, transport, fruit, plant and flower growing, petroleum research and exploration services, poultry farming, other dairy and ice cream industries, cattle, sheep and goat farming, trade and repairs, telecommunications, cereal growing, other services, hotels and accommodation, fruit and vegetable canning, fintech (Table 7.2). The particularity of the sectors recording a relatively strong rise in their added values maintain stronger inter-industry links with the destination sectors for AI in Senegal, telecoms and fintech.

[7] Business As Usual.

[8] Laboratory research.

Table 7.2 Change in value added (in percentage points relative to the BAU scenario), 2027

	Cereal crops	Growing tubers and vegetables with dry pods	Fruit, plant and flower-growing nurseries	Peanuts and other oilseed products	Other agriculture, forestry and logging activities	Cattle, sheep and goat breeding	Poultry farming	Other breeding activities	Fishing, fish farming and aquaculture
Sim	64.24	56.54	65.28	51.87	56.54	64.22	64.10	57.10	58.10
	Mining and quarrying	Slaughtering, processing and preserving	Manufacture of edible fats and oils	Grain milling	Fruit and vegetable preserves	Manufacture of dairy products and ice cream	Other food industries	Other non-food industries	Civil engineering
	84.97	58.63	90.70	58.04	60.30	63.99	51.7	71.16	55.66
Sim	Trade and repair	Hotel and accommodation	Transport	Telecommunications	Petroleum exploration and research services	Fintech	Other market services	Non-market services	
	64.947	62.46	71.07	62.03	66.90	60.23	62.90	−0.33	

Source Authors

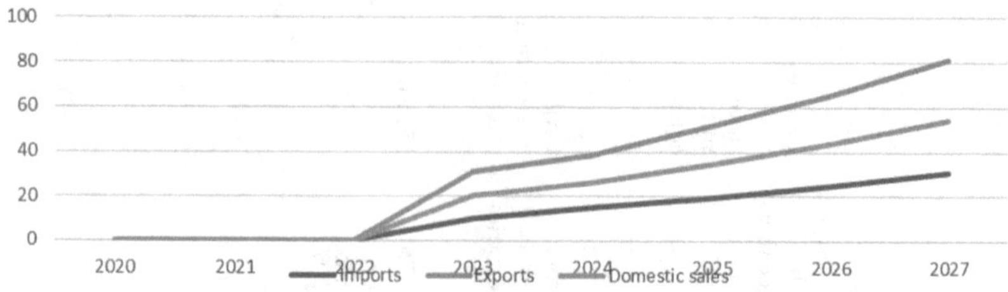

Fig. 7.2 Change in exports, imports and domestic sales (in percentage points relative to the BAU scenario), 2020–2027 (*Source* Authors)

Impact on Foreign Trade

Most of the increase in production was directed towards foreign sales, with total exports recording a significant jump. Domestic sales also increased significantly. Conversely, imports increased at a less proportional rate than exports (Fig. 7.2).

Impact on Factor Remuneration

Increased public investment in AI and greater budgetary investment in R&D and human capital accumulation boost the return on private capital and improve the return on public capital (Fig. 7.3).

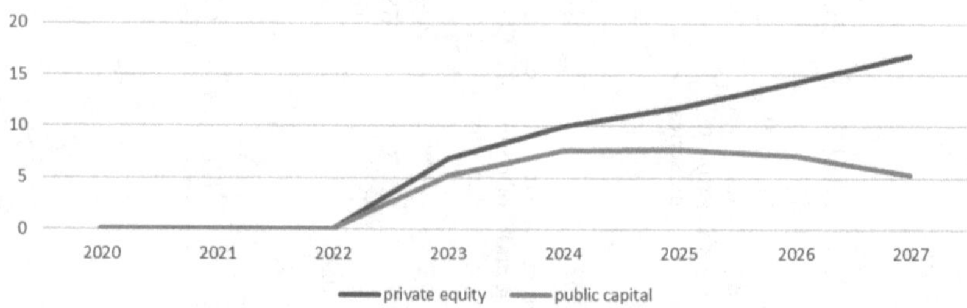

Fig. 7.3 Change in the rate of return on capital (in percentage points relative to the BAU scenario), 2020–2027 (*Source* Authors)

Table 7.3 Variation in wage rates and labour demand (in percentage points relative to the BAU scenario), 2027 (to be brought to the appendix)

Year	*No qualified men*	*Little qualified men*	*Medium qualified men*	*Very qualified men*	*No qualified women*	*Little qualified women*	*Medium qualified women*	*Highly qualified women*
Salary rate	19.402	9.428	11.479	3.797	18.986	9.316	8.791	4.073
Request for work	0.176	13.314	5.08	7.812	0.93	13.032	4.936	13.019

Source Authors

Impact on Labour Demand and Wage Rates

When more weight is given to AI, R&D (excluding AI), and human capital, labour demand tends to increase in all segments of the labour market (Table 7.3). As a result of the increase in public investment flows devoted to AI, R&D (excluding AI) and human capital, demand for highly skilled labour is rising sharply, but in the women's segment and significantly in the men's. Substantial increases in demand are also seen in the labour market's low-skilled male and female segments, given the relatively high weight of this category alongside the unskilled in the economy.

Impact on Nominal Incomes, Consumer Prices and Well-Being

The level of household well-being, measured by the equivalent change, is determined by the incomes they receive, consumer prices and the composition of their consumption basket. Nominal incomes rise for all household strata. Consumer prices move in the opposite direction. As a result, well-being increases for all household categories (Table 7.4). The increase is relatively stronger for lower and pure middle-class households in Dakar, pure and upper-middle-class households in other urban centres, and lower and lower middle-class households in rural areas, where prices have fallen relatively more while nominal incomes have risen.

Table 7.4 Change in nominal incomes, consumer prices and well-being (in percentage points relative to the BAU scenario), 2027

Households	*Nominal income*	*Price per consumption*	*Wellness*
DaKar lower class	20.475	−14.062	34.736
DaKar's lower middle class	20.548	−13.781	34.132
DaKar's pure middle class	19.988	−14.036	34.107
DaKar's upper middle class	19.712	−14.075	33.823
DaKar upper class	19.096	−13.079	31.494
ACU lower class	19.903	−13.767	33.607
ACU lower middle class	19.821	−13.785	33.498
Pure ACU middle-class	19.916	−14.127	34.031
Upper-middle class ACU	19.713	−14.135	33.948
ACU upper class	19.382	−12.797	31.345
Rural lower class	19.687	−14.557	34.531
Rural lower middle class	19.536	−14.713	34.733
Rural pure middle-class	19.877	−14.061	33.857
Rural upper-middle class	19.67	−14.235	33.964
Rural upper class	19.456	−14.21	33.851

Source Authors

Conclusions and Policy Lessons

AI development can have both positive and negative effects on economic growth. If AI accumulation increases due to improved productivity in goods and services, it can lead to short-term household benefits. However, if companies and other actors start using AI as a substitute for human labour, it can have detrimental effects on household utility in the short term. It's important to note that the long-term impact of AI development on household welfare is not always positive. On the other hand, positive effects can be observed when AI contributes to the improvement of human capital, research and development, and various types of physical capital. This trial aimed to simulate the hypothetical impact of AI on economic growth, the labour market and household welfare. In this work, we use a dynamic recursive CGE model to evaluate the hypothetical impact of an AI strategy in Senegal. We draw on the latest developments in the endogenous growth literature to model the impact of AI on the Senegalese economy. To this end, TFP is endogenised and expressed as a function of R&D, AI, human capital, infrastructure and public capital externalities in market sectors. The results show:

- Since GDP has increased significantly, a combination of AI, laboratory research (non-AI R&D), and human capital offers a good option for strong, sustainable wealth creation.
- The sectors of the Senegalese economy most responsive to AI are food fats manufacturing, mining, other non-food industries, transport, fruit, plant, and flower growing, oil research and prospecting services, poultry farming, other dairy and ice cream industries, cattle, sheep, and goat farming, trade and repairs, telecommunications, cereal growing, other services, hotels and accommodation, fruit and vegetable canning, and fintech.
- Exports grew more than proportionately to imports.
- Due to increased public investment flows into AI, R&D (excluding AI) and human capital, demand for highly skilled labour is rising sharply in the highly skilled segments, particularly among women. The same is true of the low-skilled segments of the labour market for men and women, given the relatively high weight of this category in the labour market.
- The increase in well-being is relatively greater for lower-class households and those in the lower and pure middle classes in Dakar, the pure and upper middle classes in other urban centres, and the lower and lower middle classes in rural areas.

Hence, several policy lessons can be learned:

- As IA is supposed to induce GDP increase, then an increase in TFP will impact the value added of the sectors most sensitive to AI and, given the interactions between branches, on the rest of the economy and, consequently, growth. Moreover, this option would pave the way for and/or consolidate new, highly technology-intensive niches for the Senegalese economy, such as Fintech, biotechnology and so on. In particular, Senegal should strive to create a business climate conducive to the emergence of AI start-ups and/or companies. In particular, the development of fintech could be a powerful lever for modernising the economy and improving competitiveness. Indeed, fintech, a component of the digital economy, could be one of the driving sub-sectors of the economy and contribute to GDP growth. Numerous companies in the ICT/BPO (Information and Communication Technology/Business Processing Outsourcing) sector, decentralised financial systems and banks are already engaged in several activities at varying degrees of maturity, such as mobile applications, online banking, digitisation of platforms and business intelligence.

- As IA is highly intensive in skilled labour, a successful AI strategy requires improving the supply of skills essential to adopting such technology. The effects on the labour market will be felt due to a greater demand for qualifications and, consequently, skills to be combined with capital incorporating a significant dose of AI.
- All in all, a public policy backed by an IA strategy, as in Canada or Mauritius, would substantially raise TFP and, consequently, the added value of economic sectors and growth. It would also have an impact on the labour market. What's more, this option would pave the way for and/or consolidate new, highly technology-intensive niches for the Senegalese economy, such as the expanding sectors of Fintech, biotechnology, etc.

References

African Union. (2020). *Digital Transformation Strategy for Africa (2020–2030)*. African Union.

Aghion, P., Jones, B. F., & Jones, C. I. (2019). Artificial intelligence and economic growth. In *The economics of artificial intelligence: An agenda*. University of Chicago Press.

Annabi, N., Cockburn, J., & Decaluwé, B. (2004, June). A dynamic sequential CGE model for poverty analysis. *Advanced MPIA training workshop in Dakar, Senegal* (pp 10–14).

Blanchflower, D. G., & Oswald, A. J. (1994). Estimating a wage curve for Britain: 1973–90. *Economic, Journal, Royal Economic Society, 104*(426), 1025–43.

Boccanfuso, D., Cabral, F., Cissé, F., Diagne, A., & Savard, L. (2007, May). « Strategies to reduce poverty in Senegal: A modeling analysis by CGE microsimulé ». *L'Actualité Economique, 83*(4).

Bronzini, R., Piselli, P. (2009). Determinants of long-run regional productivity with geographical spillovers: The role of R&D, human capital and public infrastructure. *Regional Science and Urban Economics, 39*, 187–199.

Burfisher, M. E. (2021). *Introduction to computable general equilibrium models*. Cambridge University Press.

Chen, C., Hu, Y., Karuppiah, M., & Kumar, P. M. (2021). Artificial intelligence on economic evaluation of energy efficiency and renewable energy technologies. *Sustainable Energy Technologies and Assessments, 47*, 101358.

Chu, Y.-H., Hsu, S.-M., Chang, C.-C., & Hsu, S.-H. (2020). An economy-wide assessment of artificial intelligence investment on manufacturing: A case study of Taiwan's semiconductor and ICT industries. *Modern Economy, 11*, 1040–1052.

Etscheid, J. (2019). Artificial intelligence in public administration: A possible framework for partial and full automation. In I. Lindgren, M. Janssen, H. Lee, A. Polini, M. P. Rodríguez Bolívar, H. Jochen Scholl, & E. Tambouris, *Electronic government, 18th IFIP WG 8.5 International conference, EGOV 2019 San Benedetto Del Tronto, Italy, September 2–4.*

Gillham, J., et al. (2018). *The macroeconomic impact of artificial intelligence.* PwC.

Hanson, K. T. (2023). Technological leapfrogging and innovation: Re-imagining evaluation approaches and practice in Africa. In *Public policy and technological transformations in Africa: Nurturing policy entrepreneurship, policy tools and citizen participation* (pp. 67–84). Springer.

Lu, C.-H. (2021). The impact of artificial intelligence on economic growth and welfare. *Journal of Macroeconomics, 69*, 103342.

Ondiek, J. O., & Onyango, G. (2024). Blockchain technologies in digital governance: The Kenyan experience with promoting public accountability. In *The Routledge International Handbook of Public Administration and Digital Governance* (pp. 112–124). Routledge. https://doi.org/10.4324/9781003458081

Turing, A. (1950). *Computing machinery and intelligence* (Vol. 59, no. 236). Oxford University Press.

CHAPTER 8

Artificial Intelligence and Public Accountability in Africa

Gedion Onyango and Japheth Otieno Ondiek

Introduction

Disruptive technological change is faster than ever in this century, and has become the new norm in public life. Citizens are increasingly expecting similar distruptive digital experiences from the government as the private sector. In doing so, automation of functions is being adopted in the public sector to improve efficiency and enhance service delivery processes. This is where *AI for Government* comes in, aiming to improve, among others, public accountability in processes pertaining to the *politics of resource allocation and public welfare*, which we can simply label as *public policy*. As public innovation accelerates, Artificial Intelligence (AI) is increasingly

G. Onyango (✉)
London School of Economics and Political Science, London, UK
e-mail: onyangojr@gmail.com

University of Johannesburg, Johannesburg, South Africa

J. O. Ondiek
University of Nairobi, Nairobi, Kenya

G. Onyango (ed.), *Designing Artificial Intelligence for Public Policy and Governance in Africa*, Studies in National Governance and Emerging Technologies, https://doi.org/10.1007/978-3-031-83445-5_8

crucial for transforming public sector and its engagement with citizens and various stakeholders (Ondiek & Onyango, 2024; Webb, 2019; Young et al., 2019). AI is presumed to reduce government costs and enhance organisations' operational systems, including in developing contexts of public administration like those in Africa (Gimpel & McBride, 2023; Houy et al., 2019; Mishra et al., 2024; Plantinga, 2024). This has been anchored on the potential of AI to enable increased productivity by government employees or create a blended workforce in the public sector. However, these can be both concerning and exciting because of the complex political dynamics (Onyango, 2025) and the AI regulatory gap (Almeida et al., 2021) in public institutions. In recent years, automation, machine learning, and digitalisation have become critical components of the digital transformation of Africa's public sector organisations (Brand, 2022; Butcher et al., 2021; Onyango & Ondiek, 2022). Within this context, AI for Government describes a scenario where governments rapidly use AI to streamline administrative processes, improve service delivery, and maximise budget allocation. However, as already detailed in *Chapter 3* and elaborated differently by other chapters in this volume, the government may also grapple with realities of incorporating AI in public administration, because these technologies also raise ethical and accountability concerns that require careful consideration. As such, *governmentalities* in public policy processes, mainly governments, non-governmental organisations, on the one hand, and on the other hand researchers and donor projects, seek new approaches to oversee and guide the development and use of AI to realise its social and financial potential (Plantinga, 2024). Many believe that governance mechanisms must be improved to properly direct the development and application of AI in a socially and environmentally sustainable way. This raises the question of how public governing institutions can effectively respond to emerging challenges to ensure that AI for Government benefits individuals, businesses, and society.

Following this frame of thought, this chapter explores how AI can promote public accountability mechanisms in the African public sector. Or how AI for Government can improve public accountability. The burgeoning research indicates that advanced technologies in their various forms have enabled citizen engagement in government activities, improving public accountability where there are stark challenges with public transparency and openness, like in the African public administration (Thinyane, et al., 2023; Ondiek & Onyango, 2023). Even so, the role of advanced technologies in public accountability has been primarily fronted with regard to the impact of social media and other technologies like Blockchain. Thus, the AI's role in this regard is only emerging (Niyitunga, 2024).

This chapter is a moderate attempt to contribute to the growing body of research on the role of AI in enabling accountability mechanisms in line with principles of ethical decision-making and transparency in the Kenyan and South African public sector. In the end, our discussion offers policy recommendations for governance practitioners and decision-makers on leveraging AI systems to improve public accountability standards in public administration. It is shown that realising artificial intelligence in African public administration brings opportunities and obstacles unique to a country's contexts and sector of application. The rest of the chapter is structured as follows: The next section reviews the literature on the adoption complexities of AI in public sector institutions, focusing on the role of collaborative frameworks. The next look into the nexus between public governance and AI. This section dissects different models of AI applications before delving into methods, discussion, and conclusion sections.

AI Adoption Complexities: The Need for a Collaborative Framework in Public Accountability

Adopting artificial intelligence (AI) is a complex and evolving process that may vary significantly across legal systems and contexts of application. This means that embedding AI in the public sector requires a more harmonious transition models and processes. One of such an endeavour may need a robust and inclusive collaborative public governance frameworks. Collaborative models, emphasising co-production and co-desigining approaches could be most preferable because of the several layers of cultures, norms and histories in adopting AI for public accountability. Wirtz et al. (2020) and Gasser and Almeida (2017) present an example of such a layer. Despite various collaborative frameworks, AI should comprise critical perspectives that can be compressed into the modular frameworks presented in Table 8.1.

As observed by most contributions in this volume, such frameworks should be anchored on ethical practices and human rights aspects of

Table 8.1 Layers of collaborative governance perspective

Layers	*Essence*
AI technology and services	Understanding the variety of AI technologies and their contexts is crucial for developing context-specific governance and governance mechanisms for various technologies and levels of intervention (technical, organisational, and policy). Collaborative frameworks would be critical to identifying these context-specific models and mechanisms
AI challenges	This layer considers AI's various societal, ethical, and regulatory impacts and risks and informs policy mechanisms by illuminating the broader legal, ethical, and societal challenges. This would require bringing various stakeholders together
Regulation	This should define the challenges and responsibilities that AI regulation and coordination should address. Designing such regulatory frameworks should be steeped in a broad-based understanding and definitions of principles of engagement so as not to marginalise a particular group
Collaborative layer	This is where stakeholder goals and opposing interests are balanced. The operations should promote cost–benefit analyses of values and interests and help stakeholders reach a consensus
Public policy	This includes the application of hard and soft governance mechanisms, such as regulations, legislation, social, and legal norms, ethical principles, and codes of conduct, in addition to organisational and technical practices like standards, certifications, and data management tools. Policy implementation should consider the different contexts, underlying politics, technical layer implementation levels, and the different forms of cooperation between various actors and stakeholders. Building trust, shared values, and motivation among many stakeholders is crucial

Source Authors' summary

public administration that are essential in promoting public accountability. Integrating AI into public administration and accountability mechanisms requires adequate planning and intervention strategies to ensure efficient allocation of the resources needed and training. Such an effort demands a practical collaborative framework both within and outside the public sector. In other words, to realise AI-enabled public accountability, there is a need for AI governance for the public sector anchored on stakeholder consultation, effective and ethical public procurement processes and other governance frameworks that emphasise values of openness, justice, and human-centricity (Floridi, et al. 2018). To promote public accountability, AI systems should not reinforce or amplify existing prejudices and disparities that have undermined public accountability dimensions, particularly those related to human rights and democracy in African public administration (Onyango, 2024).

As such, clear roles and duties among stakeholders in AI development, algorithmic modelling, deployment, and supervision are necessary for accountability. Thanks to the current transparency approach embedded in the formation of AI systems and models, stakeholders may evaluate the reasoning behind AI decisions and identify any biases, prejudices, or mistakes in the process (Cath, 2018). This human-centricity strongly emphasises how human rights, values, and dignity should come first when designing and using AI. The legal, cultural, and institutional settings influencing AI regulations differ significantly throughout states and policy sectors. While some nations have developed comprehensive AI specific policies, others use already-existing laws and regulations like the Data Protection Acts and Communications Acts, which have become part of the African countries' administrative state. Regulations pertaining to liability, algorithmic accountability, and data protection are common components of AI regulatory frameworks. However, gaps and discrepancies still make cross-border AI deployment and interoperability difficult. Furthermore, because AI technologies are dynamic, regulatory frameworks must be continuously adjusted and improved to handle new risks and issues commonly found at the heart of public accountability, like gender inequality and further marginalisation of historically neglected populations. This would need to be done more collaboratively and with a learning attitude.

However, there is a need for consciousness around institutional cultural variables that could stand in the way. Evidence has shown an underlying apathy towards the integration of new technologies such as AI in the public sector (Onyango and Ondiek, 2021). In the similar fashion, AI in the public sector could face resistance and trepidation primarily around the significant change in work and loss of jobs. Furthermore, leaders and top government officials may lack the knowledge and skills necessary to effectively implement AI due to a lack of discernable toolkits providing a blueprint for the successful implementation and adoption of AI. The result of this may exacerbate already delicate public accountability mechanisms. It is critical to galvanise collaborative approaches around AI application in the public sector, especially concerning improving accountability mechanisms. Partnerships with various organisations are essential in tracking the use of services by citizens from multiple government agencies and institutions and are becoming a major practice in the public sector. This collaborative approach and AI will likely converge, leading to new public administration models in the public sector. The optimism to apply AI in public administration is balanced by the government's goal of providing timely and quality services to citizens and introducing new service delivery strategies in the public sector.

From the ongoing policy efforts, African governments are set to harness AI systems through collaborative approaches. This has involved building the capacity for ICT skills and creating digital governance blueprints as a vital step towards designing the policy frameworks (Onyango & Ondiek, 2021). All these efforts have been built around partnerships with non-governmental and business organisations and are critical because of a significant AI skills gap between the public sector, businesses, and government institutions. Public administration stands to benefit from learning from the experiences of the private and civil society sectors (see also *Chapter 5* in this volume). In addition, there are negligible considerations of skills for AI in government, including prerequisite skills and knowledge in AI and data-based initiatives, hence a call for comprehensive training, which civil society and the private sector are in a better position to offer. In short, collaborative public governance protects the broader public interest through innovative ways of doing things beyond traditional organisational methods (Osborne, 2006). The result is reduced risks and a balance of the interests of various stakeholders in society while maintaining human values undergirding public accountability.

The existing models for AI governance have yet to be co-created with stakeholders or tested empirically; they remain purely theoretical. These proposed elements are meant to aid policymakers in developing AI governance. Public administrations have a unique responsibility to consider societal needs and values and to ensure that governance, norms, guidelines, and sanctions are balanced and compatible to ensure public accountability. This should also consider how AI can be utilised in different contexts and for various purposes with different outcomes. Public administrators act as mediators between different social interests and ideals, with a personal stake in promoting public good within an effective public accountability mechanism. There is a clear and urgent need for empirical experiments and studies on how new forms of governance and the operationalisation of key principles of good AI governance can be successfully implemented. Most existing literature on public governance of AI focuses on defining governance targets and mechanisms but needs more empirical support for understanding public accountability issues surrounding AI. The potential solutions to the technology's deployment in various settings or actual instances of stakeholder participation and public discussion leading to the development of AI governance. In diverse technological, administrative, and social contexts, policymakers and public administrations can use empirical studies and experiments as useful benchmarks for functional and non-functional practices in public accountability and AI governance (Sun & Medaglia, 2019). The next section outlines the methodological process adopted for the study and introduces the two cases discussed. The subsequent section interprets the cases, analyses AI implementation in Kenya and South Africa and proposes a framework based on the cases analysed.

Data

The chapter is based on a documentary analysis of the use of AI in public administration, focusing on accountability and decision-making. The aim was to explore the potential benefits of AI in addressing these issues. Due to limited AI literature in the African context, the efforts of Kenya and South Africa in implementing AI in the public sector were reviewed. Both countries have made commendable steps to develop AI legislation and implementation plans for AI in the public sector. This case study design allows for a contextualised exploration of the dynamics of AI and public accountability in both countries. The units of analysis considered in this analysis are the government ministries and departments applying AI applications. Literature sources were reviewed, including ministerial briefings, AI legislative drafts, AI articles, and ICT policy briefs by public officials. This involved identifying meaning units from documentary searches, speeches, and public administrators who have used the systems, re-contextualising, and identifying homogeneous groups (themes) through drawing realistic conclusions. Data analysis included theoretical deviations, categorisation, and thematic analysis based on public accountability indicators like ethics, human rights, transparency, etc.

AI Implementation in Kenya and South Africa

Kenya

There are no AI specific laws, legislations, or regulations that directly regulate the application of AI in Kenya currently. However, since April 2024, the Ministry of ICT and Digital Economy has been in close consultation with donors and other actors such as Deutsche Gesellschaft für Internationale Zusammenarbeit (GIZ) GmbH, which has led to the recent launch of the National AI Strategy Development Process. Part of this conversation has been around the proposed AI Bill, 2023, "the Robotics and AI Bill", which is intended to promote the regulations and democratisation of AI. This proposal has not yet received official government support for gazettement, nor has the private sector and stakeholders approved its tabling. Similarly, the Kenyan government established Distributed ledger technologies and an AI task force in 2019 to explore and analyse disruptive technologies that are transforming the ICT landscape. In addition, the Kenya Bureau of Standards (KEBS) has published the Draft Information Technology Artificial Intelligence Code of Practice to help organise and develop the use of AI responsibly and to protect citizens' rights in developing AI systems in 2024. Even though the draft has shown progressive standardisation towards implementing AI in both the public and private sectors, it is still regarded as a regulatory standard and cannot be fully claimed to provide a conclusive direction for AI needed for public accountability.

Notably, the Ministry of ICT and Digital Economy (ICT) is working with stakeholders and the public to draft the National AI strategy, which is currently being drafted in 2024 sessions. Even though there are no specific AI regulations requirements for the application of AI in different sectors, other laws that currently impact AI landscapes in place include the Data Protection Act of 2019, which highlights that data subjects have rights to decisions based on their data through automated processing. This legislation establishes a comprehensive regulatory framework for implementing AI accountability measures using public sector data. The 2018 Computer Misuse and Cyber Crimes Act offer crucial guidelines for infrastructure-based AI systems, while the 2022 Consumer Protection Act safeguards citizens from the misuse of AI products and systems in non-competitive processes. Although these developments demonstrate positive strides in leveraging AI for the public sector, there is still a lack of direct AI laws specifically focused on public administration accountability.

In Kenya, AI is used in various industries, including fintech, transportation, health, and education. The government has been putting itself in a position to benefit from the technologies of the Fourth Industrial Revolution (4IR), which includes artificial intelligence. The Blockchain and Artificial Intelligence Taskforce were established by the government in 2018 to offer guidance on the optimal application of AI (GoK, 2019). The task force's major suggestions include creating laws that advance AI while upholding human rights, creating an environment for AI research, assessing the hazards associated with AI, and implementing mitigation strategies. Even though AI adoption in the public sector has yet to be effected, many AI applications have been developed to address these demands in Kenya's agricultural industry. Among these is the ThirdEye project, which uses drones to track soil requirements and detect pests and illnesses in crops. It permits early detection, saves crops, and detects subtle changes in crops that are difficult for humans to notice (Martijn de Klerk, 2019).

Notable other applications are *Eska* and *Nuru*. AI is used in these applications to identify crop diseases and pests. For instance, Eska analyses crop pictures and provides real-time data on crop health. Farmers can plan thanks to vital signs, which use satellite information to estimate patterns of rain and drought. *Arifu* provides farmers with important information, such as what kind of fertiliser is best for their land, via an AI chatbot via SMS, WhatsApp, and Facebook Messenger. By contrast, Farm Drive extends financing to farmers based on farm data, including location, crop size, and crop quality, to assess creditworthiness (Arifu, 2021). Similarly, the Office of the Data Protection Commissioner (ODPC) has introduced an AI chatbot to improve service delivery and interaction with the public. The system was created to enable data privacy and protect user details, conforming to high data integrity standards and improving service delivery. These are some examples of emerging AI tools public sector institutions use to improve decision-making and improve service delivery for citizens.

Artificial intelligence plays a significant role in deciding whether to approve loans for borrowers in fintech or digital lending apps. In this instance, artificial intelligence (AI) using machine learning is used to assess a borrower's micro-behavioural data and information gleaned from the borrower's device, such as contacts, SMSs, SD card content, gallery, and download apps, to ascertain the borrower's likelihood of default (Nieburg, 2021). Fintech, specifically digital lending applications, utilise this data to verify a borrower's credit score and identify appropriate loans. Since Fintechs don't require security from borrowers like banks and other traditional financing institutions, they rely on this information (Onyango, 2023). AI is becoming more prevalent in healthcare. Early disease identification and improved access to high-quality healthcare, especially in rural regions, are made possible by partnerships between the government and AI firms like Ilara Health. AI-driven chatbots, such as Totohealth, offer tailored healthcare information to mothers and children, lowering maternal and newborn deaths (TotoHealth, n.d.). Artificial Intelligence is being used to solve problems in the medical field. For instance, it is utilised in rural areas to detect disorders like women's cervical cancer. There are further uses for it. Among these is AfyaRekod, which healthcare professionals utilise to get up-to-date health information about patients and deliver the necessary medical care (AfyaRekod, n.d.). In 2020, this application underwent additional development to combat the COVID-19 pandemic.

In Kenya, AI is utilised extensively in the field of education. One of these is Angaza Elimu, an e-learning platform funded by UNICEF that uses AI to give pupils a customised learning experience tailored to their needs. It allows students to track their progress and provides them with learning notes and assignments tailored to their own learning experiences (Angaza Elimu, n.d.). Additionally, it allows instructors to evaluate their pupils' aptitude and provide them with specialised learning materials. Another tool in the education space is M-Shule, an SMS-based platform that gives businesses access to data, assessment, and learning resources (M-shule, n.d.). In the areas of AI and privacy administration, e.g., education, labour, and healthcare, AI systems involve the utilisation and analysis of data to a deeper extent that may breach privacy. The question, therefore, remains: To what extent can individual data be analysed for use? It, therefore, becomes very complex to take action on AI privacy in Kenyan content where the data protection law doesn't give proper direction on AI applications and related privacy acts. With the advent of big data, the Kenyan government, by virtue of public service, has harnessed a lot of individual data from public service portals, e.g., E-citizens, Huduma Digital Centers, Health records, I-Tax and, lately, Huduma Number. Apart from the conventional methods of big data collection through other streams without individual awareness, a lot of data is collected, stored, and analysed through algorithmic analysis for specified or unspecified missions. Citizens can, therefore, raise transparency and ethical questions, including: What personal information does AI use in citizens' delivery of services? What are the chances that AI systems might use inaccurate, irrelevant, or outdated data, and how reliable are the data sources?

South Africa

The AI landscape in South Africa is undergoing a major shift with the development of *The National Artificial Intelligence (AI) Policy Framework for South Africa (a first step in developing the National AI Policy)* in August 2024. "The policy framework emphasises the importance of human-centred AI, ensuring that AI applications augment human decision-making rather than replace it. By safeguarding professional responsibility and promoting human values, the framework ensures that AI development aligns with societal and ethical considerations" (DCDT, 2024, p. 1). This journey towards effective integration of AI into public institutions is embedded in critical values underpinning how and what public services should be organised and administered, underscoring public accountability concerns.

Currently, AI regulation is enforced through the enactment and legislation of the Electronic Communications Act, the Protection of Personal Information Act (POPIA), the Electronic Communications and Transactions Act, and the Consumer Protection Act. Consistent efforts have been made through the expansion of AI knowledge centres led by the South Africa Centre for AI Research (CAIR) and the AI institutions of SA to draft more specific AI regulations and regulatory frameworks. Parallel efforts through the South African Department of Communication and Digital Technology (DCDT) introduced a discussion Document in 2024 to outline government AI priorities and an AI-focused legislative framework, leading to the aforementioned policy framework in August 2024. Even though South Africa has yet to implement a national approach to AI regulations, private sectors and businesses in South Africa have seen significant adoption and uptake of AI in their workplace. They are currently adopting existing legislation that somehow contributes to the regulations of AI-related developments for the public sector.

South Africa is aggressively investigating how artificial intelligence (AI) might change governance. The country is dedicated to advancement and has a thriving, innovative ecosystem. AI tools are starting to find their way into government operations, albeit their broad acceptance is still developing. Their goals are to increase public service delivery, address national issues, and boost efficiency. Cities in South Africa are making headway in adopting technology-driven approaches to urban planning and administration. By enabling data-driven decision-making, more transparent and accountable governance, innovation-led growth and development, better service delivery, and ultimately, an improved quality of life for citizens, technology is being used to support the creation of more efficient, resilient, and sustainable cities. To encourage e-government in the city, the City of Tshwane has developed a mobile application and web page that lets citizens request services and pay bills online. The platform offers several advantages, such as enhanced information accuracy and more convenient and transparent interactions with the city (e-Tshwane Benefits, n.d.).

The history of farming in South Africa is extensive. With its roughly 2.5% GDP and 10% export contribution, agricultural production is vital to the country's economy. However, industry has several difficulties, such as low productivity and climate change-related issues, including droughts and unpredictable weather that affect agricultural production. Farmers have other problems, such as market access, land tenure, and credit availability, particularly in the nation's more isolated regions. The industry may need help to balance using sustainable practices and ensuring that food is affordable and available to everyone. With AI data analysis, farmers can maximise the sustainability and efficiency of their farming methods. Farmers can collect real-time data on their crops, such as information on crop growth, soil health, water usage, and pest presence, using sensors, drones, and satellites. AI systems may then evaluate this data, and the findings can advise farmers on how to use resources best and increase agricultural yields (Mwaijande, 2023).

Creating an AI research and development program that encourages collaborations between academics, industry, government, and civil society is a priority for the Human Sciences Research Council (HSRC). Their goal is to ensure AI technologies are created and applied to meet the difficulties faced by South Africa and the Global South. In addition to expressing enthusiasm for working together on this project, the participants emphasised the significance of data sharing, accessibility, and closing the digital gap to guarantee that artificial intelligence's advantages are shared fairly (HSRC, 2023). In the direction of a more data-driven and effective approach to public service, the application of AI in South African and Kenyan administrations is groundbreaking. However, implementation should be done responsibly, prioritising human oversight, transparency, and ethical issues. An emphasis on inclusivity and strict laws will be essential as these nations navigate the rapidly changing AI landscape to guarantee that AI advances the common good and gives citizens more power. Drawing from the cases above, the next section discusses and analytically formulates AI framework analysis for public accountability in South Africa and Kenya.

AI Framework and Public Accountability: A Discussion

Public Accountability as Ethical Principles and Transparency

Accountability in AI is defined as answerability under three conditions: authority recognition, interrogation, and power limitation (Novelli et al., 2024). It includes seven components and four objectives: compliance, reporting, oversight, and enforcement. Imperfect delegation in AI systems, such as distributed responsibility and induced acceptance, undermines human accountability (Loi & Spielkamp, 2021). In addition, there is universal agreement on five ethical principles, which are also critical in creating AI applications for public accountability in public administration. These include transparency, justice and fairness, non-maleficence, responsibility, and privacy, but significant disagreement exists on how these values are interpreted and implemented, including in African public administration (Jobin, et al., 2019; Onyango, 2024). AI integration should enable instead of undoing ongoing efforts to entrench public ethics, transparency, and related values in public administration. In other words, AI integration should be complementary rather than the primary enabler of public accountability principles. Gains made by public accountability reforms should be captured and integrated into how AI functions. Undoubtedly, public ethics and accountability are issues the South African and Kenyan public sectors have been grappling with for some time now. Therefore, caution should be given when integrating AI without considering its impact on these challenging realisations of ethical and public integrity values in public service. Otherwise, there could be a likely systematic problem going into the future, as anticipated in various National Development Plans and sustainable governance agendas of the United Nations' Agenda 2030 and the African Union's Agenda 2063.

There should be emphasis on the importance of transparency in AI systems to allow for rational interpretation, focusing on trustworthiness (Felzmann et al., 2019). Kenya Bureau of Statistics (KEBS) AI code of Practice, drafted in April 2024, emphasises the need for transparency, explainability, controllability, and trust to address engineering challenges, mitigation, and threats. Transparency, as part of the accountability constructs, concerns issues around understandability, which involves clear definitions and explanations. Public transparency and auditing are both ethically beneficial and required for democratic self-government. Discussions aimed at developing AI national policies in Kenya and the South have recognised that AI deployment in the public sector creates techno-legal entanglements that affect responsibility, necessitating a new approach to AI-supported decision-making accountability (Gualdi & Cordella, 2021). Looking at the AI policy proposals in both countries, explicit accountability mechanisms are necessary to address the possibility of biased consequences from AI systems in public sector decision-making processes. How to go about this should be conducted in an extensively collaborative fashion to integrate other critical values such as representation, equality, and responsibility (Ondiek & Onyango, 2025). Accountability and social cohesion reforms dealing with, for example, corruption and ethical public leadership in Kenya and South Africa have focused on deepening representation and equality and responsibility to improve public and political accountability mechanisms. A framework for integrating AI into the public sector should harmonise rather than exacerbate these challenges.

Regulatory Oversight

In mid-September 2024, the Kenyan government announced the introduction of regulatory mechanisms to curb AI-generated disinformation.

While speaking at the launch of the Fifth National Action Plan on Open Government Partnership (OGP) in Nairobi, President William Ruto highlighted the measures the government is taking to curb the misuse of advanced technologies like Artificial Intelligence (AI). "We are also implementing a regulatory regime that forestalls the abuse of new technologies, including artificial intelligence, which leads to disinformation that threatens our democracy", he said Ruto expressed that the Fifth National Action Plan under the Open Government Partnership is expected to further Kenya's goals of promoting transparency, public participation, and accountability in governance (Ajibade, 12 September 2024).

The need for regulatory monitoring of AI applications in open government is a critical problem, especially for countries like Kenya and South Africa, where issues around public accountability overlaps with deficits in the trustworthiness of the government. This has become more challenging with the growth of misinformation and disinformation. While some urge for the creation of an independent commission to govern algorithms, like in the case of Kenya proposing to create an "Ombudsman" office for future dealings with AI misuse, others support the creation of a worldwide AI regulatory body to develop a consistent framework (Erdélyi & Goldsmith, 2018). South Africa anticipates dealing with these issues within the existing cybercrime, digital regulation, and AI national policy. Studies like Loi and Spielkamp (2021) emphasise the need for public accountability and transparency in using AI in government, recommending that these be enforced through auditing, which requires a specific regulatory framework. Medaglia et al. (2021) emphasise the importance of governance research, trustworthy AI, impact assessment methodologies, and data governance in the context of AI in government.

Establishing or strengthening regulatory bodies with a special focus on AI applications in open government is critical to ensuring accountability and adherence to specified norms (Hill, 2020). Such an approach to regulating AI integration should create detailed standards, conduct rigorous audits, and enforce AI accountability regulations (Chelvachandran, et al., 2020). The task of these specialised institutions on AI regulation should include overseeing AI systems' development, implementation, and impact on government activities and ensuring openness, fairness, and ethical use (Engstrom & Haim, 2023). Furthermore, these agencies must be able to communicate with key parties, apply corrective actions as needed, and continuously update regulatory frameworks to keep up with technological changes and social demands (Scherer, 2015). A more concerted oversight among various actors should build robust mechanisms for establishing public trust, minimising possible damages, and maintaining accountability in the context of AI applications within open government projects currently being implemented in Kenya and South Africa to improve public accountability.

Public Auditability

In January 2023, South Africa's Independent Regulatory Board for Auditors released a statement on the *Artificial Intelligence Risk Mitigation* when AI tools, especially GPT-3. In this statement, it was recognised that:

> The use of GPT-3 and other AI tools in the audit profession can be used to create false evidence and fabricated working papers, which can lead to inaccurate conclusions and misstatements in financial statements. This can have serious consequences for both the auditors and the organisations they audit. In addition, the use of these tools can also lead to ethical violations, such as fraud and misrepresentation, leading to disciplinary action or legal penalties. (IRBA, 12 January 2023)

At the same time, the South African Revenue Service (Sars) has utilised AI to improve its auditing capabilities in auditing taxpayers' filled tax reports. However, this has also raised concerns about whether this AI-enabled auditing generates reports on the filing of tax by Members of Parliament, tenderpreneurs (those awarded government contracts or tenders because of their unique contacts within the government), senior government officials and other calibre of public officials accused of not making such reports. In other words, AI-enabled auditing needs specialised AI auditing tools to audit its implementation and improve public accountability. Such an effort should not be left to the concerned government institutions alone but should include all actors. Therefore, as discussed by Bloch-Wehba (2019), public audibility in AI implementation in public administration should emphasise access to government information and procedures in increasing algorithmic transparency. Transparency, outcome monitoring, and increased governance are among the techniques which include algorithmic accountability. Shah (2018) suggested ensuring algorithmic accountability. While South Africa and Kenya could be navigating these contours to employ AI effectively in areas such as tax filing and other public services, there is a need to consider algorithmic accountability and public access. This can be partially achieved through a framework that promotes data stewardship, the opening of restricted data and algorithms, and trustworthy information exchange (Janssen et al., 2020).

Awareness Programs and collaborative Fact-Checking

In the emerging AI implementation strategies, there has been an emphasis on public sensitisation besides skill training for public officials. The ongoing AI discussions in Kenya and South Africa's AI strategy underscore the need to raise awareness of AI risks, underlying biases, and regulation requirements. Several scholars have stressed the importance of educational initiatives to increase public knowledge of the ethical ramifications of artificial intelligence. Education and awareness should also deal with defining and labelling misinformation and disinformation. This can be done through a compulsory AI course on critical dimensions of misinformation and disinformation that AI can generate. Fact check centres are needed in the public sector to ascertain the correct information. For example, the Department of Government Communication and Information Systems (GCIS) in South Africa has established procedures to check facts generated by social media and other advanced technologies. However, fact-checking, public sensitisation, and empowering public officials is not only a preserve for the government. Instead, there are non-state actors like https://africacheck.org/ that complement the role of the state agencies in fact-checking. In 2022, the Media Council of Kenya and the United Nations Development Programme (UNDP) established the iVerify Network of Fact-Checking Desks. This initiative aims to enhance cooperation in verifying information and encourages collaboration among various stakeholders. According to Ms Esther Koimett, the Principal Secretary of the State Department of Broadcasting and Telecommunications within the Ministry of ICT, Innovation, and Youth Affairs, these "campaigns have seen an explosion of disinformation, misinformation, and hate speech, especially at political rallies. We believe the iVerify platform will assist in restoring law and order using social media to share accurate and balanced information" (Media Council of Kenya, 01 July 2022). Fact-checking and raising awareness empowers users to take responsibility for the type of information they generate through AI or share on social media. Sensitisation and fact-checking tools sensitive to local values and narratives can promote this awareness and are vital for establishing more accountable AI regulations. Bryson (2019) and Borenstein & Howard (2021) argue that such initiatives are crucial for teaching AI ethics to aspiring professionals, which specifically advocate for the inclusion of AI ethics in school curricula. The role of public administrations in guiding AI developers and users toward ethical practices is emphasised by Sigfrids et al. (2022) and Nieminen et al. (2019). These scholars collectively support a comprehensive, inclusive, and institutionalised approach to AI governance, encouraging the integration of AI ethics into educational programs and the development of relevant initiatives.

Conclusions: Overcoming AI Implementation Challenges in Public Administration

In order to adjust to changing behaviours and new opportunities contained in AI, the Kenyan and South African governments need to take an adaptive and agile approach to the rapid pace of technological change. As already discussed extensively by contributions in Part I of this volume, there is no limit on how smart AI can be leveraged. It is clear that some of the capabilities (individual, institutional, environmental) that are not possible with AI today may become feasible. Artificial Intelligence frameworks and strategies must be flexible enough to evolve with changing contexts and capabilities. Technologies used for Artificial Intelligence are dynamic, and their interactions with human beings in complicated public administration systems will evolve with time. Long-term contracts that lock the public sector into current technologies as well as ways of doing work should, therefore, be avoided by both Kenyan and Southern governments. Similarly, there must be regular reviews for strategic plans to monitor the implementation of AI and assess if the assumptions made during planning still hold.

The government should establish technical, ethical, and legal frameworks at the design stage and monitor the level of compliance during AI implementation. This is because AI is a general-purpose technology, and as such, it has the potential to transform the impact on how service delivery and public administration are performed. Ethical guidelines for AI that are trustworthy articulate a series of principles that secure and foster robust and ethical Artificial Intelligence. With disruptions, AI trajectories are defined by uncertainty, risks, and complexities (Mateos-Garcia, 2018). Because of this, shaping decision-making in the public sector calls for the development of a rigorous framework to realise the potential of Artificial Intelligence and transform public sector administration. Articulating clear principles for artificial intelligence will enhance an environment that is aligned with the goals and values of society articulated in the principles. To achieve maximum impact with the principles, embedding them in the processes and institutions shaping the decision-making process in the government is important. The development of transparent and accountable structures is likely to enable governments to achieve the potential of AI in transforming public administration, hence building citizens' confidence. Failure by citizens to trust the government to use AI ethically will make them avoid services that involve the application of AI, hence opposing their introduction. As such, there could be a need to address public concerns by enabling accountability scrutiny and fair processes that AI may avail in governance engagements.

In summary, a great deal of promise exists for increased creativity, effectiveness, and responsiveness if AI is integrated into public sector organisations. Achieving AI's potential while reducing risks calls for a concentrated effort to create inclusive implementation methods and standards held to high standards. The values of ethical, transparent, and good administration must be upheld by regulatory frameworks, and users, deployers, and developers of AI applications must all be held accountable for the results of their work. We can use AI's revolutionary power to advance public good and equitable and sustainable development by cultivating a culture of responsibility and trust. While using AI to improve public service delivery may be the primary objective of the government, government agencies should also consider their role in shifting the technological frontier and the adoption of an approach of "entrepreneurial state" to spur innovation and growth using available tools to take risks and shape markets to achieve their vision.

References

AfyaRekod. (n.d.). *AfyaRekod*. Retrieved from https://afyarekod.com/

Ajibade, A. (2024, September 12). *Kenya announces regulatory measures to curb AI-driven disinformation*. TechnoPoint Africa. https://techpoint.africa/2024/09/12/kenya-announces-regulatory-measures/

Almeida, P., Santos, C., Jr., & Farias, J. (2021). Artificial intelligence regulation: A framework for governance. *Ethics and Information Technology, 23*. https://doi.org/10.1007/s10676-021-09593-z

Angaza Elimu. (n.d.). Retrieved from https://angazaelimu.com/about

Arifu. (2021). *Digital training benefits farmers*. Retrieved from Arifu.com: https://www.arifu.com/digital-training-benefits-farmers-and-agricultural-institutions/

Bloch-Wehba, H. (2019). *Access to algorithms* (Fordham Law Review, Vol. 88, 2020, Texas A&M University School of Law Legal Studies Research Paper No. 20-25). Available at SSRN: https://ssrn.com/abstract=3355776

Brand, D. (2022). Responsible artificial intelligence in government: Development of a legal framework for South Africa. *JeDEM—eJournal of eDemocracy and Open Government, 14*, 130–150.

Borenstein, J., & Howard, A. (2021). Emerging challenges in AI and the need for AI ethics education. *AI and Ethics, 1*(1), 61–65.

Butcher, N., Wilson-Strydom, M., & Baijnath, M. (2021). *Artificial intelligence capacity in sub-Saharan Africa: Compendium report.*

Bryson, J. J. (2019). The Past Decade and Future of AI's Impact on Society. In *Towards a New Enlightenment? A Transcendent Decade* (Vol. 11). Turner. https://www.bbvaopenmind.com/wp-content/uploads/2019/02/BBVAOpenMind-Joanna-J-Bryson-The-Past-Decade-and-Future-of-AI-Impact-on-Society.pdf

Cath, C. (2018). Governing artificial intelligence: Ethical, legal and technical opportunities and challenges. *Philosophical Transactions of the Royal Society A: Mathematical, Physical and Engineering Sciences.* https://doi.org/10.1098/rsta.2018.0080

Chelvachandran, N., Trifuljesko, S., Drobotowicz, K., Kendzierskyj, S., Jahankhani, H., & Shah, Y. (2020). Considerations for the governance of AI and government legislative frameworks. In *Cyber defence in the age of AI, smart societies and augmented humanity* (pp. 57–69). Cham: Springer International Publishing.

DCDT. (2024). *South Africa National Artificial Intelligence Policy Framework (Towards the development of South Africa National Artificial intelligence policy).* Department of Communications and Digital Technologies. https://fwblaw.co.za/wp-content/uploads/2024/08/South-Africa-National-AI-Policy-Framework.pdf

Engstrom, D. F., & Haim, A. (2023). Regulating government AI and the challenge of sociotechnical design. *Annual Review of Law and Social Science, 19*, 277–298. https://doi.org/10.1146/annurev-lawsocsci-120522-091626

Erdélyi, O. J., & Goldsmith, J. (2018). Regulating artificial intelligence: Proposal for a global solution. In *Proceedings of the 2018 AAAI/ACM Conference on AI, Ethics, and Society* (pp. 95–101).

e-Tshwane Benefits. (n.d.). Retrieved from City of Tshwane: https://www.e-tshwane.co.za/eTshwane/service-benefits;jsessionid=poBR063oqBVtb1gr4xGjYmSjE1UXhHNlOHBsZgEtf3Rk0r3M6VWr!1617678506

Felzmann, H., Fosch, V., & Tamò Larrieux, A. (2019). Transparency you can trust: Transparency requirements for artificial intelligence between legal norms and contextual concerns. *Big Data & Society, 6*, 1–14. https://doi.org/10.1177/2053951719860542

Floridi, L., Cowls, J., Beltrametti, M., Chatila, R., Chazerand, P., Dignum, V., ... & Vayena, E. (2018). AI4People—an ethical framework for a good AI society: Opportunities, risks, principles, and recommendations. *Minds and Machines, 28*(4), 689–707. https://doi.org/10.1007/s11023-018-9482-5

Gasser, U., & Almeida, V. (2017). A layered model for AI governance. *IEEE Internet Computing, 21*, 58–62. https://doi.org/10.1109/MIC.2017.4180835

Gimpel, L., & McBride, K. (2023). *Contextualizing the challenges and motivating factors associated with the usage of AI in and by the public sector: Initial insights from Rwanda's Mbaza Chatbot Project*. Available at SSRN 4327495.

Government of Kenya. (2019). *Distributed ledgers and artificial intelligence taskforce, emerging digital technologies for Kenya: Exploration*. Ministry of Information Communication Technology. Retrieved from https://www.ict.go.ke/blockchain.pdf

Gualdi, F., & Cordella, A. (2021). Artificial intelligence and decision-making: The question of accountability. In: Bui & X. Tung (Eds.), *Proceedings of the 54th Annual Hawaii International Conference on System Sciences, HICSS 2021*. Proceedings of the Annual Hawaii International Conference on System Sciences. IEEE Computer Society Press, Virtual, Online, (pp. 2297–2306). ISBN 9780998133140.

Hill, A. D. (2020). Regulatory accountability for AI governance mechanisms: Coordinating multiple regulators. *SSRN Electronic Journal*.

Houy, C., Hamberg, M., & Fettke, P. (2019). Robotic process automation in public administrations. In *Digitalisierung von Staat und Verwaltung* (pp. 62–74). Gesellschaft für Informatik eV.

HSRC. (2023). *Navigating the impacts of generative AI in South Africa: Challenges, opportunities and ethics*. Retrieved from https://hsrc.ac.za/news/latest-news/navigating-the-impacts-of-generative-ai-in-south-africa-challenges-opportunities-and-ethics/

IRBA. (2023, January 12). *Artificial intelligence audit RISKS MITIGAtion*. Independent Regulatory Board for Auditors. https://www.irba.co.za/upload/report_files/02.-AI-Audit-Risks-Mitigation.pdf

Janssen, M., Hartog, M., Matheus, R. D., Aaron, Y D., & Kuk, G. (2020). Will algorithms blind people? The effect of explainable AI and decision-makers' experience on AI-supported decision-making in government. *Social Science Computer Review, 40*. https://doi.org/10.1177/0894439320980118

Jobin, A., Ienca, M., & Vayena, E. (2019). The global landscape of AI ethics guidelines. *Nature machine intelligence, 1*(9), 389–399.

Loi, M., & Spielkamp, M. (2021). *Towards accountability in the use of artificial intelligence for public administrations* (pp. 757–766). https://doi.org/10.1145/3461702.3462631

Martijn de Klerk, J. V. (2019). *ThirdEye Kenya: Flying sensors to support farmers' decision making*. Retrieved from https://www.futurewater.nl/wp-content/uploads/2020/01/ThirdEyeKenya_FinalReport_Final.pdf

Mateos-Garcia, J. C. (2018). *The complex economics of artificial intelligence*. Available at SSRN 3294552.

Medaglia, R., Gil-Garcia, J. R., & Pardo, T. (2021). Artificial intelligence in government: Taking stock and moving forward. *Social Science Computer Review, 41*. https://doi.org/10.1177/08944393211034087

Media Council of Kenya. (2022, July 01). *New fact-checking tool to counter fake news*. Retrieved from https://mediacouncil.or.ke/media-center/mck-newsroom/news/new-fact-checking-tool-counter-fake-news

Mishra, A. K., Tyagi, A. K., Dananjayan, S., Rajavat, A., Rawat, H., & Rawat, A., (2024). Revolutionizing government operations: The impact of artificial intelligence in public administration. In *Conversational artificial intelligence* (pp. 607–634). Wiley.

M-shule. (n.d.). Retrieved from https://m-shule.com/

Mwaijande, F. A. (2023). Digitalisation of agricultural policy and policy performance in Tanzania. In: G. Onyango (Eds.), *Public policy and technological transformations in Africa*. Information technology and global governance. Palgrave Macmillan, Cham. https://doi.org/10.1007/978-3-031-18704-9_8

Nieburg, O. (2021). *Will AI risk analysis really expand access to credit in Africa*. Retrieved from https://www.theafricareport.com/107432/will-ai-risk-analysis-really-expand-access-to-credit-in-africa/

Nieminen, M. P., Gotcheva, N., Leikas, J., & Koivisto, R. (2019). *Ethical AI for the governance of the society: Challenges and opportunities*. Conference on Technology Ethics.

Niyitunga, E. B. (2024). The role of artificial intelligence in promoting digital public participation for successful peacebuilding in Africa. *African Journal of Peace and Conflict Studies (formerly Ubuntu: Journal of Conflict and Social Transformation), 13*(1), 25–49.

Novelli, C., Casolari, F., Rotolo, A., Taddeo, M., & Floridi, L. (2024). Taking AI risks seriously: A new assessment model for the AI act. *AI & Society, 39*(5), 2493–2497.

Ondiek, J. O., & Onyango, G. (2023). Strengthening citizen agencies in policymaking through social media. In *Public policy and technological transformations in Africa: Nurturing policy entrepreneurship, policy tools and citizen participation* (pp. 257–278). Palgrave Macmillan.

Ondiek, J. O., & Onyango, G. (2024). *Blockchain Technologies in digital governance: The Kenyan experience with promoting public accountability*. Routledge.

Ondiek, J. O., & Onyango, G. (2025). Open government partnership initiatives and policy effectiveness in Kenya. In *Routledge handbook of public policy in the Global South* (pp. 475–491). Routledge.

Onyango, G. (Ed.). (2023). *Public policy and technological transformations in Africa: Nurturing policy entrepreneurship, policy tools and citizen participation*. Palgrave Macmillan. https://doi.org/10.1007/978-3-031-18704-9

Onyango, G. (2024). DHR-PA—Democracy and human rights in public administration in Africa. *Politics & Policy, 52*(2), 426–449. https://doi.org/10.1111/polp.12584

Onyango, G. (2025). e-Whistleblowing: Civictech and GovTech Innovations in Nigeria and Kenya. In D*igitalisation and public policy in Africa: GovTech and CivicTech Innovations* (pp. 251–275). Palgrave Macmillan.

Onyango, G., & Ondiek, J. O. (2021). Digitalization and integration of sustainable development goals (SGDs) in public organizations in Kenya. *Public Organization Review, 21*, 511–526. https://doi.org/10.1007/s11115-020-00504-2

Onyango, G., & Ondiek, J. O. (2022). Open innovation during the COVID-19 pandemic policy responses in South Africa and Kenya. *Politics & Policy, 50*(5), 1008–1031.

Osborne, S. P. (2006). The new public governance. *Public Management Review, 8*(3), 377–387. https://doi.org/10.1080/14719030600853022

Plantinga, P. (2024). Digital discretion and public administration in Africa: Implications for the use of artificial intelligence. *Information Development, 40*(2), 332–352.

Scherer, M. U. (2015). Regulating artificial intelligence systems: Risks, challenges, competencies, and strategies. *Harvard Journal of Law & Technology*. https://doi.org/10.2139/SSRN.2609777

Shah, H. (2018). Algorithmic accountability. *Philosophical Transactions of the Royal Society A: Mathematical, Physical and Engineering Sciences, 376*, 20170362. https://doi.org/10.1098/rsta.2017.0362

Sigfrids, A., Nieminen, M., Leikas, J., & Pikkuaho, P. (2022). How should public administrations foster the ethical development and use of artificial intelligence? A review of proposals for developing governance of AI. *Frontiers in Human Dynamics*. https://doi.org/10.3389/fhumd.2022.858108

Sun, T. Q., & Medaglia, R. (2019). Mapping the challenges of Artificial Intelligence in the public sector: Evidence from public healthcare. *Government Information Quarterly, 36*(2), 368–383. https://doi.org/10.1016/j.giq.2018.09.008

Thinyane, M., Siebörger, I., Khene, C. (2023). Technology-mediated transparency, accountability, and participation in the realisation of citizen-centred health interventions: Case sof MobiSAfAIDS in Southern Africa. In: G. Onyango (Eds.), *Public policy and technological transformations in Africa*.

Information technology and global governance. Palgrave Macmillan, Cham. https://doi.org/10.1007/978-3-031-18704-9_13

TotoHealth. (n.d.). *Totohealth*. Retrieved from https://totohealth.org/aboutus#:~:text=About%20Us,age%20or%20stage%20of%20pregnancy

Webb, M. (2019). *The impact of artificial intelligence on the labor market*. Available at SSRN 3482150. https://doi.org/10.2139/ssrn.3482150

Wirtz, B. W., Weyerer, J. C., & Sturm, B. J. (2020). The dark sides of artificial intelligence: An integrated AI governance framework for public administration. *International Journal of Public Administration, 43*(9), 818–829. https://doi.org/10.1080/01900692.2020.1749851

Young, M. M., Bullock, J. B., & Lecy, J. D. (2019). Artificial discretion as a tool of governance: A framework for understanding the impact of artificial intelligence on public administration. *Perspectives on Public Management and Governance, 2*(4), 301–313.

CHAPTER 9

Improving Public Safety in the City of Johannesburg Using Artificial Intelligence

Lewis Edwin Chigova and Costa Hofisi

Introduction

Since member countries of the United Nations agreed on Goal 11 of the Sustainable Development Goals to "make cities and human settlements inclusive, safe, resilient and sustainable" (United Nations, 2015), tools that maintain high levels of safety and security are increasingly becoming essential (Yoshinaga et al., 2022). Current practitioner and research discussions show city authorities harnessing Fourth Industrial Revolution (4IR) tools such as artificial intelligence (AI) (Baker, 2021; Benyera, 2021; Na et al., 2022; OECD, 2021). Undoubtedly, AI plays a massive role in cities (Ahmed et al., 2021). Studies on the use of AI demonstrate that it can support decision-making in cities (Berntzen et al.,

L. E. Chigova (✉) · C. Hofisi
North-West University, Vanderbjilpark, South Africa
e-mail: lewisec47@gmail.com

C. Hofisi
e-mail: Costa.Hofisi@nwu.ac.za

G. Onyango (ed.), *Designing Artificial Intelligence for Public Policy and Governance in Africa*, Studies in National Governance and Emerging Technologies, https://doi.org/10.1007/978-3-031-83445-5_9

2018; Bokhari & Myeong, 2022; Pomerol, 1997), has the potential to address social challenges successfully (Ndung'u & Signe, 2020), deliver public services better and faster (Benyera, 2021), ensure the proper execution of the city services (Ahmed et al., 2021), and address criminal justice needs (Rigano, 2019). Hence, Ndung'u and Signe (2020) emphasise the costs of failing to recognise and capitalise on the opportunities presented by mobilising 4IR tools like AI. This chapter complements burgeoning research examining the prospects for cities that harness AI to ensure public safety. Current work on AI traces its roots to private sectors such as engineering, manufacturing and communication technologies (Omar et al., 2017; Rigano, 2019). Today, AI is part of intelligent/digital/innovative technologies linked to the 4IR[1] that solve public sector problems. Since the 4IR has become a buzzword for city authorities and researchers in South Africa, studies on how tools linked to it, such as AI, can be deployed in different sectors to address societal challenges are necessary.

Studies like Na et al. (2022) underpins AI as the core innovation in the 4IR era. Contemporary research is increasingly focusing on AI's capability to perform several public administration tasks (Benyera, 2021). One such task that requires further scholarly discussion is AI's ability to help local governments provide public safety and security in cities. Many studies link the use of AI as a 4IR technology to the establishment of smart cities (Allam & Dhunny, 2019; Batty, 2018; Fashoro & Barnard, 2021; Kassens-Noor & Hintze, 2020; Shava & Vyas-Doorgapersad, 2021; Srivastava et al., 2017; Ullah et al., 2020; Yigitcanlar & Kamruzzaman, 2020). Srivastava et al. (2017) believe that AI "is what makes a smart city 'smart." Allam and Dhunny (2019) argue that AI allows for better urban governance as policymakers can make informed decisions and formulate adequate and responsive policies. Gatzweiler (2020) and Yigitcanlar et al. (2020) underscore that AI has significant potential to address the challenges of urbanisation in our time. In cities with high crime rates, a fresh impetus for more studies is added for scholars to explore the benefits of AI

[1] The 4IR is defined by Ochara (2021, p. 2) as Comprising a broad range of not only traditional ICTs but also AI (AI), robotics, Internet of things (IoT), cloud computing, big data, fifth-generation mobile technology (5G), blockchain, 3D printing, robotics, or virtual/augmented reality (AR/VR), and machine learning technologies that are fundamentally changing the way society and its institutions organise work and relate to each other.

to ensure public safety. Hence, Srivastava et al. (2017) reason that cities equipped with AI systems perfectly blend man and machine, operating to keep them safe and secure.

Against this background, Batty (2018) emphasises the need for a real push to demonstrate how AI can be used in urban analysis and city science, urban planning and design, and a concerted effort to explore the limits of AI in our understanding of cities, in how new ways of automating functions within cities, and within a broader context can be invented. This chapter explores the utility of AI in maintaining public safety in the City of Johannesburg (CoJ). Using the CoJ as a case study, it examines the Technological Acceptance Model and the Diffusion of Innovation Theory as theoretical frameworks. The chapter is structured as follows: the first section begins with a conceptualisation and contextualisation of AI, followed by a discussion of the three specific areas in which AI can be utilised to improve the safety of cities. It then presents its theoretical framework, focusing on the Technological Acceptance Model and the Diffusion of Innovation Theory. The fourth section of the chapter explores the challenges and opportunities that arise from using AI in the CoJ, considering the specific context and unique challenges facing this urban area. Finally, the chapter concludes with a discussion of the recommendations.

Literature Review

Conceptualisations of AI in literature have evolved over the years in parallel to new advancements and inventions. In the formative years, John MacCarthy, one of the pioneers of AI, defined it as "the science and engineering of making intelligent machines" (Rigano, 2019, p. 1; Srivastava et al., 2017). When MacCarthy coined the term AI, discussions were mainly associated with the communication, technology, engineering, and manufacturing sectors (Omar et al., 2017). Srivastava et al. (2017) view AI as a field with roots in mathematics, psychology, computer science, linguistics, philosophy, neuroscience, and artificial psychology. A rapid rise in AI studies is linked to digital innovations emerging from the Industrial Revolution (IR) 4.0. Thus, the current conceptualisations of AI show a departure from the narrow engineering-based definition provided by John McCarthy in 1979 to more broad definitions. Rigano (2019, p. 1) defines AI as a machine's ability to independently perceive and respond to its environment and perform tasks that typically require human intelligence and decision-making processes without direct human intervention. Similarly, AlSheibani et al. (2018) view AI as a broad subject with a range of terms such as 'machine intelligence,' 'intelligent agents,' 'intelligent behaviour,' 'intelligent systems', and 'algorithms' in defining it. The study characterises AI within the context of the two definitions presented by Rigano (2019) and AlSheibani et al. (2018). Louw and Dube (2021, p. 1033) observe that AI in the age of the 4IR has become an important and critical topic of study due to its versatility, which cuts across multidisciplinary and multidimensional fields, practices, and organisations. Globally, AI attracts interest because it can address social challenges such as city crime and safety issues. As Ndung'u and Signe (2020) and Louw and Dube (2021) contend, AI as a 4IR technology is transformational.

Srivastava et al. (2017) argue that government disinterest has long hindered research into the development of AI. A review of extant studies links the increasing interest in the public sector to the 4IR discourse. These studies illustrate that 4IR is changing the functions of public entities, with AI being a key technology in this transformation. For example, Mhlanga et al., (2021, p. 1003) explain that the 4IR is the contemporary unfolding environment in which evolving technologies and developments like the Internet of Things (IoT) and AI are changing the functions of public entities. Koekemoer and Von Solms (2021) reason that the 4IR builds on digital advances such as AI. Na et al. (2022) view AI as the key technology in the 4IR. Hence, AI is a transformational tool for responsive city governance. For many years, government institutions have been slammed for their bureaucratic practices and approaches regarding delivering public sector goods and services, which could be more effective, effective, and efficient to the needs of a country's citizenry (Louw & Dube, 2021; Onyango, 2023). Thus, innovative technologies, especially in public safety and security, are becoming necessary in response to pervasive bureaucratic practices in government institutions. Policy discussions by practitioners and scholarly research responding to social problems show the increasing use of advanced data processing and global AI technologies for crime prevention (Stone, 2020). This increasing use of advanced data processing and global AI technologies for crime prevention indicates the positive impact AI can have in reshaping public sector goods and services.

The use of AI in enhancing community safety has been a topic of recent discussion (Rigano, 2019; Srivastava et al., 2017; Williams, 2021). The research indicates that AI could serve as a valuable resource to improve public safety, especially in areas facing substantial resource constraints, such as South African law enforcement agencies (Stone, 2020). The potential for AI to provide critical tools for crime prevention interventions and the transformation of societies has been highlighted. For instance, Misuraca and Van Noordt (2020) posit that AI allows city authorities to tap into the rapid advances in computing power, the increasing availability of data, and new algorithms. They further postulate that breakthroughs in AI provide immense opportunities to transform societies and represent critical technologies of the century for citizens and governments. The opportunities brought are costly to ignore as it is becoming evident that AI systems have graduated with ever-present and ubiquitous fixtures in our communities (Baker, 2021; Williams, 2021). However, it is also noted that many cities, including the CoJ, are only beginning to explore the full extent of AI's benefits, particularly in tools like facial recognition and machine learning. Williams (2021) observes that even though AI has expanded its frontier into citizens' daily lives, many cities, such as the CoJ, are only commencing to scratch the surface regarding the technology's benefits. Undoubtedly, the development of AI systems, such as facial recognition and machine learning, presents valuable tools to address safety issues in the CoJ (Baker, 2021).

More so, Williams (2021) notes the likelihood of more innovations in AI in the next few years and an increased reliance on AI to help further save time and, most importantly, lives. These AI innovations can enable local authorities such as the CoJ to fulfil the aspirations of the White Paper of Safety and Security through aiding "targeted crime and violence prevention programmes" and "coordinating crime and violence prevention activities" (Civilian Secretariat of Police, 2016b). More AI studies show that assistive technology increasingly benefits public safety professionals and communities (Williams, 2021). Hence, all future exploits to improve city public safety must be anchored on AI technologies and emerging digital innovations. Currently, the challenges to providing safer communities in the CoJ cannot be separated from the city's uptake, mobilisation, and use of AI tools.

Understanding AI Use in Cities

This chapter integrates and discusses the Technological Acceptance Model (TAM) and the Diffusion of Innovation Theory and their applications as frameworks for understanding AI use in maintaining city safety. Fred D. Davis developed the TAM in 1989. It focuses on answering the question, "What causes people to accept or reject a technology?" (Davis, 1989). The TAM is an influential theoretical tool that explains the significant factors when users adopt new devices or technologies (Na et al., 2022). According to Davis (1989), two variables are critical in adopting the technology: perceived ease of use and perceived usefulness. In line with Davis (1989), this study adopts these two variables from the TAM as theoretical frameworks to explore the plausibility of using AI to ensure public safety in the CoJ. The TAM theoretical framework is critical for this study because it highlights issues regarding perceptions of AI. Perception is crucial in adopting AI applications since many pressing problems arise. Sun and Medaglia (2019) and Ahn and Chen (2022) agree that positive perception and understanding of the new technologies might facilitate successful integration and use. Many doubts and misconceptions may impede the adoption and full use of AI technologies. Of importance to note in the TAM model is the advancement and emphasis that various external factors form users' perceptions of usefulness and ease of use regarding new technology, and those factors indirectly impact whether users embrace new technology as well as their attitudes towards it (Davis, 1989; Na et al., 2022).

The Diffusion of Innovation Theory was developed by Everett Rogers (1995). According to Orr (2003), Rodgers's scholarly work has grown into a standard textbook and reference on diffusion studies, offering an insightful explanation of the conditions that indicate innovation will reach the much-hyped tipping point. Rogers (2003) defines "diffusion as the process by which an innovation is communicated through certain channels over time among the members of a social system." The Diffusion of Innovation Theory (DOI) explains how, why, and at what rate new technology spreads (AlSheibani et al., 2018; Rogers, 1995). Therefore, DOI theory is considered an appropriate framework for exploring the use of AI as a 4IR tool that can make the CoJ safe. This study follows Rogers' (2003, p. 1) premise that "adopting a new idea, even with many obvious advantages, is often very difficult." The DOI theory assumes that the application of innovations such as AI at the local government level depends on certain factors like individual characteristics (for example, of the leader), internal features and external aspects (of the organisation) (Rogers, 1995). The DOI theory determines five attributes of an innovation that may be essential for adoption: relative advantage, compatibility, complexity, trialability, and observability. The DOI theory allows this paper to examine the environmental and organisational contexts in which innovations occur, their nature, enabling antecedents, and underlying contingencies (De Vries et al., 2016). Such an examination is critical to this chapter's objectives, considering that AI innovations have distinctive features that impact their adoption, dissemination, and acceptance.

Methods and Materials

The study for this chapter explored the potential applications of AI in enhancing public safety in urban areas by investigating and analysing various sources of information. This included a comprehensive literature review to examine existing research on AI and its role in enhancing public safety in cities. Relevant literature sources that included peer-reviewed articles, book chapters, and online data material relating to AI were used to support the discussion of findings. In addition to the literature review, the study analysed various documentary materials about public safety in the CoJ. These include South African public policies and national development plans; the government released official statistics, media reports, and government and CoJ-released materials. Using these sources enables the study to gather valuable insights and information regarding the current state of public safety in the CoJ and the potential benefits that AI could bring to the city. Content analysis was used to analyse the data. The qualitative research approach adopted in this study is well-suited for exploring complex issues and gaining a comprehensive understanding of the potential of AI in enhancing public safety in urban areas. The analysis of various sources of information helps to provide valuable insights and recommendations that can inform the development of policies and strategies for improving public safety in the CoJ.

AI Use in South Africa

Although adopting AI to make cities safe and secure has become an increasingly dominant global phenomenon, the national government and provincial governments in South Africa have been included. Nationally,

Section 152 (1d) of the 1996 Constitution of South Africa mandates local governments to provide a safe environment. A review of the South African policy frameworks shows the national government's compassion for digital technologies. For example, adopting technology is a crucial pillar of South Africa's National Development Plan 2030 (NDP 2030), the country's development blueprint. The NDP 2030 sets the tone for the adoption of technologies such as AI as follows:

> Technology for preventing and investigating crime should be prioritised in order to avoid it from happening in the first instance and to expedite investigations through increased forensic capacity, better crime, scene investigation and analysis of current and future threats to safety. (National Planning Commission, 2012, p. 388)

In light of the policy direction set out by the NDP 2030, AI is a 4IR technology that can be harnessed to improve public safety in South African cities. Government-underwritten policy discussion documents add a fresh impetus and support to digital technologies in local government and, more recently, the 4IR discourse. The NDP 2030, the 2020 Foresight Exercise Report, the Decadal Plan for Science, Technology and Innovation 2022–2031, White Paper on Policing, White Paper on Safety and Security, White Paper on Science, Technology and Innovation, National Integrated ICT Policy and various policy interventions necessitated explicitly by the COVID-19 pandemic emphasise the importance of digital innovations and moving towards new technologies. A policy review on South Africa's NDP 2030 by Chigova (2021) exposes how the proposed Decadal Plan for Science, Technology, and Innovation 2022–2031 aims to ramp up the aspirations of the NDP 2030 while incorporating new critical technological issues linked to the fourth industrial revolution. Chapter 12 of the NDP 2030 speaks to building safer communities using, for example, technology to prevent and investigate crime (National Planning Commission, 2012, p. 388). Despite the policy cognisance by the government, evidence of the use of AI in South Africa shows two main problems: the opaque nature of current data collection and processing activities and a lack of coherent policy direction on the use of emerging technologies in crime prevention (Stone, 2020).

Mobilising AI to Make the COJ Safe

The CoJ is one of the biggest metropolitan cities in Africa. The city needs help with making it safe and secure for its citizens. The CoJ in the Integrated Development Plan 2021–2026 notes that "the citizens of Johannesburg suffer from high levels of insecurity" (CoJ, 2021, p. 183). According to the 2022 Numbeo Crime Index, South Africa is ranked the third most dangerous country globally, and Johannesburg is the fourth most dangerous city globally. The CoJ (2015) admits that, like many other rapidly changing cities worldwide, the city faces several challenges to urban safety in its Johannesburg City Safety Strategy. The CoJ Draft Integrated Development Plan 2020/2021 reiterates that safety and security remain ongoing concerns in the city (CoJ, 2020).

Regarding safety and security concerns, the CoJ Integrated Development Plan 2021–2026 calls for adopting 4IR, AI and intelligent systems (CoJ, 2021). In this context, AI (AI) stands as part of solutions that can assist in fighting crime in the CoJ and making it safe. According to the consulting firm Ernest and Young (2020), AI technologies promise to improve safety across this spectrum. Ernest and Young (2020) further stress that can help reduce, prevent, and respond to crimes, for example, by creating a unique opportunity to establish safer communities. The White Paper on Safety and Security aims to facilitate the objectives of the NDP 2030 of "building safer communities" by using technologies as one of its strategies to promote "a society where all people live in safe environments, play a role in creating and maintaining a safe environment, feel safe from crime and violence and conditions that contribute to it, and have equal access and recourse to high-quality services when affected by crime and violence…" (Civilian Secretariat of Police, 2016b). In addition, Stone (2020) argues that the public's demand for safety in South African cities may be arguably construed as meaning that communities are prepared for mainstream surveillance technology equipped with AI-based intelligence. The demands emanate from the perception that Johannesburg is a dangerous system (CoJ, 2021).

Against this background, Rigano (2019) and Idder and Coulaux (2021) concur that criminal justice systems in cities are turning to AI to improve their outcomes, cut crime, and reduce justice-related delays. Due to the macro and micro social-economic challenges in South Africa, criminal activities in cities like the CoJ are growing faster and undermining public safety. Considering these challenges, the auditing firm Ernest and

Young (2020) underscores that as threats to public safety mutate quicker, AI holds the promise of levelling the playing field for local governments. Research by Rigano (2019) shows AI evolving into a permanent part of safe city ecosystems. Idder and Coulaux (2021) noticed that AI is used in city law enforcement as a prevention and prediction tool and a crime-solving and recidivism tool. Thus, AI can provide COJ authorities with support in preventive policing, criminal investigations, crowd, and traffic control, and combating terrorist threats (Ernest & Young, 2020).

In 2019, the CoJ launched the Integrated Intelligence Operations Centre (IIOC) Reaction Unit as part of its Smart City Programme to serve as the city's 'nerve centre' for municipal data (CoJ, 2020). The system coordinates a network of surveillance cameras that keep a beady eye on the inner city, selected public places, streets, and highways (CoJ, n.d.). The city's expansion of broadband network services supports opportunities for the CoJ to use more AI-supported tools. The IIOC obtains real-time data to proactively address various incidences ranging from crime, fire safety, traffic management, by-law enforcement, and service delivery issues (CoJ, 2021, p. 185). The following are areas where AI can be used in cities.

AI in Preventive Policing in the CoJ

The 2016 White Paper on Policing provides for using technologies such as AI to support proactive policing, improve efficiency in crime investigation, and analyse current and future trends (Civilian Secretariat of Police, 2016a). In cities such as the CoJ, where certain areas, such as the inner city, are notorious for high criminal activity, AI provides opportunities for preventive policing. Rigano (2019) reasons that AI offers continuous monitoring algorithms to assess movement and predict emergent suspicious and criminal behaviour across a network of cameras. The scope and extent of preventive policing require CoJ authorities to have tools capable of predictive analysis. According to Rigano (2019), Predictive analysis is a complex process that uses large volumes of data to forecast and formulate potential outcomes. AI tools in the CoJ respond to South Africa's 2016 White Paper on Safety and Security, reiterating the criticality of integrated data and information management systems that enhance the effectiveness of crime and violence prevention operations (Stone, 2020).

In the CoJ, where criminals reign supreme and threaten the safety of citizens, AI applications offer immense possibilities to policing and justice systems that can improve public security. These applications include video analytics for integrated facial recognition, detecting individuals in multiple locations via closed-circuit television or across various cameras (Rigano, 2019). Rigano (2019) argues that object and activity detection abilities necessitated by AI could prevent crimes through movement and pattern analysis, recognise crimes in progress, and help investigators identify suspects.

The CoJ (2020) claims that the extensive surveillance camera network anchored on the IIOC is helping to minimise crime and grime in the inner city. For a city with ambitions to be an innovation-driver smart city, the CoJ aims to mobilise digital technologies to improve the safety and security of its inhabitants (Mzekandaba, 2018). According to Rigano (2019), with technology such as cameras, video, and social media generating massive volumes of data, AI could help city authorities detect crimes that would otherwise go undetected. Policing powers can monitor high crime places without having personnel on the ground or even pick criminal activities in crowded places through close video analysis. Hence, CoJ officials can ensure excellent public safety by investigating potential illegal activity, thus increasing community confidence in law enforcement and criminal justice (Rigano, 2019). Critically, AI can drive the discourse for the CoJ as it aims to become an innovative, world-class city that is safe to live in and do business in.

AI in Smart Policing Johannesburg

The CoJ (2020) notes that with the collaboration between IIOC, where a constellation of city-owned CCTV cameras is monitored, the strategic deployment and quick reaction time, muggers, armed robbers, and hijackers are finding themselves in handcuffs and behind bars. If the authorities in the city properly build on the use of AI technologies, there is no doubt that crime will subside. Crimes statistics covering the period April–June 2022 by the South African Police Services show that Johannesburg had five police stations in the top 20 police stations that recorded the highest numbers of contact crimes, with Johannesburg Central and Alexandra police stations being the second and third in South Africa (South African Police Services, 2022). According to the South African Police Services (2022) According to the data, contact crimes increased in three police stations: Johannesburg Central (5.1%), Alexandra (5.3%), and Jeppe (20.3%), compared to the same period in 2021. This evidence shows that the CoJ can reduce the policing gaps through AI-supported smart policing.

When supported by advanced AI technologies, policing officials in the CoJ can analyse large volumes of criminal justice-related records and predict potential criminal recidivism (Rigano, 2019). More so, Rigano (2019) stresses that by using AI and predictive policing analytics integrated with computer-aided responses and live public safety video enterprises, law enforcement will be better able to respond to incidents, prevent threats, stage interventions, divert resources, and investigate and analyse criminal activity. In addition, AI technology can provide law enforcement with situational awareness and context, thus aiding in police well-being due to better-informed responses to possibly dangerous situations Rigano (2019). Ernest and Young (2020) observe that AI has been used for facial and image recognition, managing crime scenes, and detecting criminal behaviours. Hence, if city policing authorities optimise AI to ensure society's safety, criminal elements' capacity to threaten citizens' safety is curtailed.

AI in Criminal Investigations

Williams (2021) postulates that AI assists in image and video analysis, saves investigators valuable time, and reduces errors. Williams further stresses that it aids crime analysts by pouring through vast amounts of data and making connections that can empower policing. Such capacity is helpful for authorities operating in a mega city like CoJ. Problems of migration, planning, inequalities, and population growth make policing a complex responsibility. The mushrooming of unplanned settlements makes criminal investigations difficult, particularly tracing people who break the law. In such a problem, Rigano (2019) argues that AI has the potential to provide investigative assistance and allow criminal justice officials to maintain public safety better. South Africa's White Paper on Policing supports using AI technologies to offer information-sharing solutions across the criminal justice system, including in e-docket and case management systems (Stone, 2020).

The challenge is that despite many upsides, AI has a disturbing element: bias in facial recognition technology that seeps into the criminal justice system (Kaiser, 2024). In developed countries, such as the United States of America, Kaiser (2024) notes that several people of colour have been falsely identified as suspects in criminal investigations that used facial recognition software. Kaiser further stresses that in some cases, AI bias resulted in wrongful arrests and charges.

AI in Traffic Control, Streets, and Public Places Surveillance

South Africa highly demands suitable traffic congestion solutions that reduce road accidents (Olayode et al., 2020). Likewise, cities like the CoJ are increasingly turning to AI-aided surveillance to police public spaces (Kwet, 2021). Evidence from countries such as China affirms AI as a critical tool for city traffic management. Olayode et al. (2020) indicate that AI effectively combats traffic congestion. According to Hao and Swart (2022), AI tools that work through a constellation of more than 5000 cameras installed in the CoJ use motor vehicle licence plate recognition to monitor movement and track delinquent individuals on city roads. This is part of the local authority's 'safe city' projects, which include linking cameras to form city-wide networks using AI to index, sort and interpret data pooled into centralised surveillance-based 'nerve centres' (Kwet, 2021). The challenge in the CoJ is that AI-aided tools are yet to be used to provide real-time input to traffic control, streets, and public places surveillance. Until that stage, real benefits accrue when real-time AI data support city officials' decisions, planning and response actions. As the foundation for AI mobilisation is being laid, the expectation is that, with time, the application of AI expands to produce tangible outcomes in the fight to improve public safety.

Challenges and Concerns of AI in Cities

AI usage in the public sector attracts much scrutiny. Like any technology, AI comes with challenges and concerns, raising many ethical issues in cities. Even though there is overwhelming evidence of the capacities and advantages of AI use in cities, how it is used creates concerns. According to the consulting organisation Deloitte (2021), an underlying question in using AI-supported technologies to make cities safe is: What society are we aiming to build? In South African cities, for example, Hao and Swart (2022) have argued that AI usage and impact risk repeating the patterns of colonial history. Similarly, Benyera (2021) cautions against instruments such as AI, hypothesising they are an extension of colonialism or part of neo-colonialism. Hao and Swart (2022) since colonial bequests flourish in South Africa, the unconstrained placement of AI surveillance in the CoJ offers just one case study of how a technology that promised to bring societies into the future threatens to send them back to the past. Hao and Swart (2022) argue that AI creates a new form of apartheid, that is, digital apartheid. Benyera (2021) corroborates and explains that AI will present the same consequences to the victims of coloniality in the same way colonial systems, such as apartheid, in the name of security and the rule of law.

Kwet (2021) laments that AI-linked technologies are being deployed in the CoJ without full public transparency. This is a huge concern because it raises negative perceptions towards AI from the citizens who are supposed to benefit from safe communities. According to Baker (2021), if AI systems are left unmonitored, they can negatively affect the community law enforcement serves. Similarly, Stone (2020) reiterates that it cannot be denied that deploying surveillance technologies linked to AI in public spaces threatens people's constitutional rights to privacy and freedom of movement. It presents a moral and legal dilemma where several trade-offs can be observed. For example, critical issues arise, such as if citizens' desire to "feel and be safe" in the CoJ can be sacrificed to the omnipresent eye and hand of private security corporations or a "surveillance state" (Duncan, 2018; Stone, 2020). Deloitte (2021) exposes doubts and uncertainties about AI's impact on communities and cities: the most fundamental concern is privacy.

Omar et al. (2017) allude to issues and specific reasons that lead to challenges in AI adoption and its rejection. As buttressed in the theories discussed above, perceptions usually underpin the reasons. For instance, Omar et al. (2017) share that top leadership might be worried that AI carries a massive cost and is at significant risk since its adoption results are hard to determine and involve a high level of uncertainty with possibilities of unfavourable outcomes. Furthermore, faced with scarce resources, limited budgetary space, competing demands and a highly expectant citizenry, local authorities, such as the CoJ, might not be better positioned to finance the adoption of AI-enabled technologies in their areas because AI needs technological advancement and state-of-the-art facilities (Omar et al., 2017). The current use of AI in the CoJ is associated with unclear data collection and processing actions and a deficit of policy direction, resulting in government officials and the wider public needing more guidance on acceptable practices (Stone, 2020). Stakeholders are under pressure to deal with the high crime environment prevailing in the city. The CoJ partnerships with private companies like Vumacom in deploying thousands of surveillance cameras raise several legal questions (Hao & Swart, 2022). These are questions about the scope and extent of their operations and accountability issues. The overriding challenge stems from the need for a legal framework that regulates the time of surveillance, use, and sharing of collected data.

Further, AI technologies are often presented as producing intelligent decisions free from bias or prejudice; it must also be highlighted that their operationalisation does not occur in a vacuum (Stone, 2020). Their use is mainly offered as objective and somehow neutral, which in most cases is far from the truth. As Stone (2020) underscores that the reality is that all technologies are informed by and respond to the unwritten rules of their social, political, and economic context. In the absence of coherent guiding frameworks and robust accountability mechanisms, AI technologies are prone to abuse and manipulation and end up being used to infringe on citizens' liberties and rights. In extreme circumstances, they can be used to defeat the ends of justice by criminals and threaten not to improve public safety.

Key Recommendations for Responsible AI Use in City Safety

Misuraca and van Noordt (2020) highlight that the possible benefits of AI technologies are enormous, but risks must not be overlooked, whereas democratic values and human rights are underscored. The study advises that in a constitutional democracy like South Africa, operationalising AI technologies into practice in cities requires an approach that recognises the complexity of the context in which they are deployed and the meticulousness essential to lessen likely human rights violations (Stone, 2020). In addition, as Idder and Coulaux (2021) cautioned, CoJ authorities must remember that AI is just a tool which is as good as its user. In that context, the article recommends to users, such as the CoJ, the importance of evaluating likely negative externalities of AI used in criminal justice to avoid counterproductive consequences such as bias and errors.

While the policy framework in South Africa, such as the NDP 2030, White Paper on Policing, and the White Paper on Security and Safety, appreciate the centrality of AI-linked technologies, the Government of South Africa must avail resources. Shava and Vyas-Doorgapersad (2021) underscore that despite the many benefits of digital technologies, AI-based tools in local municipalities in South Africa are constrained by capacity gaps. It is recommended that the national and provincial governments support to ensure enough capacitation of local government. In addition, AI use must be regulated to enable its responsible application in the public sector. Finally, since AI technologies are likely to become permanent tools for ensuring public safety in cities, the government must complement the White Paper on Policing proposals by providing coherent legislative and regulatory frameworks for optimising the use of AI technologies across law enforcement (Rigano, 2019; Stone, 2020). In addition, cities must enact complementary by-laws that spell out the framework for using, sharing, and storing data. The frameworks must also regulate private actors in the city using AI tools. These frameworks are necessary for checks and balances. Since studies have pointed out that AI can be biased, institutions and mechanisms in the CoJ must be monitored to avoid prosecuting innocent residents mistakenly identified.

Further, the aspiration that AI technologies must be used responsibly in cities can always be emphasised. One recommended approach is continuous engagement between the CoJ, private players, and the residents in using AI tools, as community safety is often a shared responsibility. Most importantly, community buy-in and participation might lessen perceptions of AI deployment as a renewed Apartheid tactic aimed at surveillance of profiled areas and perpetuating ulterior motives. In addition, CoJ must have clear regulations on the collection, processing, access, and storage of data to ensure accountability and maintain transparency.

Conclusion

This chapter explored AI as a 4IR tool for ensuring public safety and security in Johannesburg. It demonstrated that AI could be harnessed to improve public safety in the CoJ through preventive policing, smart policing, criminal investigations, traffic control, and street and public place surveillance. The chapter located the use of AI to the CoJ public safety aspirations SDG 11 and within South Africa's robust policy frameworks. Public policy documents such as the NDP 2030 and White Papers on Policing, Safety, and Security emphasise the importance of safe cities and support the use of AI-supported technologies. This inquiry used the TAM Model and DOI Theory as theoretical frameworks to show: (1) that perceptions and views of stakeholders' influence are central to the adoption and acceptance of AI technologies in the CoJ and (2) The factors and attributes that drive the successful implementation of AI in cities.

The opportunities and benefits of using AI technologies to make the CoJ safe are apparent. However, AI use in cities necessitates reflections on balancing the opportunities and challenges it presents. Hence, it is recommended that ethical issues relating to AI usage in cities must be addressed in line with the country's constitutional provisions. Finally, future studies must examine how people living in high-crime cities perceive AI-enabled surveillance. For example, these studies can involve surveys and longitudinal studies on the perceptions of people who face difficult trade-offs of a surveillant state on the one hand and a desire to live in safe cities.

References

Ahmed, S., Hossain, M., Kaiser, M. S., Noor, M. B. T., Mahmud, M., & Chakraborty, C. (2021). Artificial intelligence and machine learning are used to ensure security in smart cities. In *Data-driven mining, learning and analytics for secured smart cities* (pp. 23–47). Springer.

Ahn, M. J., & Chen, Y. C. (2022). Digital transformation toward AI-augmented public administration: The perception of government employees and the willingness to use AI in government. *Government Information Quarterly, 39*(2), 101664.

Allam, Z., & Dhunny, Z. (2019, January). On big data, artificial intelligence and smart cities. *Cities, 89*, 80–91.

AlSheibani, S., Cheung, Y., & Messom, C. (2018). *Artificial intelligence adoption: AI-readiness at firm-level*. Retrieved from https://researchmgt.monash.edu/ws/portalfiles/portal/273209396/254798983_oa.pdf

Baker, E. M. (2021). *I've got my AI on you: Artificial intelligence in the law enforcement domain* (Masters dissertation). University of Texas.

Batty, M. (2018). *Artificial intelligence and smart cities* (Vol. 45, pp. 3–6). Sage.

Benyera, E. (2021). *The Fourth Industrial Revolution and the recolonisation of Africa: The coloniality of data*. Taylor & Francis.

Berntzen, L., Johannessen, M. R., & El-Gazzar, R. (2018). *Smart cities, big data and smart decision-making-understanding "big data" in smart city applications*. Paper presented at the ICDS 2018, The Twelfth International Conference on Digital Society and eGovernments.

Bokhari, S. A. A., & Myeong, S. (2022). Use of artificial intelligence in smart cities for smart decision-making: A social innovation perspective. *Sustainability, 14*(2), 620.

Chigova, L. E. (2021). The National Development Plan 2030: A focus on innovation issues. *Journal of Public Administration, 56*(4.1), 1069–1073.

City of Johannesburg. (2015). *Joburg City Safety Strategy: Working towards a safer Joburg*. Retrieved from http://www.jicp.org.za/wp-content/uploads/2016/11/2015-JCCS.pdf

City of Johannesburg. (2020). *JMPD'S focused IOC Reaction Unit already leading to decrease in inner-city crime*. Retrieved from https://www.joburg.org.za/media_/Pages/Media/Mayoral%20Newsletter/Mashaba%20On%20Point%20June%202019/JMPD%E2%80%99s-focused-IOC-Reaction-Unit-already-leading-to-decrease-in-inner-city-crime.aspx

City of Johannesburg. (2021). *The City of Johannesburg integrated development plan 2021–26: Rebuilding a resilient Joburg our plan, our future!* Retrieved from https://www.joburg.org.za/documents_/Documents/2021-016%20Final%20IDP/2021-26%20FINAL%20IDP%2021May%202021.pdf

City of Johannesburg. (n.d.). *IIOC provides for intelligent policing using CCTV cameras*. Retrieved from https://www.joburg.org.za/media_/Pages/Media/Newsroom/IIOC-provides-for-intelligent-policing-using-CCTV-cameras.aspx

Civilian Secretariat of Police. (2016a). *White Paper on policing*. Retrieved from http://www.policesecretariat.gov.za/downloads/bills/2016_White_Paper_on_Policing.pdf

Civilian Secretariat of Police. (2016b). *White Paper on Safety and Security*. Retrieved from http://www.policesecretariat.gov.za/downloads/bills/2016_White_Paper_on_Policing.pdf

Davis, F. D. (1989). Perceived usefulness, perceived ease of use, and user acceptance of information technology. *MIS Quarterly, 13*, 319–340.

Deloitte. (2021). *Surveillance and predictive policing through AI*. Retrieved from https://www2.deloitte.com/fi/fi/pages/public-sector/articles/urban-future-with-a-purpose/surveillance-and-predictive-policing-through-ai.html

De Vries, H., Bekkers, V., & Tummers, L. (2016). Innovation in the public sector: A systematic review and future research agenda. *Public Administration, 94*(1), 146–166.

Duncan, J. (2018). *Stopping the spies: Constructing and resisting the surveillance state in South Africa*. NYU Press.

Ernest & Young. (2020). *How AI is establishing itself as the newest public safety officer*. Retrieved from https://www.ey.com/en_gl/consulting/how-ai-is-establishing-itself-as-the-newest-public-safety-officer

Fashoro, I., & Barnard, L. (2021). Assessing South African government's use of social media for citizen participation. *The African Journal of Information Systems, 13*(1), 3.

Gatzweiler, F. W. (2020). Advancing urban health and wellbeing through collective and artificial intelligence: A systems approach 3.0. In *Urban health and wellbeing programme* (pp. 33–38). Springer.

Hao, K., & Swart, H. (2022). *South Africa's private surveillance machine is fuelling a digital Apartheid*. Retrieved from https://www.technologyreview.com/2022/04/19/1049996/south-africa-ai-surveillance-digital-apartheid

Idder, A., & Coulaux, S. (2021). *Artificial Intelligence in criminal justice: Invasion or revolution?* Retrieved from https://www.ibanet.org/dec-21-ai-criminal-justice

Kaiser, L. (2024). *AI systems initially trained on images of young white males, and are most biased against women of color*. Retrieved from: https://www.buffalo.edu/news/tipsheets/2024/ub-ai-expert-facial-recognition-expert-ifeoma-nwogu.html

Kassens-Noor, E., & Hintze, A. (2020). Cities of the future? The potential impact of artificial intelligence. *AI, 1*(2), 12.

Koekemoer, S., & Von Solms, R. (2021). Does the 4th Industrial Revolution provide solutions for sustainable basic service delivery in South African municipalities? *Journal of Public Administration, 56*(2), 339–351.

Kwet, M. (2021). *The city surveillance state: Inside Johannesburg's Safe City Initiative*. Retrieved from https://saiia.org.za/wp-content/uploads/2021/03/Policy-Briefing-231-kwet-FINAL.pdf

Louw, V., & Dube, I. (2021). The nexus between service delivery, Artificial Intelligence and the Fourth Industrial Revolution. *Journal of Public Administration, 56*(4.1), 1030–1038.

Mhlanga, D., Ndhlovu, E., & Hofisi, C. (2021). Assessment of the 4IR challenges of radical innovation in service delivery in Africa. *Journal of Public Administration, 56*(4.1), 1002–1017.

Misuraca, G., & Van Noordt, C. (2020). *AI Watch-Artificial Intelligence in public services: Overview of the use and impact of AI in public services in the EU* (JRC Working Papers [JRC120399]).

Mzekandaba, S. (2018). *Joburg banks on nerve centre to enhance service delivery*. Retrieved from https://www.itweb.co.za/content/O2rQGqAplDzMd1ea

Na, S., Heo, S., Han, S., Shin, Y., & Roh, Y. (2022). Acceptance model of Artificial Intelligence (AI)-based technologies in construction firms: Applying the Technology Acceptance Model (TAM) in combination with the Technology–Organisation–Environment (TOE) framework. *Buildings, 12*(2), 90.

National Planning Commission. (2012). *National Development Plan 2030: Our future—Make it work*. The Presidency

Ndung'u, N., & Signe, L. (2020). *The Fourth Industrial Revolution and digitization will transform Africa into a global powerhouse* (pp. 61–73). Foresight Africa.

Ochara, N. M. (2021). *Governance mechanisms for Fourth Industrial Revolution artifacts in higher education institutions: A systems perspective*. Retrieved from https://papers.ssrn.com/sol3/papers.cfm?abstract_id=3814133

OECD. (2021). *Development Co-operation Report 2021: Shaping a just digital transformation*. Retrieved from https://www.oecd-ilibrary.org/development/development-co-operation-report-2021_ce08832f-en

Olayode, O., Tartibu, L., & Okwu, M. (2020). Application of Artificial Intelligence in traffic control system of non-autonomous vehicles at signalized road intersection. *Procedia CIRP, 91*, 194–200.

Omar, S. A., Hasbolah, F., & Ulfah, M. (2017). The diffusion of artificial intelligence in governance of public listed companies in Malaysia. *International Journal of Business, Economics and Law, 14*(2), 1–9.

Onyango, G. (2023). Crafting policy technologies (PolicyTechs): An introduction to policy digitalisation pathways in Africa. In *Public policy and technological transformations in Africa: Nurturing policy entrepreneurship, policy tools and citizen participation* (pp. 1–26). Palgrave Macmillan.

Orr, G. (2003). *Diffusion of innovations, by Everett Rogers (1995)*. Retrieved from https://www.academia.edu/1988400/Diffusion_of_innovations_by_Everett_Rogers_1995_

Pomerol, J.-C. (1997). Artificial intelligence and human decision making. *European Journal of Operational Research, 99*(1), 3–25.

Rigano, C. (2019). Using artificial intelligence to address criminal justice needs. *National Institute of Justice Journal, 280*, 1–10.

Rogers, E. M. (1995). Diffusion of innovations: Modifications of a model for telecommunications. In *Die diffusion von innovationen in der telekommunikation* (pp. 25–38). Springer.

Rogers, E. M. (2003). *Diffusion of innovations* (5th ed.). Free Press.

Shava, E., & Vyas-Doorgapersad, S. (2021). Information Communication Technology (ICT) and smart service delivery in the Fourth Industrial Revolution: A case of the City of Johannesburg. *Journal of Public Administration, 56*(4.1), 986–1001.

South African Police Services. (2022). *Police Recorded Crime Statistics Republic of South Africa First Quarter of 2022/2023 Financial year April to June 2022*. Retrieved from https://www.saps.gov.za/services/downloads/April-2022_23-presentation.pdf

Srivastava, S., Bisht, A., & Narayan, N. (2017). *Safety and security in smart cities using artificial intelligence—A review*. Paper presented at the 2017 7th International Conference on Cloud Computing, Data Science & Engineering-Confluence.

Stone, K. (2020). *Responsible use of artificial intelligence for crime prevention in South Africa*. Policy Action Network. Retrieved from https://policyaction.org.za/sites/default/files/PAN_TopicalGuide_AIData2_CrimePolicing_Elec.pdf

Sun, T. Q., & Medaglia, R. (2019). Mapping the challenges of Artificial Intelligence in the public sector: Evidence from public healthcare. *Government Information Quarterly, 36*(2), 368–383.

Ullah, Z., Al-Turjman, F., Mostarda, L., & Gagliardi, R. (2020). Applications of artificial intelligence and machine learning in smart cities. *Computer Communications, 154*, 313–323.

United Nations. (2015). *Sustainable development goals*. United Nations.

Williams, J. (2021). *Public safety and smart cities: How assistive AI will help*. Retrieved from https://www.openaccessgovernment.org/public-safety-and-smart-cities-how-assistive-ai-will-help/111615/

Yigitcanlar, T., Desouza, K. C., Butler, L., & Roozkhosh, F. (2020). Contributions and risks of artificial intelligence (AI) in building smarter cities: Insights from a systematic review of the literature. *Energies, 13*(6), 1473.

Yigitcanlar, T., & Kamruzzaman, M. (2020). Smart cities and mobility: Does the smartness of Australian cities lead to sustainable commuting patterns? In *Smart cities and innovative urban technologies* (pp. 21–46). Routledge.

Yoshinaga, T., Fukuda, Y., Jp, P., Watanabe, Y., & Hiroike, A. (2022). Video analytics AI for public safety and security. *Infection, 2*, 1.

CHAPTER 10

AI, Governance, and Public Policy: Examining the 2024 South African Elections

Mandla J. Radebe

Introduction

Today, there is an increasing focus on integrating Artificial intelligence (AI) with other related 4IR technologies to potentially transform democratic electoral processes in developing and middle-income countries like those in Africa. However, while AI offers promising advancements, it also raises significant concerns. Scholars like Stevenson (2024) have explored the impacts of AI on voter registration, predictive analytics, election monitoring, accessibility, and voter participation by analysing secondary literature. As already discussed in other chapters in this volume, these analyses have also shown that the more pressing issue pertains to the need for accountability, equity, and transparency in algorithmic decision-making. Many argue that addressing these concerns is essential to mitigating legal and moral reservations about AI's use in elections

M. J. Radebe (✉)
Department of Strategic Communication, University of Johannesburg, Johannesburg, South Africa
e-mail: mradebe@uj.ac.za

G. Onyango (ed.), *Designing Artificial Intelligence for Public Policy and Governance in Africa*, Studies in National Governance and Emerging Technologies, https://doi.org/10.1007/978-3-031-83445-5_10

(Stevenson, 2024). This aspect of *AI for Government* underscores the need for policymakers to critically reflect on the intersection of technology and democracy, particularly in contexts where AI's influence could undermine meaningful self-determination, especially in Africa, where external forces often drive AI deployment (Timcke & Hlomani, n.d.). AI presents a greater potential, pointing to the need for effective policy and regulatory mechanisms to bolster governance processes and address emerging deficits. Notably, AI's influence is becoming pervasive across various policy sectors in Africa, including health, transportation, and education (Putranto & Aristawidya, 2023), and its impact on elections is no exception (Omondi et al., 2024).

The 2024 elections are notably the first to occur within the context of rapidly advancing AI, including generative AI technologies. Concerns about the recurrence of political disinformation, as seen in previous UK and U.S. elections, are growing. These fears are not unfounded, given the rapid development of AI technologies like large language models, which have the potential to be misused to undermine democratic processes (Hawes et al., 2023). AI tools can be employed to disrupt elections, including creating and spreading misinformation, manipulating public opinion, targeting voters with personalised content without informed consent, hacking election systems, and disrupting civil society activities surrounding elections (Hawes et al., 2023). These threats highlight the legitimate concerns about AI's potential to jeopardise electoral integrity.

As political discourse increasingly takes centre stage on social media during election cycles, the opportunity for malicious actors to disseminate misinformation and erode trust in the electoral process grows, particularly with the rise of large language models (Dmonte et al., 2024). The manipulation of social and political algorithms, as seen in the 2016 U.S. elections using bots to undermine electoral outcomes (Howard et al., 2018), calls for heightened vigilance. The debate around AI regulation continues in this context of rampant fake news. Scholars like Marsden et al. (2020) advocate for co-regulation, suggesting that regulatory responsibilities should not only rest with national governments or supranational bodies like the European Union but also involve self-regulation by companies.

Conversely, Kan (2024) emphasises that AI's impact on human rights necessitates regulations and policies that protect these rights and uphold democratic values. A comprehensive framework for AI technologies' ethical and legal management should be implemented at national and international levels (Kan, 2024). Many jurisdictions have recognised the need for policies that ensure AI remains "trustworthy" (Manheim & Kaplan, 2019). Additionally, some scholars argue that, given the negative environmental consequences of global supply chains, greater state regulation is needed rather than empowering transnational corporations as global governors (Dauvergne, 2022).

As AI continues to reshape various aspects of society, its role in modern elections has become increasingly critical, offering both opportunities for innovation and risks for manipulation. Indeed, AI presents unparalleled opportunities to enhance the election through *inter alia* data analysis, voter targeting, and personalised messaging. In short, it threatens the integrity of democratic processes (Yu, 2024). However, this underscores the critical need to develop robust governance frameworks and public policies, not only to foster public trust (Robles & Mallinson, 2023) but, more importantly, to manage AI technologies in accordance with democratic values and human rights principles (Kan, 2024).

In this context, this chapter explores how AI technology impacted the 2024 South African elections, examining its effects within the broader framework of global developments and the unique political landscape of the country. The chapter delves into the dual-edged nature of AI in this electoral cycle—while it can enhance democratic engagement and streamline electoral processes, it also poses significant threats through the spread of misinformation, manipulation of public opinion, and cyber vulnerabilities. Understanding the impact of AI on the 2024 South African elections requires a nuanced analysis that considers both the technological advancements shaping modern democracies and the specific socio-political context in which these elections occurred. Ultimately, the chapter seeks to identify the policy issues South Africa must grapple with to address these challenges effectively. Therefore, in light of the above background, this chapter's main question is to what extent AI technology impacted the 2024 South African elections and what policy conundrums must be addressed to manage this. The hypothesis explored is that while AI-driven technologies possess positive potential for society, they also have the potential to pose a substantial threat to democracy. There is an ongoing debate about policy and governance concerning ethics, disinformation, and misinformation (Alibašić, 2024).

Many countries in the Global North have swiftly responded to the increased visibility of AI's risks, looking beyond its benefits to emphasise the need for appropriate regulation to ensure AI is "trustworthy"—in other words, legal, ethical, and robust (Smuha, 2021). The chapter begins with a discussion of the South African context leading up to the elections, addressing issues such as the historical overview of misinformation and disinformation in the country, the political landscape in South Africa concerning the Russia-Ukraine war, Gaza, BRICS issues, and the country's digital landscape, including internet penetration and social media usage. AI-driven threats to democracy in the 2024 South African elections are explored, focusing on concerns such as low voter turnout, the hidden influence of AI, and policy dilemmas. The chapter concludes with an analysis of future implications and recommendations.

The South African Context: Pre-2024 Elections

Historical Overview of Misinformation and Disinformation in South Africa

The fabrication of information is not a new phenomenon; misinformation, disinformation, and propaganda have been integral aspects of human communication since the Roman Empire, significantly amplified with the invention of the printing press (Posetti & Matthews, 2018). During the height of apartheid in South Africa, particularly from the early 1970s to the early 1990s, the South African government orchestrated a sophisticated and clandestine global propaganda and lobbying campaign aimed to garner support for the regime and counteract opposition by influencing key opinion formers in Western capitals (Posetti & Matthews, 2018). Post-apartheid, there have been numerous disinformation scandals, such as the one in 2018 that led to the closure of the UK-based public relations firm Bell Pottinger, exposed as a central player in what was described as a "large-scale fake news propaganda war in South Africa". Bell Pottinger, in collaboration with an India-based marketing firm, was accused of orchestrating a secret campaign to incite racial polarisation and discredit critics of President Zuma and the Gupta family, who financed the operation. This disinformation campaign involved websites, tweets amplified by bots, misleading online advertisements, covert exploitation of Facebook and Wikipedia, and hacks and malicious leaks (Posetti & Matthews, 2018). Also, in 2018, Australia's Border Protection and Immigration Minister, Peter Dutton, caused a diplomatic row by responding to problematic journalism inspired by far-right propaganda about land redistribution plans in South Africa. Dutton controversially proposed creating a special visa category to fast-track asylum claims for white South African farmers, which further fuelled misinformation (Posetti & Matthews, 2018).

The spread of misinformation and politically motivated disinformation in Africa has a long history. The widespread adoption of mobile phones and the popularisation of apps like WhatsApp have made misinformation more pervasive across the continent (Madrid-Morales et al., 2021). Social media platforms, particularly Facebook and WhatsApp, have become major viral misinformation and disinformation sources. Wasserman and Madrid-Morales (2019) argue that exposure to fabricated political news stories in countries like Kenya, Nigeria, and South Africa is perceived to be higher than in the United States. In South Africa, many online users have shared political news stories they believed at the time to be fabricated (Wasserman & Madrid-Morales, 2019). This is exacerbated by high media freedom, self-regulation, an open and participatory media culture, and a well-established digital media landscape in South Africa (Madrid-Morales et al., 2021).

Moreover, anti-migrant sentiments in South Africa have been largely fuelled and disseminated through social media. Chenzi (2021) argues that the proliferation of social media platforms, which have become substitute news sources for a growing number of South Africans despite their imperfections, has driven much of the fake news in the country. Misinformation and disinformation campaigns in Africa have certainly been used to influence political agendas, and governments have attempted to respond with countermeasures. Despite a lack of robust policies, countries with high exposure to disinformation often experience low levels of trust in social and national media (Wasserman & Madrid-Morales, 2019). Disinformation, particularly through fake news spread via social media, has undeniably become a significant and ongoing problem in South Africa (de Wet & Marivate, 2021).

Political Landscape in South Africa: Russia-Ukraine, Gaza, and BRICS Issues

South Africa's non-aligned stance on the Russia-Ukraine conflict, coupled with its decision to take Israel to the ICJ, has strained relations with Western superpowers. This tension became evident when U.S. Ambassador to South Africa, Reuben Brigety, made unsubstantiated allegations that South Africa had supplied weapons and ammunition to Russia.

These accusations were followed by economic threats, including discussions about South Africa's potential exclusion from the African Growth and Opportunity Act (AGOA). On 9 June 2023, four senior U.S. Congress members—Democrats Gregory Meeks and Chris Coons, and Republicans James Risch and Michael McCaul—addressed a letter to high-ranking officials in the Biden administration. The letter concerned an upcoming forum in South Africa focused on enhancing trade between sub-Saharan African countries and the U.S. It urged South Africa to condemn Russia explicitly, warning that failure could result in reduced U.S.-South Africa trade. The letter was released shortly before the U.S.-Africa Business Summit in Gaborone, Botswana, under the Corporate Council of Africa, established in 1993 to promote U.S.-Africa trade. This move was intended to pressure the Biden administration and African governments, compelling them to influence South Africa to avoid jeopardising their trade relations with U.S. corporations (Radebe & Prashad, 2023).

Several African countries, including South Africa, Namibia, and Senegal, refused to condemn Russia's actions, with some attributing the conflict to Western and NATO policies. South African President Cyril Ramaphosa emphasised that, despite external pressures to adopt a confrontational stance against Russia, South Africa would advocate for dialogue as the only viable solution to the conflict (Ajala, 2022). South Africa's close political ties with Russia and reluctance to condemn the invasion have made some question whether its neutrality is merely declarative (Brosig, 2024).

South Africa's approach to Israel has also created friction with the West. The government's announcement on 29 December 2023 that it would approach the ICJ under the Genocide Convention concerning "acts committed by Israel" in Gaza has drawn significant criticism from Western nations. South Africa's case is based on serious concerns about the plight of civilians in Gaza, highlighting the indiscriminate use of force and the forcible displacement of residents. The government argued that the ongoing reports of international crimes, including crimes against humanity and war crimes, justified this legal action. Moreover, there have been reports of acts potentially meeting the threshold of genocide as defined by the 1948 Convention on the Prevention and Punishment of Genocide, occurring amidst the ongoing violence in Gaza. South Africa's prominent role as a founding member of BRICS has further heightened tensions with the West. The BRICS alliance, particularly in the context of the 15th BRICS summit held in South Africa, where Russian President Vladimir Putin was notably absent due to an International Criminal Court arrest warrant for war crimes in Ukraine, reflects a growing challenge to the U.S.-led global order. BRICS has increasingly positioned itself as a counterbalance to Western hegemony, with Russia and China playing significant roles in this geopolitical shift. However, India's strategic partnerships with five of the six new BRICS members also signal a nuanced approach (Kumar, 2023). The alliance is characterised by a shared sense of historical grievances and a commitment to reforming global governance in favour of developing countries, advocating for inclusive global growth and recalibrated international relations (Cooper & Thakur, 2023). Consequently, BRICS is viewed by the West as a potential counter-hegemonic force challenging the established U.S.-led global order (Özekin & Sune, 2023).

Despite South Africa's young democracy, which has shown resilience since the 1994 democratic breakthrough, the 2024 elections were considered the most contested since the end of apartheid. With the African National Congress (ANC) experiencing a significant drop-in electoral support, falling to an unprecedented low of 40%, and the lowest voter turnout recorded since 1994 at 58.5% (Tregenna & Radebe, 2024), concerns about electoral interference have emerged. Recent analyses by the Centre for Information Resilience suggest that accounts on X (formerly Twitter) praising Russia's invasion of Ukraine have been mobilising support for Jacob Zuma's new party, raising additional concerns about the integrity of the electoral process and the risk of foreign interference (Bloomberg UK, 2024).

The potential for AI technologies to create and disseminate disinformation has become a focal point in discussions about election integrity. In March 2024, controversy erupted when Zuma's daughter posted a deepfake video on X, in which a fabricated message from Donald Trump urged South Africans to vote for Zuma to ensure their voices would be heard. Similarly, the Economic Freedom Fighters (EFF), then South Africa's third-largest political party, attempted to use deepfake technology, featuring the voice of Eminem, in a post that was later debunked by Africa Check (Africa Check, 2024). These incidents prompted Meta to roll out anti-hate speech and misinformation campaigns on its platforms before the South African elections (Siddo, 2024). While initial concerns about election-related violence or vote rigging were focused on the ANC's potential attempts to retain power, the reality shifted towards fears of international interference, particularly in the context of AI. Allegations that Russia was employing a top-down approach to spreading disinformation in South Africa, including electoral interference and support for extraconstitutional claims to power (Schmidt, 2024), suggest possibilities of external forces with an interest in undermining the democratic process in the country.

South Africa's Digital Landscape: Internet Penetration and Social Media Use

Over the past two decades, South Africa has undergone significant technological and political transformations, profoundly impacting its digital environment (Donati, 2023). As of 2024, approximately 45.34 million people in South Africa, representing 74.7% of the population, are Internet users. This figure places South Africa above the global internet adoption rate of 66.2%, reflecting its advanced digital landscape (McInnes, 2024). South Africa also boasts one of the highest internet usage rates globally, with the average user between 16 and 64 spending over nine hours online daily. South Africans are among the most active social media users worldwide. While the global average time spent on social media is 2 hours and 23 minutes per day, South Africans spend an average of 3 hours and 41 minutes daily on these platforms. The primary motivations for social media use in South Africa include staying in touch with friends and family (65.9%), reading news stories (46.4%), finding inspiration for activities and purchases (44.6%), seeing what is trending (42.0%), and discovering content such as articles and videos (39.3%) (McInnes, 2024). Social media also plays a significant role in consumer behaviour, with a higher percentage of South African users (78%) researching a brand's social media presence before making a purchase compared to the global average of 73.9%. This trend underscores the importance of social media in shaping consumer decisions in the country. Additionally, concerns about the impact of misinformation in South Africa are high since internet users are more likely to use social media as a news source than the global average, with 46.5% citing reading news stories as a primary reason for their social media engagement (McInnes, 2024).

The impact of fake news on voter behaviour remains a complex issue, but various studies highlight its potential influence. For instance, during the 2020 U.S. elections, research indicated that political alignment and the type of news consumed significantly affected voters' trust in the electoral process. Facebook users were more prone to consuming fake and hyper-partisan news, whereas those who directly accessed news websites predominantly consumed mainstream news sources (Stachofsky et al., 2023). Similarly, research on the 2021 Czech parliamentary elections introduced a model to measure citizens' resilience to disinformation and its impact on voting behaviour, revealing that dissatisfaction with a political party could increase susceptibility to disinformation targeting that party (Syrovátka et al., 2023). In the context of the 2018 Mexican presidential elections, false information about a scandal involving Ricardo Anaya, a candidate from the National Action Party, was widely circulated. Although Anaya was later exonerated, the study found that the retraction of fake news led to post-election regret among voters with lower internal political efficacy. Conversely, those with higher political knowledge and internal political efficacy were less affected by the retraction and less likely to experience regret (Iida et al., 2024). During the 2017 Kenyan elections, despite the prevalence of disinformation, fake news, and cyber propaganda, which cast doubt on the election's integrity and contributed to post-election conflicts, most interviewed individuals stated that this extensive propaganda did not influence their voting decisions (Maweu, 2019).

Instances where cybersecurity was utilised to subvert the electoral processes encompass pivotal events such as the 2016 U.S. Presidential Election, where intelligence revelations pointed to Russian hackers breaching the Democratic National Committee's network to disclose sensitive emails. Similarly, in Ukraine's 2014 Presidential Election, malware was leveraged to manipulate the official outcomes, with the strategic intent to portray a far-right candidate as the victor. Moreover, in the context of the 2017 Estonia Electronic Voting System, a substantial cyber onslaught targeted governmental entities, including the election infrastructure, amidst escalating tensions with Russia. Furthermore, during the 2017 French Presidential Election, a scheme unfolded wherein attackers divulged many emails and documents, evidently aiming to influence the electoral results (Yu, 2024). These studies underscore the varied tactics employed and the repercussions of fake news, cyber-attacks, and disinformation on electoral outcomes. These influences are intricately shaped by factors such as political alignment, media consumption habits, and individual political efficacy. These instances also highlight the global nature of the threat, with entities worldwide partaking in cyber operations to sway electoral results in foreign countries (Yu, 2024). They fundamentally question the kind of policy responses regulators in countries such as South Africa must contemplate and tackle.

AI-Driven Threats to Democracy in the 2024 South African Elections

The 2024 South African elections unfolded amidst significant concerns regarding the potential for foreign interference, a subject that garnered considerable attention in the media. These concerns were amplified by the increasing role of technology in manipulating electoral processes, as reflected in various news outlets, including *TechCentral*'s article, "'Hacking the electorate': The tech threat to the 2024 election" (2 November 2023), *Business Insider Africa*'s "Russian observer accuses the West of interfering in South Africa's election" (31 May 2024), *IOL*'s "SACP warns of foreign interference to remove ANC from power" (3 July 2024), and *Bloomberg*'s "South Africa's Ramaphosa Warns ANC of Foreign Meddling in Vote" (31 January 2024). Indeed, the online sphere was inundated with articles discussing the potential implications of AI on electoral processes, as illustrated in the comprehensive list provided in Table 10.1.

Between January and May 2024, leading up to the South African elections, a series of online articles surfaced, shedding light on three significant themes in the electoral landscape: foreign interference through AI, the possible manipulation of electoral procedures using AI, and the proliferation of misinformation and disinformation in the context of AI. Generative AI tools, such as deepfakes, were flagged as significant risks by the South African Electoral Commission (IEC), which prepared to tackle AI-generated misinformation ahead of the May elections. Deepfakes were of particular concern, as they could be used to create realistic but fabricated videos or audio clips to mislead voters and tarnish reputations. To combat this, the IEC partnered with civil society organisations and tech companies to raise awareness and provide fact-checking tools like "Padre" (Naki, 2004). While deepfakes were prominent in the discussions, many disinformation efforts relied on traditional tactics such as sharing out-of-context images and fabricated claims about vote rigging and political endorsements. For example, AI-generated videos, including one featuring Donald Trump endorsing a South African political party, were shared widely but identified as fake. Despite the limited number of

Table 10.1 Some articles on AI and elections

	Article	*Publications*	*Themes*
1.	Deepfakes in South Africa: Protecting your image online is the key to fighting them (February 22, 2024)	The Conversation	Manipulation
2.	Artificial Intelligence and the integrity of African elections (March 26, 2024)	International IDEA	Maintaining trust, transparency, and fairness
3.	South Africa: Cheap politics and deep fakes—The use of AI-generated content ahead of South Africa's election (April 5, 2024)	All Africa	Disinformation and/or hate speech and manipulation
4.	How meta is preparing for the 2024 South African elections (April 12, 2024)	Meta	Fact checking and harmful content
5.	AI and the 2024 South African elections (May 9, 2024)	EISA	Disinformation and manipulation
6.	Pro-Russian accounts fuel polarisation as South Africa's elections near (May 9, 2024)	African Digital Democracy Observatory	Interference
7.	Can Artificial Intelligence on steroids hijack an election? (May 12, 2024)	Daily Maverick	Manipulation
8.	South Africa's pivotal 2024 election: Maintaining democratic processes and trust amid digital challenges 30 years since the fall of apartheid (May 24, 2024)	Oxford University	Mis-disinformation
9.	Elections will reveal SA's exposure to digital influence as a service (May 28, 2024)	ISS	Manipulation
10.	The WIRED AI Elections Project (May 30, 2024)	Wired	Manipulation

(continued)

Table 10.1 (continued)

Article		*Publications*	*Themes*
11.	AI can make African elections more efficient—But trust must be built and proper rules put in place (June 17, 2024)	The Conversation	Good and bad of AI
12.	Harnessing Artificial Intelligence (AI) for Transparent Elections: A New Dawn for African Democracy (June 20, 2024)	NEPAD	Transparency
13.	The role of artificial intelligence in African elections (July 03, 2024)	Centre for Human Rights	Ethical concerns
14.	Expectations versus reality: The use of generative AI in South Africa's 2024 election (July 18, 2024)	Polity	Disinformation and manipulation

Source Author

such AI-driven campaigns, the misuse of generative AI was recognised as a growing threat (Dube, 2024). In addition to disinformation, AI was employed to manipulate voter sentiment by creating psychological profiles to craft persuasive political messages. This ability to micro-target voters raised concerns about the ethical implications of using AI in political campaigning. Despite these challenges, AI was also utilised for positive purposes, such as voter education through bots that provided essential election information (EISA, 2024).

Furthermore, a significant apprehension in these articles concerned foreign intervention, particularly from Russia, portrayed in the Western-aligned media as the main culprit in disinformation endeavours during elections. The year 2024, according to these articles, witnessed evident signs of coordinated efforts to sway voter behaviour, with social media platforms emerging as pivotal battlegrounds for such influence operations. Given perceived Russia's historical engagement in spreading misinformation, notably observed during the Ukraine conflict, the implications of such activities within the context of South Africa's historical ties with Russia and ongoing political dynamics amplified concerns. The reporting on the conflict in Ukraine and the underlying biases present in South African online commercial media, which often heavily lean on Western sources, inevitably export Western norms, standards, hegemonic narratives, and worldviews, notwithstanding (Radebe, 2022).

Moreover, these articles raised the issue of rampant dissemination of disinformation on platforms like WhatsApp, characterised by minimal content regulation, facilitated the rapid circulation of false narratives. The widespread connectivity across South Africa, with a substantial user base exceeding 45 million individuals, underscored the gravity of the situation and the swift propagation of misleading content. These narratives underscore the inherent challenges South Africa is encountering in safeguarding its democratic processes against the multifaceted threats posed by both domestic and international actors harnessing AI for perception manipulation. Calls for the establishment of a regulatory framework guiding AI integration in elections, emphasising the imperative of African ownership of technological infrastructures to safeguard democratic values, were echoed as critical recommendations. Moreover, the imperative for cultivating a nuanced comprehension of AI technologies among African nations indicated a pressing necessity for capacity-building initiatives and heightened awareness to navigate the intricate landscapes introduced by AI within electoral frameworks.

In their report on how foreign actors use digital techniques to undermine democracy, Tenove et al. (2018) emphasise mass misinformation and propaganda campaigns, micro-targeted manipulation, and trolling operations as common tactics employed. Additionally, foreign actors often seek to undermine fair opportunities for citizen participation, vibrant public deliberation, and the effectiveness of democratic institutions and rules. Domestic actors frequently facilitate this interference, who inadvertently or deliberately act as de facto partners in these efforts. The success of such tactics is often attributable to deficits in digital literacy, shortcomings in the design and policies of social media platforms, high levels of political polarisation, and the absence of robust international laws and practices to address cyber-attacks and information operations (Tenove et al., 2018).

The pre- and post-COVID-19 era has been marked by a surge in fake news, largely driven by technological advancements. These developments pose a significant threat to democratic processes. Despite efforts to combat the spread of fake news, it continues to challenge social media platforms, citizens, lawmakers, governments, and businesses alike.

According to Mtsweni et al. (2023), the spread of misinformation in South Africa is predominantly driven by male users of mobile devices in affluent regions such as the Western Cape and Gauteng. While social media has played a crucial role in supporting democratic discourse, this positive influence has been increasingly undermined by the proliferation of "misinformation, propaganda, and controversy" on platforms like Facebook and X, which disseminate both legitimate political discourse and fake news in equal measure (Chirwa & Manyana, 2021: 59).

While social media can create spaces for diverse political viewpoints, especially in contexts where there is unequal access to resources—as seen in the 2024 South Africa elections, which saw a record number of small political parties contesting—it also facilitates the spread of disinformation that can undermine democratic norms. Numerous studies have established clear linkages between social media disinformation and the erosion of democratic processes, highlighting how government and political party disinformation can weaken key democratic principles (Hunter, 2023).

For example, the trend of fake news in South Africa gained significant momentum during the COVID-19 pandemic, prompting the government to create a special platform for combating fake news related to issues like the sale of alcohol, cigarettes, and vaccination (see www.gov.za). This trend continued into the 2024 election year, exacerbated by more advanced technologies such as generative AI, which not only threaten democracy but also hold potential for its protection and consolidation. Examples of election-related fake news include a fabricated voice note attributed to former Sports, Arts, and Culture Minister Zizi Kodwa, falsely discussing the state of the South African economy, which circulated widely on social media and was later debunked by a media statement (Patel, 2024). Another instance involved a doctored video purportedly showing President Cyril Ramaphosa snubbing former President Thabo Mbeki at the funeral of renowned photojournalist Dr Peter Magubane in January 2024. Similarly, ANC Secretary-General Fikile Mbalula and EFF leader Julius Malema were targets of manipulated videos that circulated on social media.

The prevalence of misinformation in political competition has enabled candidates and their media allies to spread false information about policy issues, leading to public confusion and blurring the line between truth and fiction. This deliberate misinformation aims to mislead the public and sow discord (Ogwezzy-Ndisika et al., 2023). Foreign actors drive some of these efforts with geopolitical agendas seeking to influence the election outcome. For instance, several studies from the Global North have analysed the threats posed by countries like China and Russia in election manipulation, suggesting that these major powers actively engage in such practices to further their strategic interests (Chechelashvili et al., 2023; Vićić & Gartzke, 2024). The South African elections illustrate the growing threat that AI-driven technologies and social media disinformation pose to democratic processes. As these tools become more sophisticated, there is an urgent need for robust policy mechanisms to safeguard democracy against both domestic and foreign manipulation.

Low Voter Turnout and the Hidden Influence of AI

While it may be premature to draw definitive conclusions about potential interference in South Africa's 2024 elections, the low voter turnout raises concerns about the deliberate sowing of confusion, which may have led many to abstain from voting. This phenomenon could potentially be linked to the subtle influence of AI-driven disinformation campaigns. The 2024 elections in South Africa revealed a striking correlation between voter turnout and racial demographics. The overall voter turnout was 58.5%, but the participation varied significantly across different racial groups: turnout was highest in predominantly white areas at 71%, followed by Indian regions at 64%, coloured areas at 58%, and African areas at 55% (Scholtz, 2024). This disparity in voter participation had a tangible impact on the election results, with traditionally ANC strongholds experiencing notably lower turnout. This raises the question: could the prevalence of misinformation and disinformation have contributed to this uneven voter engagement?

The influence of fake news on voters is multifaceted. Some voters may gullibly accept everything they encounter. In contrast, others, overwhelmed by the sheer volume of disinformation, may become sceptical of even legitimate information, ultimately disengaging from the electoral process altogether. This widespread confusion could be a significant factor behind the low voter turnout, particularly among the ANC's core constituencies, who failed to attend the polls. There is speculation that this outcome may have been partially orchestrated by international actors seeking to undermine the ANC as the ruling party. This underscores the need for further investigation into the potential role of AI-driven disinformation in shaping electoral outcomes, particularly in contexts where voter engagement is already vulnerable to manipulation.

Policy Conundrum

In the lead-up to and during the 2024 elections, various social media platforms were criticised for failing to adequately moderate overtly right-wing content that was anti-migrant, ethnonationalist, and racist. For instance, the slogan "mabahambe" (loosely: let them go) used by the Patriotic Alliance, along with videos of its leader Gayton McKenzie chasing "Zimbabweans" at the border, circulated widely without being checked or removed. These examples highlight the significant limitations of current content moderation strategies on social media platforms. Relying solely on algorithms to moderate content has proven to be insufficient. While effective in some contexts, AI-based models often underperform when confronted with examples of out-of-distribution that differ from the training data. Moreover, existing detection tools for hate speech have been found to lack fairness, as biases in the training datasets or the absence of various dialects can lead to skewed classification results (Singhal & Bedi, 2024). Another major weakness in moderation is that content on platforms like TikTok and YouTube frequently migrates to offline platforms such as WhatsApp, where it can circulate without any oversight or moderation.

Given these challenges, it is essential to address issues of fairness and inequality by ensuring that AI decisions are fair and non-discriminatory. This is a critical ethical challenge in the deployment of AI technologies. Additionally, AI systems must align with human values and avoid conflicts of interest, mainly when profit maximisation is at stake. Questions surrounding AI decisions' responsibility, appealability, and explainability are crucial for maintaining transparency and trust. AI ethics, therefore, requires a collaborative approach involving policymakers, AI companies, and individuals to guide the development, deployment, and use of these technologies (Straight et al., 2024). Indeed, it is evident that AI has the potential to be misused to spread misinformation, manipulate voter opinions, and exacerbate cybersecurity vulnerabilities. The risks associated with AI-generated disinformation, cyber-attacks on election infrastructure, and the ethical concerns of voter manipulation through psychological profiling have been well documented (Yu, 2024). In this context, the regulation of AI becomes an urgent and critical issue.

Governments and policymakers must design and develop effective strategies to combat the growing threat of digital interference. Key measures that could be implemented include digital literacy training for citizens to reduce confusion and design and policy reforms by social media platforms that emphasise accessible content moderation within the country. These platforms should also ensure the availability of adequate human resources for this task. For example, many countries in the Global South, particularly Africa, have expressed concerns about the lack of human contact when attempting to raise issues or complaints with platforms like Facebook (Meta). Furthermore, governments must collaborate with international regulators, such as the African Union (AU) and the European Union (EU), to address cyber interference effectively (Tenove et al., 2018).

Another critical area for regulators to address is the development of policy initiatives to protect privacy, particularly for vulnerable populations (Aral & Eckles, 2019). To mitigate the impact of fake news and societal polarisation, especially during elections, some scholars have advocated for a "responsibility-based approach" for social media platforms. In this framework, social media providers should be encouraged to minimise societal risks through responsible actions in human rights, education, and transparency of algorithmic decisions (Reisach, 2021). To this end, the discourse on regulating social media platforms must extend beyond the U.S. and EU, given the global impact of these companies, particularly in the Global South. This is especially important considering the power asymmetry, as many countries in the Global South lack significant bargaining power (Takhshid, 2021).

Conclusion: Future Implications and Recommendations

South Africa's 2024 elections were not merely a reflection of local political dynamics but were also deeply intertwined with global trends. For instance, the country had to navigate diplomatic tensions with the U.S. following public allegations made by the U.S. ambassador that arms or related technologies were loaded onto a Russian ship. At the same time, it was docked at South Africa's Naval Base (Ray & Walsh, 2023). Furthermore, South Africa's stance on the Russia-Ukraine war, including the view that it could have been avoided had NATO heeded warnings from within its own ranks (Alden, 2023), and the country's non-alignment, perceived as resistance to Western imperialism, highlighted these global influences. These complexities coincided with South Africa hosting the 15th BRICS Summit, where Putin's expected attendance placed the country in an invidious position (van der Westhuizen, 2024).

This chapter began with the premise that AI has the potential to disrupt democracies and that, although conclusive evidence is still forthcoming, the 2024 South African elections were likely influenced by the manipulation of AI technologies. This is argued to be a severe threat to democratic processes. The prevalence of fake news in South Africa is driven by high internet and mobile device penetration, extensive use of social media platforms like Facebook and X, and messaging platforms such as WhatsApp, coupled with high media freedom (Madrid-Morales et al., 2021). In this context, it is argued that the low voter turnout, which primarily affected the ruling ANC, leading to its drop below 50% for the first time since the advent of democracy in 1994, may be attributed to deliberate sabotage. Although it is still premature to attribute these influences on AI and possible manipulations akin to the Cambridge Analytica scandal (Hinds et al., 2020; Ondiek & Onyango, 2023), there is a genuine need for caution. For this reason, policymakers must proactively consider ways to combat the negative aspects of AI while encouraging its positive potential to safeguard democracy.

AI, built on big data and integrated with the pervasive devices and sensors of the Internet of Things, now permeates almost every facet of society, including political discourse and democratic decision-making. Therefore, it is imperative to insist on the principles of the rule of law as a foundation for policy formulation and regulation (Nemitz, 2018). While the coexistence of the positive and negative aspects of AI in society is undeniable, policies must safeguard the interests of the public, particularly the vulnerable, including countries in the Global South. Failing to anchor new technologies in the rule of law could lead to further compromises in democratic processes and a flagrant disregard for legal norms, as observed in the Facebook-Cambridge Analytica scandal. Thus, the relationship between technology and democracy must be understood in the context of the power concentration of big tech companies (Nemitz, 2018), making it imperative to regulate these entities to ensure they produce technologies for the public good. While AI technologies undoubtedly have positive aspects, such as enhancing the quality of democratic processes by helping policymakers understand public opinion, identifying controversial issues, and influencing policy planning and implementation (Milano et al., 2014), as well as empowering civil society to improve political participation (Savaget et al., 2019), we must remain vigilant to the dangers they pose. These dangers carry the potential for significant negative consequences for democracy. Given the observed impact of AI during the COVID-19 pandemic, civil unrest, and elections in South Africa, policymakers need to seriously engage in mitigating the negative aspects of AI. The proposed AI policy framework for South Africa, released by the Department of Communications and Digital Technologies in August 2024, provides a solid starting point. This framework acknowledges the need to balance the effective and beneficial exploitation of AI's advantages against ethical, social, and economic imperatives.

While policymakers and advocates in liberal democracies may prioritise safeguarding citizens' rights due to concerns over the political takeover of the justice system and partisan control of law enforcement, which have limited legal protections against AI-related violations (Konopczyński & Fellowship, 2024), countries in the Global South, such as South Africa, have a different set of priorities. These include safeguarding sovereignty, protecting data privacy, and addressing data colonialism and imperialism, where the U.S., for example, is seen as reinventing colonialism in the Global South through the domination of digital technologies (Kwet, 2019). While advocating for equality from a Global South perspective is crucial, it is equally important to recognise that the companies and countries leading in AI technologies are often developing these technologies not for benevolent purposes but to remain competitive and extract profit, particularly from consumers in the Global South. Policymakers in the Global South must remain aware of this reality. Therefore, their policy interventions should align with the social economy discourse, which advances the idea of social and economic well-being for the entire global population, ensuring that wealth distribution is equitable to reduce the gap between the rich and the poor (Rascão, 2023). It is incumbent upon policymakers to drive the AI technology discourse premised on inclusivity and development for all.

References

Africa Check. (2024). Will the real slim shady please stand up? *Eminem video endorsing South African opposition party EFF and bashing the ruling ANC is a deepfake*. Africa check. (May 22, 2024). https://africacheck.org/factchecks/meta-programme-fact-checks/will-real-slim-shady-please-stand-eminem-video-endorsing

Ajala, O. (2022). The case for neutrality: Understanding African stances on the Russia-Ukraine conflict. *Journal of Military and Strategic Studies, 22*(2), 129–153.

Alden, C. (2023, September). The Global South and Russia's invasion of Ukraine. In *Ukraine* (p. 359).

Alibašić, H. (2024). *The post-factual polity: Ethical, governance, administrative, and policy crises in the disinformation era*. IAP.

Aral, S., & Eckles, D. (2019). Protecting elections from social media manipulation. *Science, 365*(6456), 858–861.

Bloomberg UK. (2024). *Pro-Russia X Accounts Tout Zuma's South African Party*. CIR Says. (May 22, 2024). https://www.bloomberg.com/news/articles/2024-04-02/zuma-russia-x-accounts-backing-russia-support-zuma-s-mk

Brosig, M. (2024). Aligned or non-aligned: South Africa's response to the war in Ukraine. *Global Policy, 15*, 757–761.

Chechelashvili, M., Berikashvili, L., & Malania, E. (2023). Foreign interference in electoral processes as a factor of international politics: Mechanisms and counteraction. *Foreign Affairs, 33*, 52–62.

Chenzi, V. (2021). Fake news, social media and xenophobia in South Africa. *African Identities, 19*(4), 502–521.

Chirwa, C., & Manyana, Z. (2021). The rise of Fake news: Surveying the effects of social media on informed democracy. *The Thinker, 88*(3), 59–66.

Cooper, A. F., & Thakur, R. (2023). The staying power of the BRICS. In *International organization and global governance* (pp. 307–320). Routledge.

Dauvergne, P. (2022). Is artificial intelligence greening global supply chains? Exposing the political economy of environmental costs. *Review of International Political Economy, 29*(3), 696–718.

de Wet, H., & Marivate, V. (2021, September). *Is it fake? News disinformation detection on south african news websites*. 2021 IEEE AFRICON, pp. 1–6. IEEE.

Dmonte, A., Zampieri, M., Lybarger, K., & Albanese, M. (2024). *Classifying human-generated and AI-generated election claims in social media*. arXiv preprint arXiv:2404.16116.

Donati, D. (2023). Mobile Internet access and political outcomes: Evidence from South Africa. *Journal of Development Economics, 162*, 103073.

Dube, T (2024, March 20). *Doctored video does not show Trump backing new South African party*. AFP, Fact Check. https://factcheck.afp.com/doc.afp.com.34LT2UZ (Accessed 8 September 2024).

Electoral Institute for Sustainable Democracy in Africa (EISA). (2024). *AI and the 2024 South African elections*. https://www.eisa.org/ai-and-the-2024-south-african-elections/

Hawes, B., Hall, D. W., & Ryan, M. (2023). *Can artificial intelligence be used to undermine elections?*

Hinds, J., Williams, E. J., & Joinson, A. N. (2020). "It wouldn't happen to me": Privacy concerns and perspectives following the Cambridge Analytica scandal. *International Journal of Human-Computer Studies, 143*, 102498.

Howard, P. N., Woolley, S., & Calo, R. (2018). Algorithms, bots, and political communication in the US 2016 election: The challenge of automated political communication for election law and administration. *Journal of Information Technology & Politics, 15*(2), 81–93.

Hunter, L. Y. (2023). Social media, disinformation, and democracy: How different types of social media usage affect democracy cross-nationally. *Democratisation, 30*(6), 1040–1072.

Iida, T., Song, J., Estrada, J. L., & Takahashi, Y. (2024). Fake news and its electoral consequences: A survey experiment on Mexico. *AI & Society, 39*(3), 1065–1078.

Kan, C.H. (2024). Artificial intelligence (AI) in the age of democracy and human rights: normative challenges and regulatory perspectives. *International Journal of Eurasian Education and Culture, 9*(25), 145–166.

Konopczyński, F., & Fellowship, R. C. (2024). *AI policy in EU illiberal democracies*.

Kumar, P. (2023). 15th BRICS summit: Key takeaways and their relevance. *The Round Table, 112*(5), 549–550.

Kwet, M. (2019). Digital colonialism: US empire and the new imperialism in the Global South. *Race & Class, 60*(4), 3–26.

Madrid-Morales, D., Wasserman, H., Gondwe, G., Ndlovu, K., Sikanku, E., Tully, M., ... & Uzuegbunam, C. (2021). Comparative approaches to mis/disinformation| motivations for sharing misinformation: A comparative study in six Sub-Saharan African countries. *International Journal of Communication, 15*, 20.

Manheim, K., & Kaplan, L. (2019). Artificial intelligence: Risks to privacy and democracy. *Yale Journal of Law & Technology, 21*, 106.

Marsden, C., Meyer, T., & Brown, I. (2020). Platform values and democratic elections: How can the law regulate digital disinformation? *Computer Law & Security Review, 36*, 105373.

Maweu, J. M. (2019). Fake elections? Cyber propaganda, disinformation and the 2017 general elections in Kenya. *African Journalism Studies, 40*(4), 62–76.

McInnes, K. (2024). *South African digital & social media statistics 2024*. https://www.meltwater.com/en/blog/social-media-statistics-south-africa (Accessed July 29).

Milano, M., O'Sullivan, B., & Gavanelli, M. (2014). Sustainable policy making: A strategic challenge for artificial intelligence. *AI Magazine, 35*(3), 22–35.

Mtsweni, J., Ndlovu, L., Mthethwa, S., & Mkuzangwe, N. (2023). Measuring misinformation trends on social media in South Africa using Machine Learning. In *International Conference on Artificial Intelligence and its Applications* (pp. 128–133).

Naki, E. (2004, March 4). Elections 2024: IEC ready to fend off deep fakes. *The Citizen*. https://www.citizen.co.za/news/south-africa/elections/elections-2024-iec-ready-to-fend-off-deep-fakes/ (Accessed 8 September 2024).

Nemitz, P. (2018). Constitutional democracy and technology in the age of artificial intelligence. *Philosophical Transactions of the Royal Society A: Mathematical, Physical and Engineering Sciences, 376*(2133), 20180089.

Ogwezzy-Ndisika, A. O., Amakoh, K. O., Ajibade, O., Lawal, T. O., & Faustino, B. A. (2023). Fake News and General Elections in Nigeria. In *Nigerian media industries in the era of globalization* (p. 61). Bloomsbury.

Omondi, M., Adesanya, A. A., Otieno, G., Kioko, M., & Ogieomo, E. Y. (2024). *Elections in Africa: Trends, diversity, and emerging technologies*. Co-Creation Hub. https://govote.ng/wp-content/uploads/2024/09/Election-in-Africa-I.pdf

Ondiek, J., & Onyango, G. (2023). Realising digitalised electoral process in Africa: Public policy implications from Kenya's electoral technology systems. In *African Governance in the Digital Age* (Tayarisha Working Paper Series, No: 2023/005). University of the Witwatersrand, Johannesburg. https://wiredspace.wits.ac.za/server/api/core/bitstreams/ee26f3ec-0111-4259-abbc-16436877b0bf/content

Özekin, M. K., & Sune, E. (2023). Contesting hegemony: The rise of BRICS and the crisis of US-led Western hegemony in the MENA region. *The Korean Journal of International Studies, 21*(3), 409–446.

Patel, F. (2024, June 11). Zizi Kodwa dismisses 'fake voice note' about SA economy. *Citizen online*. https://www.citizen.co.za/news/zizi-kodwa-fake-voice-note-sa-economy/ (Accessed 2 September 2024).

Posetti, J., & Matthews, A. (2018). A short guide to the history of 'fake news' and disinformation. *International Center for Journalists, 7*(2018), 201.

Putranto, R. P. A., & Aristawidya, N. S. (2023, December). *The influence of AI technology in election modernisation on Indigenous tribal people. International Conference for Democracy and National Resilience (ICDNR 2023)*, pp. 323–328. Atlantis Press.

Radebe, M. J. (2022). New features of media imperialism: The South African online media and the coverage of the Ukrainian war. *Communicare: Journal for Communication Sciences in Southern Africa, 41*(2), 75–89.

Radebe, M. J., & Prashad, V. (2023, June 25). *The United States cannot tolerate an independent South Africa*. Peoples Dispatch.

Rascão, J. (2023). Challenges of the democracy of the future, in the digital society (from theory to practice). *American Journal of Humanities and Social Sciences Research.*

Ray, C. A., & Walsh, M. (2023). *Russia's alleged arms shipment in South Africa.*

Reisach, U. (2021). The responsibility of social media in times of societal and political manipulation. *European Journal of Operational Research, 291*(3), 906–917.

Robles, P., & Mallinson, D. J. (2023). Artificial intelligence technology, public trust, and effective governance. *Journal of Information Technology & Politics, 20*(2), 196–211.

Savaget, P., Chiarini, T., & Evans, S. (2019). Empowering political participation through artificial intelligence. *Science and Public Policy, 46*(3), 369–380.

Schmidt, A. (2024). *Russian disinformation in Africa: Threat to democracy and reinforcement of authoritarianism and corruption.* [Master's thesis, Université catholique de Louvain]. UCLouvain Thesis Repository. https://thesis.dial.uclouvain.be/server/api/core/bitstreams/bd2d6eda-56d0-44dd-b0cf-b7f9e06ed347/content

Scholtz, D. (2024, June 7). 2024 political earthquake: How shock results unfolded. *News24.* https://www.news24.com/opinions/fridaybriefing/2024-political-earthquake-how-shock-results-unfolded-20240607

Siddo, B. I. (2024, April 12). *How Meta is preparing for the 2024 South African elections.* Meta. https://about.fb.com/news/2024/04/how-meta-is-preparing-for-the-2024-south-african-elections/

Singhal, K., & Bedi, J. (2024). Transformers at HSD-2Lang 2024: Hate speech detection in Arabic and Turkish tweets using BERT based architectures. In *Proceedings of the 7th Workshop on Challenges and Applications of Automated Extraction of Socio-political Events from Text (CASE 2024)* (pp. 190–194).

Smuha, N. A. (2021). Beyond a human rights-based approach to AI governance: Promise, pitfalls, plea. *Philosophy & Technology, 34*(1), 91–104.

Stachofsky, J., Schaupp, L. C., & Crossler, R. E. (2023). Measuring the effect of political alignment, platforms, and fake news consumption on voter concern for election processes. *Government Information Quarterly, 40*(3), 101810.

Straight, R., Lowery, J., Poehlman, D., & Yowika, W. (2024). Preparing post humanist perspectives on AI human collaboration in developing cyber ethics curricula. In *Proceedings of the ISCAP Conference ISSN* (Vol. 2473, p. 4901).

Stevenson, K. (2024). Artificial intelligence: A double-edged sword in elections. Educational Administration. *Theory and Practice, 30*(4), 1660–1667. https://doi.org/10.53555/kuey.v30i4.1724

Syrovátka, J., Hořejš, N., & Komasová, S. (2023). Towards a model that measures the impact of disinformation on elections. *European View, 22*(1), 119–130.

Takhshid, Z. (2021). Regulating social media in the global south. *Vanderbilt Journal Entertainment Technology Law, 24*, 1–56.

Tenove, C., Buffie, J., McKay, S., & Moscrop, D. (2018). *Digital threats to democratic elections: How foreign actors use digital techniques to undermine democracy*.

Tregenna, F., & Radebe, M. J. (2024). *Exploring the impact of ethnonationalism on South Africa's 2024 electoral outcome*. [Unpublished manuscript].

van der Westhuizen, J. (2024). Ukraine, the 2023 BRICS Summit and South Africa's non-alignment crisis. *Contemporary Security Policy, 45*(4), 612–626.

Vićić, J., & Gartzke, E. (2024). Cyber-enabled influence operations as a 'center of gravity' in cyberconflict: The example of Russian foreign interference in the 2016 US federal election. *Journal of Peace Research, 61*(1), 10–27.

Wasserman, H., & Madrid-Morales, D. (2019). Disinformation in the Global South. In *The Routledge companion to media disinformation and populism* (pp. 246–255). Routledge.

Yu, C. (2024). *How will AI steal our elections?* Center for Open Science.

CHAPTER 11

Reimaging Peacebuilding on the African Continent: AI an Alternative to Strengthening Institutional Capacities and Conflict Mitigation

Shaun Kinnes and Tshidi Green

Introduction

With its vast potential for development and prosperity, most African countries have continuously been plagued by violence and instability, fostering a reality of instability and conditions unconducive to development. The emergence of conflict in several pockets on the continent has ultimately fuelled contagion, resulting in entire regions falling victim to acts of genocide, terrorist attacks, sexual violence and intimidation, including the derailing of their democracies (McGuirk & Burke, 2020). Peacekeeping

S. Kinnes (✉)
University of Witwatersrand, Johannesburg, South Africa
e-mail: shaunkinnes@yahoo.com

T. Green
University of Witwatersrand, Johannesburg, South Africa

G. Onyango (ed.), *Designing Artificial Intelligence for Public Policy and Governance in Africa*, Studies in National Governance and Emerging Technologies, https://doi.org/10.1007/978-3-031-83445-5_11

forces, either sponsored by regional bodies or international organisations, have routinely intervened in the conflict to end violence while aiming to restore order and control the monopoly of force. United Nations peacekeeping forces, including regional forces such as the African Stand by Force, NATO and several private military corporations such as the Russian Wagner Group and South African security firms, Executive Outcomes and Dyck Industries, have been the main security players within the African security landscape (Pokalova, n.d.). Intervening forces have, in many instances, achieved relative success in restoring peace. Still, they have also seen peace missions fail due to poor planning, poor judgment, and a lack of knowledge of the geographical terrain where battles occasionally occur. This chapter contributes to this body of research while exploring the potential application of AI to assist with designing intervention actions in conflict mitigation. Specifically, it begins with exploring the rise of artificial intelligence (AI) technologies and how governments and peacebuilding forces could employ them to foster institutionalisation processes. As variedly shown by most chapters in this volume, when programmed effectively, AI can reduce biases, human perspectives, and human-based rationality rooted in personal experiences, resulting in high possibilities of achieving more optimised policy decisions (Plantinga, 2024). This makes AI an objective, systematic, and impartial alternative for decision-making, crucial for peacekeeping and security decisions.

In this chapter, we show how AI can assist in mitigating and eradicating the surge of terrorism, rebel groups, and civil conflict in three African states—Mozambique, Mali, and the Democratic Republic of Congo. It is based on the premise that intelligence groups and hostile enemies have traditionally seen the physical landscape as a constantly changing factor in conflict (Suharjo et al., 2024). This suggests that it is time for actors to view technology as a constantly changing landscape and should be utilised to end violence and drive stability within Africa (Kol et al., 2023). This could be particularly useful within the conflicts in Africa. Artificial intelligence could be employed in this instance, as omniscient autonomous vehicles could be utilised in cases such as the Mozambican province of Cabo Delgado, where peacekeeping efforts have faced immense challenges due to the landscape and scope of the conflict (Svicevic & Bradley, 2024). In this scenario, artificial intelligence can be employed to navigate terrain usually unconducive to conventional vehicles.

Civil conflict and domestic terrorism are the most common factors undermining the African landscape (Hunter et al., 2023). Hence, by assessing omniscient autonomous vehicles, big-data-driven modelling, wargaming, and AI-driven ISR systems, this project showcases how these AI technologies can level the playing field and tip the scales in favour of intervening forces when entering hostile territory. The research examines three African states; Mozambique, Mali, and the Democratic Republic of Congo, each demonstrating varying degrees of conflict. It explores the possibility AI presents in assisting the mitigation and eradication of the surge of terrorism, rebel groups, and civil conflict within the three states. The paper rests on the premise that intelligence groups and hostile enemies have long viewed the physical landscape as a constantly changing factor within conflict and suggests that it is time that these parties see technology as a constantly changing landscape as well, one which must be both mitigated against and employed as a means to end violence and drive stability within the African continent.

Literature Review

Recent literature within the discourse on liberal peacekeeping has alluded to the shortfalls and ineffectiveness of peacekeeping operations in Africa. Despite major pushes from regional and international organisations to expand Africa's peace and security architecture, the quantitative data does not indicate any substantive reduction of violent conflicts or their consequences. A study by Malte Brosig and Norman Sempijja (2018) examined 11 indicators that comprehensively measure security and applied them to the data relevant to various conflicts within Africa. These indicators ranged from violence against civilians, domestic unrest, battle deaths, and domestic governance to political stability. The study concluded that contrary to their intended goal, conflicts persisted despite the large-scale deployment of peacekeepers (Brosig & Sempijja, 2018). Peacekeeping missions have increased exponentially in size and scale. In 2017/2018, the UN was estimated to have spent $6.8bn on peacekeeping with three large-scale operations consisting of an accumulated 20,000 peacekeeping troops deployed in Africa alone, namely within Sudan, Somalia and the Democratic Republic of Congo (UN General Assembly, 2018).

However, quantitative research examining a wider range of security indicators has demonstrated that the increased deployment of human and financial peacekeeping capital has not effectively stopped or reduced the violence and presence of these conflicts. Yamakawa (2019) examines plausible reasons for the failure of peacekeeping missions. In his paper titled 'Peacekeeping Conditions for an Artificial Intelligence Society' (2019), he outlines three biological constraints humans have that limit and hinder our ability to unite and our propensity to wage war and engage in conflict. The paper further claims that a migration to artificial intelligence, specifically within warfare and peacekeeping, would mitigate the shortfalls associated with human error and human nature. Within his study, he attributes the rise and prevalence of war to our innate desire to ensure our survival. In this context, he argues that we are biologically designed to fend for our survival; living in a system with limited resources and limited means to sustain life propels us into competition and eventual conflict to acquire resources necessary for survival. Secondly, he argues that humans are prone to conflict because of our propensity to organise ourselves according to our ethnic, religious, cultural and socio-political identities. He attributes this self-organisation and self-mobilisation to evolution and the struggles between specifies in pursuit of resources and survival.

Lastly, he argues that humans are victims of our biases and rationality. Decisions are usually made because of our interpretation and experience of a particular situation; our perceptions and conclusions manifest our sympathetic or apathetic views towards a particular situation or scenario. We are also limited by language and the extent to which we are able to communicate and understand ideas, reason and meaning within conversations (Yamakawa, 2019). Attempts to bring rationality and sincerity into the discourses around negotiated peace suffer great difficulties and often lead to a continuation of violence and conflict. Yamakawa and scholars such as Daniel Oshler and Sharma thus promote the incorporation of artificial intelligence into systems of electronic warfare and peace processes. P. Sharma and N. E. Mastorakis' 2020 paper, titled 'Artificial Intelligence Aided Electronic Warfare Systems—Recent Trends and Evolving Applications', states that modern-day military warfare is characterised by an intricate interplay of complex and evolving technologies that enhance combat fighting by integrating electronics into warfare practices and equipment. These techniques and equipment, referred to as electronic warfare (EW), consist of highly efficient tools that assist all military and defence forces by restricting radio frequency (RF) spectrums. Though EW has significantly improved the efficiency and optimisation of resources, decision-making capabilities remain challenging for military and peace operations. Sharma et al., therefore, promote the integration of artificial intelligence (AI) into the EW security system. They deposit AI as the means to bridge the gap between war-fighting capability and effective decision-making and skills (Sharma et al., 2020).

AI-integrated EW tools enhance decision-making support, codify and analyse large data pools, promote visualisation technologies that predict evolving situations, and promote situational awareness to a capacity well beyond human algorithmic capability. They have reconstructed the nature of military technology and act as autonomous systems and can be extended to be used within threat analysis, logistics, weapon system selection, decision-making support and interpretation of intelligence (Sharma et al., 2020). Militaries across the globe have witnessed an increasing incorporation of AI into EW systems in the form of data process systems. The use of these systems is subdivided into two categories, namely operations and strategy. The former seeks to remove uncertainties, enhance tactical responsiveness, and improve planning. The latter enhances war strategies, departmental organisation, intelligence sharing and analysis, and decision-making capacity, among other objectives. Scholars and proponents of AI argue that incorporating AI into EW and, by extension, peacekeeping operations enhances the overall efficiency of warfare and reduces the risks of operational failures associated with human error and incapacity. Additionally, as Yamakawa (2019) argues, AI is arguably devoid of the risks accompanied by human nature. Unlike humans, AI systems are not dependent on resources for survival and are not driven by the insistent need to protect themselves by eliminating other threats. Furthermore, if programmed effectively, AI could be devoid of biases, human perspectives and human-based rationality rooted in human understanding of experiences. AI, therefore, provides an objective, systematic and impartial alternative to decision-making that is arguably crucial to peacekeeping and security decisions and protocol.

Daniel Olsher provides an account of an AI system that addresses the issues of human bias and human cognitive limitations in his paper titled 'New Artificial Intelligence Tools for Deep Conflict Resolution and Humanitarian Response'; Daniel examines the novel AI system, cogSolv. The AI software acts as a human simulator, in which it analyses and assesses human behaviour and viewpoints in order to create simulated responses, reactions, and decisions that mimic and reflect those of humans from various groups. CogSolv integrates real-world knowledge with the data gathered from observing human behaviour and creates models that can enhance negotiation strategies and outcomes, models that can be used for persuasion and deliberation, and provide peacekeeping decisions and strategies that are most likely to be successfully accepted and implemented (Olsher, 2013). Peacekeeping and humanitarian missions consist of multidimensional and multifaceted social, environmental, political, and economic systems. Responses are generally created and drafted by a complex network of actors who work and sometimes fail to create effective and efficient synergies that merge the various areas needed for a functional response plan and implementation process. Information is shared across various networks between different actors and, therefore, faces the great risk of communication delays, misunderstanding, or simply the erasure of data and information. Furthermore, actors involved in the response process often lack the information and knowledge relevant to the conflict and humanitarian crisis. Therefore, AI systems such as cogSolv serve to address and correct the shortfalls within the response process by creating a base for equitable, traceable, and comprehensible response process generation (Olsher, 2013).

The existing literature accounts for the need to revisit peacekeeping systems and operations, specifically the failures of liberal peacekeeping within Africa. Additionally, a substantive amount of research has emerged within recent years that promote the integration of AI into the peace and security architecture as a means to mitigate the failures of peacekeeping that have been associated with human cognitive bias and weakness. Additionally, proponents of AI-integrated EW argue that AI improves the efficiency of peacekeeping both at a strategic and operational level. Given the backdrop provided, an interesting case can be made for the advantages of AI within peace operations and conflict mitigation mechanisms within Africa. To understand the impact AI can have on peacekeeping, examining how AI networks are created and function is necessary. In their paper, Hang Zou, Qiyang Zhao and their colleagues (2024) demonstrate how Generative AI (GenAI) could be connected to wireless networks to enhance collective intelligence and build the foundations for artificial general intelligence (AGI). By doing so, they highlight the intricate ways artificial intelligence networks are formed and the opportunities these networks present. Zou and Zhao demonstrate how GenAI and large language models (LLM), which have been developed on and around generative pre-trained transformers (GPT), rely on large pools of data which is fed from various programmes agents and servers alike to develop and produce common sense reasoning, mathematical solutions and interactive engagement, etc. LLMs use a multi-agent framework in which the environment is observed, a sequence of actions is planned, a reflection from past inputs or experiences is stored and memorised, and plans are finally formulated. This multi-agent framework can be broken down to (i) perception, in which relevant information and data are gathered; (ii) action, in which all tools available to the agent are managed (iii) planning, which refers to the optimisation and creation of actions and lastly, (iv) memory, in which short-term experience is stored to generate low-term knowledge. The sophistication of LLMs has led to their adoption in fields such as robotics, healthcare, finance, and telecommunications. Therefore, they have a crucial role in enhancing artificial general intelligence (Zou et al., 2024).

Thilo Hagendorff and Katharina Wezel (2020) further expand on how AI networks function by assessing the challenges within their system operation. They highlight the methodological, societal and technological challenges which AI faces. They argue that AI systems' data collection and processing are largely manipulated to perform computations with visually presented results. This process is problematic in and of itself as the systems do not necessarily correspond with reality and are instead the result of filtering through the selection of data and the manipulation and distortion thereof. Furthermore, they critique the supervised learning model of data collection, which many AI systems rely on, as they argue that it merely perpetuates the past, therefore critiquing the reliance on 'memory' to generate plans and actions. They critique the AI system and LLM's reliance on algorithms to gather data and present trained suggestions and solutions, as algorithms are argued to lack flexibility in their application and functionality. Their critiques, which span various aspects of AI systems, rest largely on the shortfalls within the data collection, interpretation, and application in which these systems are trained and developed.

These shortfalls in its function also highlight the importance of ethical practices when utilising powerful advancements such as artificial intelligence, more especially within a conflict environment. Damian Okaibedi, Kutoma Wakunuma, and Simisola Akintoye highlight how AI promises to bring about important socio-cultural changes to Africa in sectors such as political activity, healthcare, agriculture, transportation and environmental sustainability (Eke et al., 2023). All these sectors are crucial to ending and mitigating the negative effects of artificial intelligence. Hence, ethics must guide the implementation of ethical practices when employing artificial intelligence in healthcare, political activity and the environment. Responsibility is thus closely related to pillars such as accountability and exercising control over functions and systems. Hence, it is important that AI is employed within the African battlefield to reflect the dynamics of the African people and landscape. Within this paradigm, Okaibedi, Wakunuma, and Akintoye draw on how adoption, adaptation and access should be accounted for under the umbrella of responsible AI.

Prediction is also key in informing strategies to drive resilience to conflict within the African landscape. As national treasuries develop predictive models to prepare for global economic shocks, so must African conflict planners develop models to predict conflict-caused ills such as migration, disease, and weapons flow. Vito D' Orazio and Yin Lu demonstrate how automated machine learning systems are crucial in developing predictive conflict models, which develop algorithms to predict conflict (Brandt et al., 2022). It is important to note that artificial technologies will bring about new security issues. These new security challenges include hybrid warfare and lack of arms control on artificial intelligence technologies capable of undermining national security. Jovana Marovic highlights how interference in electoral processes and disinformation may become more prevalent within this age of AI in which the world finds itself (Biscop, 2019). The Russian Federation and North Korea have become particularly good at carrying out acts of electoral interference and disinformation. North Korean disinformation campaigns against South Korea and Russian cyber-attacks against Ukraine and its European neighbours have almost become the norm, especially since the Russian invasion of Ukraine. Such activities pose great harm to the democracies of states, more especially on the African continent, as dictatorial regimes may employ artificial technologies to influence or swing elections in their favour.

Ultimately, the seeming lack of control conventions placed on dangerous AI technologies also entails that access to such technologies is too under-regulated and too easily accessible by groups and persons who seek to employ such advancement to undermine stability. Dick Zandee argues that just as nuclear and ballistic missiles are subject to arms control conventions limiting their use and accessibility, so should artificial intelligence be regulated using treaties and conventions; treaties, such as the Ballistic Missile Treaty and Conventional Forces in Europe Treaty, serve to safeguard nuclear weapons. Hence, the same arms control measures must be placed upon the artificial realm.

Benefits of AI in Mitigating Conflict in Mozambique, DRC, and Mali

The common notion of the Weberian state entails that the state maintains control over the use of force within its demarcated territory, commonly referred to as the monopoly of force. Countless African states struggle to consolidate this due to a lack of state capacity, under-resourced armed forces, and social ills, which range from unemployment to HIV/AIDS (Morgan, 2009). Stabilisation forces often enter these states lacking combat readiness, adequate weaponry, and information to conduct successful counter-offensive operations to restore peace and stability. Artificial intelligence, which has proven to be a game changer in business, education, science, and technology, can bridge the gap between military forces and armed groups seeking to undermine the state and drive instability. Therefore, it is worth investigating how armed forces could potentially employ AI to end conflict and restore stability in war-torn regions of the African continent. Decisions requiring split-second decision-making, terrain data collection, and advanced AI cyber systems could all be employed by intelligence forces as a means of studying the enemy and attaining mission success. AI has the capacity to improve (i) intelligence and data collection efficiency as well as (ii) operational and decision-making efficiency. Below is a summary of how AI could improve the effectiveness and efficiency of peacekeeping and counter-insurgency efforts within the three case studies.

Intelligence and Data Collection Efficiency

AI is vastly capable of bolstering national and military security due to AI being latent with military potential. In the first quarter of 2019, the Mozambican province of Cabo Delgado experienced the rise of a new destabilising force within the region, soon emerging from catastrophic floods and climatic events. A terrorist group by the name of Ansar al-Sunna, an ISIS-backed terrorist group, is responsible for mass murders and oil thefts within the Cabo Delgado province. Mozambican security forces struggled to contain and exterminate the extremist group and ultimately resorted to contracting the Russian-backed private military corporation 'Wagner Group'. Due to Wagner's unfamiliarity with the territorial terrain and local insurgency, the group suffered disappointing setbacks and ultimately withdrew from the region (Chirambwi, 2023).

This is a perfect case study to employ, as AI could potentially be leveraged in such an environment to ensure a positive mission outcome. Peace forces backed by the Southern African Development Community and Wagner included were often left unable to reach extremist strongholds due to unfavourable terrain and lack of road infrastructure. Artificial intelligence could be employed within this instance, as omniscient autonomous vehicles could be utilised within the Mozambican province of Cabo Delgado. Zachary S. David draws upon how these vehicles employ AI-informed software supported by ubiquitous sensors, which enables unmanned vehicles to find their way through hostile territory, so equipped they will be able to conduct sophisticated battle tactics and instantly adjust to enemy manoeuvres to exploit battlefield opportunities (Davies, 2024). In this scenario, artificial intelligence is employed to navigate terrain usually unconducive to conventional vehicles. This ultimately allows peace forces to access hard-to-reach geographical areas where extremist groups claim strongholds and are readily able to employ battlefield technologies as a means of restoring peace within the region. Vantage points may also be identified long before deployments to safeguard against ambush attacks. In several instances, SADC and Wagner's forces sought to penetrate areas where Ansar al-Sunna claimed territory. Ultimately, battlefield success may be greatly increased if forces could access areas using AI technologies such as omniscient autonomous vehicles, which furthers the twin goal of mission success and preserving life.

The Democratic Republic of Congo has long been plagued by conflict and instability. The country, which is the size of Western Europe, is one of the African continent's richest countries in terms of mineral resources. Over 122 different rebel groups wage battles against each other and against the state to challenge state legitimacy and gain access to mineral resources such as diamonds, copper, and cobalt. At times, the Congolese armed forces have struggled to level the playing field because they lack information and weaponry to stabilise rebel strongholds (Ganesan & Tyson, 2024). Intervening forces have often found the internal dynamics of the DRC exceptionally challenging. Artificial intelligence could be a vital tool if utilised correctly by military forces. A concept commonly called 'ISR' (intelligence, surveillance, and reconnaissance) is a game changer in knowing the enemy and executing counter-offensive operations. ISR is key to multi-domain situational awareness. AI-enabled ISR systems are able to process a flood of information rapidly. Zachary S. Davis draws upon how ISR may identify the build of troops, missiles and other relevant intelligence information ultimately moving faster than an adversary enhances offensive mobility and allows military forces to hit harder and faster as the element of surprise is forthcoming (Davis, 2019).

In essence, should intervening acquire such technology, the conflict scene may look vastly different within the DRC than what it is today. As intelligence forces have access to adequate information intelligence reports and satellite imaging, AI systems could rapidly process this information using ISR intelligence. This ultimately assists in planning operational deployments and raids, which could have targeted geographical areas and informed the deployment of troops and weapons systems to limit casualties and ensure mission success. ISR-driven AI may be an essential tool in identifying local strongmen, such as rebel leaders, via ISR AI software such as voice or biometric identification AI tools. This could prove to be an iron blade in the hands of military intelligence as a means of planning drone operations aimed at the elimination of warlords. The elimination of local strongmen fuels the emergence of a power vacuum within rebel groups, prompting the rise of instability given their leaderless reality. Ultimately, this provides the opportunity for further interventions for intervening forces, as instability within non-state actors, such as rebel groups, creates weakness and misdirection. This is then an intrinsic step in attaining peace. It is important to note that AI will not completely end the conflict but predominantly acts as an instrument that must complement existing military tools, weaponry, and intelligence while making the way armed forces intervene in conflict easier and more accurate. Hybrid warfare is the name of the game in today's battlefield landscape.

The emergence of artificial cyber intelligence is also a complete gamer for the security complex. Today, cyber commands employing AI can do just as much technology damage to non-state actors such as terrorist and rebel groups. Terror and rebel groups rely heavily on the black market as a means of purchasing weaponry, spreading propaganda and developing complex weapons systems. This creates a unique opportunity for intelligence forces, as the more technology these groups rely on, the more vulnerable they are to cyber disruption. Jeppe Jaconbsen and Jens Ringsmose highlight how artificial cyber intelligence may be employed to identify key players, disrupt electronic payments, and identify weapons programmes being pursued by terrorist groups. Artificial intelligence is crucial for deep learning. In 2015, US Cyber Command carried out strategic cyber bombing on ISIS-linked computer networks, ultimately derailing and dispossessing them of financial resources, geographic locations and weapons programmes (Jacobsen & Ringsmose, 2017). Mozambique, Mali, and the DRC could pursue a similar strategy. Terrorists in Mozambique and Mali and rebel groups in the DRC stand to lose a credible amount if financial streams and weapons programmes are disrupted. This would undermine recruitment and their ability to buy arms, which would cause a great dent in the supply or flow of weapons within these conflict regions. Conflict and peacebuilding would be in close reach if this were to be carried out successfully. It is imperative that a great deal of technology transfer occurs between AI-competent states and Mozambique, Mali and the DRC to ensure sufficient artificial cyber intelligence capability.

Operation and Decision-Making Efficiency

In 2022, Iranian nuclear scientist Mohsen Fakhrizadeh was killed by an unknown assassin. An AI weapon fired from a continent away and operated via a satellite virtually killed Iran's nuclear programme as well. Ultimately, a sharpshooting autonomous weapon operated by technology transfer could be an iron blade in the hands of security forces in Mozambique, Mali, and the DRC. Known leaders of actors undermining state security could be targeted via these special military technology operations, thus reducing the need for armed forces to risk their lives by potentially going into unknown hostile territories. Predictability can also be a powerful advantage in the hands of peace forces. Artificial intelligence could also predict the emergence of interstate disputes and internal conflicts. Game theorists routinely engage in activities with the objective of predicting conflict and playing out response scenarios. While effective, this activity of humans undertaking game theory is subject to human eras and miscalculations. Ultimately, AI could be employed to pre-empt conflict and fuel proactive responses to prevent conflict from breaking out even before the need to intervene using armed peace forces arises.

Artificial intelligence may also assist in dispute resolution, as it may be an effective tool for the armed forces and judges, prosecutors, and lawyers engaged in post-conflict resolution mechanisms. This is an added benefit as conflict resolution mechanisms can often be costly to resource-constrained states such as DRC, Mali, and Mozambique. As a result, AI may bring cost-saving benefits in the form of accurate decisions, minimised costs and increased revenue opportunities for Africa, according to Izouma Egeruoh-Adindu (2021). Such a cost-saving mechanism could open up funds for peace-building initiatives and post-conflict reconstruction.

In conflict landscapes in the DRC, Mali, and Mozambique, people displaced and affected by conflict rely on humanitarian aid. Ultimately, artificial intelligence can prove to be an iron blade in the streamlining of aid distribution; this comes as AI is able to optimise resources, as conventional norms of aid distribution have often failed. In the DRC, in particular, aid has often failed to reach its intended recipients due to logistical and conflict factors. AI will also prove exceptionally important in determining population density and local needs to determine the most cost-effective way to distribute aid. Ceasefires are also incredibly vital within the conflict landscape, as the ceasefire agreements perform the important task of conflict prevention toolkit. One could then assert that artificial intelligence can play a role in monitoring and evaluating ceasefire agreements. At the same time, AI will not entirely replace human labour within the ceasefire process, but it may assist in reducing harm to humans.

According to Sarah Grand-Clement, artificial intelligence can then monitor core ceasefire components such as weapons and ammunition and kinetic and non-kinetic attacks, including the buildup and movement of troops outside areas specified in the ceasefire agreement

(Grand-Clément & Cops, 2023). Hence, the following artificial intelligence technologies may be key to monitoring ceasefire guiding pillars. Sarah Grand-Clement draws upon how acoustic sensors, cameras, seismic sensors and cyber monitoring are key technologies that assist in monitoring ceasefires and preventing conflict (Grand-Clément & Cops, 2023). Acoustic sensors may assist in identifying and locating artillery sounds. At the same time, cameras specifically attached to drones may monitor the buildup or demobilisation of troops in conflict zones. In contrast, seismic sensors may sense vibrations and ground movements of large military movements such as tanks. Cyber-monitoring can also be crucial to the intelligence gathering of potential attacks on critical and digital infrastructure.

		Weapons and ammunition	Troops and combatants	Non-lethal hostile activity	Protection of civilians	Infrastructure	Humanitarian assistance	Peacekeeping duties	Prisoners and hostages	Propaganda, hate speech and other hostile media
Data acquisition	Accoustic sensors	✓✓	-	✓	-	-	-	-	-	-
	Cameras	✓✓	✓✓	✓✓	✓	✓✓	✓	✓	✓	-
	Infrasound sensors	✓✓	-	-	-	-	-	-	-	-
	Motion sensors	✓	✓	✓✓	-	-	-	-	-	-
	Radars	✓✓	✓✓	✓✓	✓	✓✓	✓✓	✓✓	✓	-
	Satellites	✓✓	✓	✓	✓	✓✓✓	✓	✓	✓	-
	Seismic sensors	✓	✓	✓	-	-	-	-	-	-
	Aerial platforms	✓✓✓	✓✓	✓✓	✓	✓✓	✓✓	✓✓	✓	-
	UAVs	✓✓✓	✓✓	✓✓	✓	✓✓	✓✓	✓✓	✓	-
	Crowdsourcing	✓	✓	✓	✓	✓	✓	✓	✓	✓✓✓
	Data scraping	✓	✓	✓	✓	✓	✓	✓	✓	✓✓✓
	Advanced binoculars	✓	✓	✓	✓	✓	✓	✓	✓	-
	Biometrics	-	✓	-	-	-	-	-	-	-
	Cyber monitoring	✓	-	✓✓	-	✓✓	-	-	-	-
	RFID	✓	-	-	-	-	-	-	-	-
Analysis	Artificial intelligence	CROSS-CUTTING TECHNOLOGIES								
	Data fusion									
Communications										

Source Sarah Grand-Clement, Exploring the use of technology for remote ceasefire monitoring and verification, UNIDIR, 2022

		Weapons and ammunition	Troops and combatants	Non-lethal hostile activity	Protection of civilians	Infrastructure	Humanitarian assistance	Peacekeeping duties	Prisoners and hostages	Propaganda, hate speech and other hostile media
Data acquisition	Accoustic sensors	✓✓	-	✓	-	-	-	-	-	-
	Cameras	✓✓	✓✓	✓✓	✓	✓✓	✓	✓	✓	-
	Infrasound sensors	✓✓	-	-	-	-	-	-	-	-
	Motion sensors	✓	✓	✓✓	-	-	-	-	-	-
	Radars	✓✓	✓✓	✓✓	✓	✓✓	✓✓	✓✓	✓	-
	Satellites	✓✓	✓	✓	✓	✓✓✓	✓	✓	✓	-
	Seismic sensors	✓	✓	✓	-	-	-	-	-	-
	Aerial platforms	✓✓✓	✓✓	✓✓	✓	✓✓	✓✓	✓✓	✓	-
	UAVs	✓✓✓	✓✓	✓✓	✓	✓✓	✓✓	✓✓	✓	-
	Crowdsourcing	✓	✓	✓	✓	✓	✓	✓	✓	✓✓✓
	Data scraping	✓	✓	✓	✓	✓	✓	✓	✓	✓✓✓
	Advanced binoculars	✓	✓	✓	✓	✓	✓	✓	✓	-
	Biometrics	-	✓	-	-	-	-	-	-	-
	Cyber monitoring	✓	-	✓✓	-	✓✓	-	-	-	-
	RFID	✓	-	-	-	-	-	-	-	-
Analysis	Artificial intelligence	CROSS-CUTTING TECHNOLOGIES								
	Data fusion									
Communications										

Key: ✓✓✓ = technology very well adapted for this activity; ✓✓ = technology moderately adapted, may not be suitable for all specific areas falling under this activity; ✓ = technology has limited and/or specific areas of applicability within this activity; - = technology not suited for this activity.

Source Sarah Grand-Clement, Exploring the use of technology for remote ceasefire monitoring and verification, UNIDIR, 2022

Another critical dimension that AI may add to the military dynamics includes wargaming. Zachary Davis highlights how wargaming may enrich battlefield simulations revolving around multi-actor interactions; AI enables wargames to add and modify game variables as a means of exploring how dynamic and uncertain conditions such as weapons, allies, and rebel intervention may affect outcomes and decision-making. AI will then be able to analyse the results of each game (Davis, 2019). During battlefield conflicts, second decision-making is often the difference that entails whether the outcome of a peace mission is either a success or failure. This factor, compounded with the excess stress and trauma of conflict, often leads to human error, which may have disastrous outcomes for conflict and peace-making/building. AI reduces the risk of such errors, and wargaming and scenario planning assist in decision-making, especially split-second decision-making. Wargaming also allows military planners to know all the uncertainties long in advance before even embarking upon the peace mission. Charles Tilly's famous dictum uttered that 'war made the state, and the state made war' (Hui, 2019). Conflict and war are factoring that Mali, Mozambique, and the DRC must grapple with as a means of attaining peace and building a strong, capable society. As Hibah Alessa denotes conflict as a growing industry, the demand for dispute resolution tools will grow simultaneously (Alessa, 2022).

Averting Risks of AI Integrated Peacekeeping

The argument has been made promoting AI as a useful alternative to the ongoing security concerns within the DRC, Mali and Mozambique. Though the advantages of such an approach leave room for great excitement, which is arguably welcomed given the dire situation of the existing peace operations within these countries, it is necessary to address the cautions around such an approach. Sharma warns that AI-based EW systems are at risk of faulty data inputs, and due to the great reliance on data, catastrophic consequences might erupt in instances where data is flawed, faulty, or misrepresented. AI software may need to be more sophisticated to differentiate between objects, and given the mandates outlined within their algorithms, they may need to be more accurate in their targets. Data reliability is, therefore, a grave concern within the application of AI systems.

Furthermore, though praised for its decision-making capability and speed, it may serve as a risk as it may accelerate decisions, which may invertedly accelerate conflicts. Prolonged negotiations and diplomatic procedures often aid in de-escalated conflict and tensions. Should this process be removed or shortened, it may prevent sufficient time for hostilities and grievances to pacify. Additionally, major decisions about warfare and the potential risk to human life cannot and arguably should not be reliable on the predictions of AI systems, as these systems, unfortunately, cannot predict outcomes without a margin of error. Though acceptable in theory and research contexts, these margins of error can be detrimental in real-life battle settings. Finally, it also warns against the risk of propagating and promoting fake news and misinformation, which could be generated by convincing AI systems. Leaders could misuse this to derail and deform public perception and prevent the successful implementation of response plans and strategies (Sharma et al., 2020).

It is also worth noting that just as security forces and states are leveraging AI's benefits to ensure security, due to the low cost of entry, non-state actors such as rebel and terrorist groups may also employ AI's benefits to achieve strategic objectives. According to Nate Allen, Matthew

La Lime, and Tomslin Samme-Nlar, AI is an enabling technology that is employed for command, control, and operational planning purposes. Hence, AI could be utilised by insurgent groups in Mali, DRC and Mozambique for increasing recruitment, financing, international communications and planning (Allen & La, 2022). Ultimately, intervening forces need to be cognizant that armed non-state actors will also employ AI to give themselves an upper hand over intervening forces. AI may also be leveraged to increase the success of terrorist operations and assist terrorist forces in identifying the weak spots of an intended target that may ensure mission success.

Another factor that may impede the success of AI in fostering peace is that AI itself may indirectly fuel conditions ripe for recruitment, leading to the expansion of armed actors in Africa. For one, AI could fuel an increase in inequality and unemployment in DRC, Mali, and Mozambique. Ekkehard Ernst, Rossana Merola, and Daniel Sammon highlight how when firms automate production, job growth is affected, as new technologies directly substitute jobs and tasks performed by workers. Hence, automation and AI will accelerate the shifts in skills that the workforce needs (Ciminelli et al., 2019).

AI also requires a necessary skill base which many Malians, Mozambicans and Congolese might not be trained in; hence, a real possibility exists that, yes, AI will close some sectors of the workforce, but new sectors will be opened but will require some skill base which governments will not have trained their citizens for, as even Ernst, Merola, and Sammon draw upon how AI brings about a complementary increase in jobs and tasks (Ciminelli et al., 2019). Ultimately, poverty, inequality and a skills mismatch may fuel conditions ripe for disenfranchised persons to see rebel groups and terrorist groups as a source of income and means to survival. Ultimately, to prevent this, Mozambique, Mali and DRC may have to consider some universal basic income grants to assist those affected by AI and prevent the increase in terrorist group recruitment.

Another worrying reality is the fact that Africa as a continent is home to many authoritarian and oppressive forms of government, constantly on the hunt for new means to suppress populations and consolidate power. Artificial intelligence for authoritarian regimes could prove to be a highly effective rule that strengthens undemocratic regimes and weakens democracy on the continent. Bibo Lin highlights how Huawei's technicians enabled and sometimes directly assisted governments in monitoring and tracking political opponents, while digital surveillance technologies in Africa have been exported from Russia, Saudi Arabia, France, the U.S., the United Kingdom, Israel, and Germany, have also supplied high-end surveillance technologies such as spyware, hacking, software, including censorship applications to fragile democracies and illiberal governments in Africa (Lin, 2023). Ultimately, illiberal governments could employ artificial intelligence against citizens protesting human rights abuses or activists and opposition politicians challenging the dictatorial regime. Tanzania, Uganda, and Burundi, including Zimbabwe, routinely employ technology to restrict citizen access to the internet, suppress voting opinions, and silence journalists.

Alina Polyakova and Chris Meserole also add how governments collect surveillance footage and eventually transmit it to intelligence services. As a preventative, Polyakova and Meserole advocate for civil bodies and democratic governments to designate regimes as digital authoritarian regimes when employing surveillance without safeguards and protections, including how digital governance code of conduct should be developed, which may have to involve civil society, governments as well as tech and AI corporations (Polyakova & Meserole, 2019). Artificial intelligence in the wrong hands or being employed where there is no clear legislative framework, norms, or standards is simply bound to end in disaster. Hence, a notion of techplomacy may have to emerge as governments and tech corporations will be forced to cooperate on issues of the dangers of technology. It is also worth noting that while AI brings tremendous benefits to Africa's conflict landscape, it is still vastly unregulated. Unlike nuclear weapons treaties and agreements, which have checks and balances, artificial intelligence lacks necessary checks and balances; this essentially translates into no measure of restraint on AI or control measures. Powerful non-state actors and autocratic regimes may largely exploit these vulnerabilities to cling to power. It is worth noting that Mali, the Democratic Republic of Congo, and Mozambique do not enjoy flourishing democracies; these are all states plagued by autocratic tendencies and large-scale human rights abuses. Hence, for this reason, before AI can be utilised in these states, adequate arms control and restrictive measures must be put in place to prevent AI from being employed as just another tool to undermine democratic consolidation.

Conclusion

Conflict in Africa has consequences such as economic downturn, human rights abuses, and displacement; hence, as these consequences are connected, solutions to address and solve issues must be interconnected. Artificial intelligence employed in conflict zones provide a precise interconnected platform solution to tackle violence and instability. Disruption, although needs planning and AI is exceptionally disruptive, stakeholder engagement and cooperation are exceptionally necessary to facilitate and harness the benefits of AI in driving down conflict and fostering peace. Thus, it is also important to note that as intervening forces aim to leverage AI for good, conflict actors will leverage AI technologies to advance their battlefield objectives. It is also important to note that while AI may be beneficial to the conflict landscapes of the Democratic Republic of Congo and Mali, the cost considerations of leveraging artificial intelligence to drive peace are also exceptionally important to take note of. Humans still need to operate and create platforms for data fusions to occur as a means of interpreting the data. Hence, the human labour that must be accounted for is both labour and budget these conflict-ridden states might not have; this then calls for the pooling of resources on a domestic level via domestic resource mobilisation and the continental pooling of resources. Split-second decision-making, information interpretation, and knowledge of the landscape are all factors that will determine the success or failure of peace operations. Hence, quantum computers, unmanned ariel vehicles, and seismic sensors are the tools of the trade for ensuring the smooth undertaking of peace missions. Kzanberg's law of technology implies that 'technology is neither good nor bad, but it is also not neutral'. Technology can be employed as a force for good if utilised correctly.

References

Alessa, H. (2022). The role of Artificial Intelligence in Online Dispute Resolution: A brief and critical overview. *Information and Communications Technology Law, 31*(3), 319–342. https://doi.org/10.1080/13600834.2022.2088060

Allen, N., & La, M. (2022, December). *Research report the downsides of digital.*

Biscop, S. (2019). EU-U.S. Consensus and NATO-EU cooperation, In *New perspectives on shared security: NATO's next 70 years* (pp. 15–18). Available at: https://carnegieendowment.org/files/NATO_int_final1.pdf

Brandt, P. T., et al. (2022). Conflict forecasting with event data and spatio-temporal graph convolutional networks. *International Interactions, 48*(4), 800–822. https://doi.org/10.1080/03050629.2022.2036987

Brosig, M., & Sempijja, N. (2018). Does peacekeeping reduce violence? Assessing comprehensive security of contemporary peace operations in Africa. *Stability, 7*(1). https://doi.org/10.5334/sta.576

Chirambwi, K. (2023). Constraints on peace research in war-torn situations: Cabo Delgado, Mozambique. *Journal of Aggression, Conflict and Peace Research, 16*. https://doi.org/10.1108/JACPR-12-2022-0766

Ciminelli, G., et al. (2019). The composition effects of tax-based consolidation on income inequality. *European Journal of Political Economy, 57*, 107–124. https://doi.org/10.1016/j.ejpoleco.2018.08.009

Davies, P. (2024). Counterintelligence and escalation from hybrid to total war in the Russo-Ukrainian conflict 2014–2024. *Intelligence and National Security, 39*, 496–514. https://doi.org/10.1080/02684527.2024.2329419

Davis, Z. S. (2019, March). *Artificial intelligence on the battlefield: An initial survey of potential implications for deterrence, stability, and strategic surprise* (pp. 1–26). Center for Global Security Research Lawrence Livermore National Laboratory.

Egeruoh-Adindu, I. (2021). Technology and the law: The impact of Artificial Intelligence (AI) on litigation and dispute resolution in Africa. In *Nigerian Yearbook of International Law 2018/2019* (pp. 413–436). Springer. https://doi.org/10.1007/978-3-030-69594-1_18

Eke, D. O., Wakunuma, K., & Akintoye, S. (2023). *Introducing responsible AI in Africa*. Springer. https://doi.org/10.1007/978-3-031-08215-3_1

Ganesan, K., & Tyson, R. (2024). *The impact of natural resources on civil conflict in the Democratic Republic of the Congo*.

Grand-Clément, S., & Cops, D. (2023). *PROJECT D-TECT: Technologies to counter the diversion of small arms and light weapons, and components of conventional weapons*.

Hagendorff, T., & Wezel, K. (2020). 15 challenges for AI: Or what AI (currently) can't do. *AI & Society, 35*. https://doi.org/10.1007/s00146-019-00886-y

Hui, V. (2019). *Does war make states? Investigations of Charles Tilly's*. Cambridge University Press.

Hunter, L. Y., et al. (2023). The Fourth Industrial Revolution, artificial intelligence, and domestic conflict. *Global Society, 37*(3), 375–396. https://doi.org/10.1080/13600826.2022.2147812

Jacobsen, J. T., & Ringsmose, J. (2017). Cyber-bombing ISIS: Why disclose what is better kept secret? *Global Affairs, 3*(2), 125–137. https://doi.org/10.1080/23340460.2017.1337471

Kol, L., Maimunah, T. D., & Midas, O. (2023). The application of artificial intelligence (AI) in peacekeeping operation. *The Journal of Defence and Security, 18*(1), 2023.

Lin, B. (2023). Beyond authoritarianism and liberal democracy: Understanding China's artificial intelligence impact in Africa. *Information, Communication & Society, 27*, 1–16. https://doi.org/10.1080/1369118X.2023.2239322

McGuirk, E., & Burke, M. (2020). The economic origins of conflict in Africa. *Journal of Political Economy, 128*(10), 3940–3997. https://doi.org/10.1086/709993

Morgan, P. (2009). *Security in international politics* [Preprint].

Olsher, D. (2013). *Cognitive/AI peacekeeping decision support models*. Proceedings of the 3rd IEEE Global Humanitarian Technology Conference, GHTC 2013. https://doi.org/10.1109/GHTC.2013.6713667

Plantinga, P. (2024). Digital discretion and public administration in Africa: Implications for the use of artificial intelligence. *Information Development, 40*(2), 332–352. https://doi.org/10.1177/02666669221117526

Pokalova, E. (n.d.) The Wagner Group in Africa: Russia's quasi-state agent of influence. *Studies in Conflict & Terrorism*, 1–23. https://doi.org/10.1080/1057610X.2023.2231642

Polyakova, A., & Meserole, C. (2019). *Exporting digital authoritarianism: The Russian and Chinese models* (Policy Brief, Democracy and Disorder Series, pp. 1–22). Available at: https://www.brookings.edu/wp-content/uploads/2019/08/FP_20190827_digital_authoritarianism_polyakova_meserole.pdf

Sharma, P., Sarma, K. K., & Mastorakis, N. E. (2020). Artificial intelligence aided electronic warfare systems—Recent trends and evolving applications. *IEEE Access, 8*(April), 224761–224780. https://doi.org/10.1109/ACCESS.2020.3044453

Suharjo, D., Ali, M. N., & Hasbullah, H. (2024). Strategy for handling conflict resolution through a territorial development approach. *International Journal of Social Science, Education Communication and Economics (SINOMICS JOURNAL), 3*(1), 185–198.

Svicevic, M., & Bradley, M. M. (2024). *Mozambique's Cabo Delgado conflict*. Routledge. https://doi.org/10.4324/9781003317647

UN General Assembly. (2018). *General Assembly approves appropriation of $6.8 billion for 14 peacekeeping operations in 2017/18*. Available at: https://press.un.org/en/2017/ga11927.doc.htm

Yamakawa, H. (2019). Peacekeeping conditions for an artificial intelligence society. *Big Data and Cognitive Computing, 3*(2), 1–12. https://doi.org/10.3390/bdcc3020034

Zou, H., et al. (2024) *GenAINet: Enabling wireless collective intelligence via knowledge transfer and reasoning* (pp. 1–7). Available at: http://arxiv.org/abs/2402.16631

Index

G. Onyango (ed.), *Designing Artificial Intelligence for Public Policy and Governance in Africa*, Studies in National Governance and Emerging Technologies, https://doi.org/10.1007/978-3-031-83445-5